FIREWORKS 4

in e

CW01669137

NICK VANDOME

COMPUTER STEP

In easy steps is an imprint of Computer Step
Southfield Road . Southam
Warwickshire CV47 0FB . England

http://www.ineasysteps.com

Notice of Liability

Every effort has been made to ensure that this book contains accurate and current information. However, Computer Step and the author shall not be liable for any loss or damage suffered by readers as a result of any information contained herein.

Trademarks

Fireworks® is a registered trademark of Macromedia, Inc. All other trademarks are acknowledged as belonging to their respective companies.

Printed and bound in the United Kingdom

ISBN 1-84078-136-X

Table of Contents

Introducing Fireworks 4

Fireworks 4 is a powerful image editing and graphics design program, that is designed primarily for Web designers. It can be used to create and edit simple images and graphics, such as buttons for Web pages, or it can handle more complex tasks such as creating rollover images and pop-up menus. This chapter shows how to obtain and install Fireworks and goes through the basic functions so that you can get up and running with the program.

Covers

Chapter One

What is Fireworks 4?

On the surface, Macromedia's Fireworks is an image editing package, of a similar nature to a program such as Adobe Photoshop. However, there are some very important differences. Firstly, Fireworks is designed specifically to work with images that are going to be used on the Web. It is closely integrated with the Macromedia Web authoring tool, Dreamweaver, and its main purpose is to give Web designers the means to create images for the Web and also manipulate existing images so that they are in the optimum condition for use on the Web. This involves creating files sizes that are as small as possible, while still retaining sufficient image quality. This means that the images will download as quickly as possible when viewed on the Web.

For more information about Dreamweaver, have a look at 'Dreamweaver 4 in easy steps'.

The term 'Web designer' can be applied to anyone who produces Web pages. You do not have to be a highly qualified professional. With programs such as Fireworks and Dreamweaver, you will be perfectly capable of producing Web sites that are comparable with those of the professionals.

But Fireworks is not just an image manipulation tool. Web designers can also create interactive features for Web pages using HTML and Javascript functions. All the designer has to do is create the elements that they want and Fireworks creates all of the code for them in the background. It is then just a case of exporting the end product into Dreamweaver, a task that Fireworks handles with ease. Some of the elements that can be created within Fireworks include:

- Add hyperlinks to images
- Create navigation bars
- Create pop-up menus
- Create simple and advanced rollover images
- Create hotspots and slices

Slicing is a technique in Fireworks whereby an image is broken down into smaller parts and then reconstructed when it is viewed in an HTML Web page. This means that different areas of an image can be edited independently of each other. For more information on slicing, see Chapter Seven.

With Fireworks it is possible to perform simple image editing tasks or create complex graphics, primarily for use on the Web. It is even possible to author an entire Web site using Fireworks, although it is more common to use it in conjunction with Dreamweaver. Overall, Fireworks is an extremely powerful tool that can make a dramatic difference to the production of Web pages.

Obtaining Fireworks 4

Fireworks is produced by Macromedia, the market leader in Web authoring software. Fireworks is their main graphic design tool for the Web and this is complemented with Dreamweaver for overall Web design and management, Flash for Web animation and Freehand for illustration creation.

Fireworks can be purchased from general software retailers, either in person or over the Web. It costs approximately £240–£270, depending on where you buy it. Alternatively, it can be downloaded from the Macromedia Web site at:

- www.macromedia.com/software/fireworks

As well as downloading the full product, it is also possible to download a fully-functioning 30-day trial version from the same site.

DON'T FORGET: It is worth shopping around when buying a program such as Fireworks, because there can be considerable differences in price between different retailers. To find some online sellers of Fireworks, and other Macromedia products, go to their Web page at www.macromedia.com/uk/buy and click on the Find a Reseller button.

Click here to buy the full functioning version of Fireworks

Click here to download the free 30-day trial version of Fireworks

HOT TIP: Fireworks and Dreamweaver can be purchased together as a combined, or studio, package. This costs approximately £350–£420 depending on where you buy it, which is a considerable saving on buying the two programs separately.

Installing Fireworks 4

If Fireworks is downloaded from the Macromedia Web site it will be loaded automatically onto your computer. If you are using a CD-ROM version it should run automatically on a PC; on a Mac it is activated by double-clicking on the Fireworks 4 installer icon. You will then be taken through the installation process and asked to enter information as required. Once the installation has been completed you may be asked to restart your computer.

It is possible to run Fireworks 4 on a PC or a Mac with 32 MB of RAM. However, this may prove irritatingly slow and some of the program's functions may not work properly. It is strongly recommended to run it on a machine that has a minimum of 64 MB of RAM. When it comes to working with images and graphics, the more RAM there is, the better.

System requirements

Windows

- Windows 95, 98, Me, XP, 2000 or NT 4 (with Service Pack 5)
- Intel Pentium processor (Pentium II or better recommended)
- 64 MB of RAM
- 100 MB of available disk space
- 800 x 600 pixel resolution, 256-colour display (1024 x 768 resolution, 16 million colours recommended)

In addition to the system requirement listed here, you will also require a mouse or digitising tablet and a CD-ROM or DVD-ROM drive in order to load and use Fireworks 4.

Mac

- Power Macintosh (G3 or higher recommended)
- OS 8.6 or above
- 64 MB of RAM
- 100 MB of available disk space
- Adobe Type Manager® 4 or later for using Type 1 fonts
- Colour monitor (1024 x 768 resolution, 16 million colours recommended)

Once you have installed Fireworks, it is a good idea to add a shortcut (Windows) or an alias (Mac) to your desktop. This is done by locating the program file and right-clicking (Windows) or Ctrl+click (Mac) and dragging the icon onto the desktop. Release and select Create shortcut here (Windows) or Make Alias (Mac) from the menu.

The first view

The Fireworks interface has been designed to match as closely as possible other Macromedia products such as Dreamweaver and Flash. This means you can switch between various programs, while remaining in a familiar environment. When Fireworks is first opened there is no document visible. To create a new document:

For more information on settings when creating new documents, see page 22.

Select File>New from the menu bar

Once a new document has been created a blank page will be visible in the Fireworks environment:

The Fireworks panels can be accessed at any time by selecting Window from the menu bar and then selecting the required panel. Each panel appears grouped with others that perform related or similar tasks. If required, each panel can be separated by clicking on the tab at the top and dragging it away from the others.

Tools panel   Preview tabs   Menu bar   Toolbars

Work area   Panels   Mini Launcher, which can be used to access the most commonly used panels

Close down any panels that you do not use regularly. If you have too many panels visible, this will mean there is less space for working in the document window.

Menu bar and toolbars

Menu bar

The menu bar is located at the top of the Fireworks screen and contains menus for accessing all of the functionality of the program. To view a menu, click on the relevant heading and then, if required, click on the arrow next to an option to view any sub-menus.

Toolbars

The Modify toolbar contains functionality for working with graphics and images. Some of these functions will be looked at in Chapter Four.

There are two toolbars available in Fireworks, the Main toolbar and the Modify toolbar. To access these:

From the menu bar, select Window> Toolbars>Main/ Modify

The functions on the Main toolbar are (from left to right):

- New. Creates a new document
- Open. Opens an existing document
- Save. Saves the currently active document
- Import. Imports a document from another format
- Export. Exports a document to another format
- Print. Prints the currently active document
- Undo. Undoes previous actions
- Redo. Replaces any actions that have been undone
- Cut. Removes a selection and copies it to the clipboard
- Copy. Copies a selection to the clipboard
- Paste. Pastes a selection that has been placed on the clipboard with either Cut or Copy

The Undo function can be performed on numerous previous actions. The number of steps to which Undo can be applied can be set in the Preferences dialog box, which can be accessed by selecting Edit>Preferences from the menu bar. For more information on Preferences, see page 21.

Tools panel

The Tools panel contains all of the most frequently used tools needed to create and edit graphics and images in Fireworks. Some of the buttons on the Tools panel have a small arrow at the bottom right-hand corner. By clicking on this a further selection of tools within this category can be selected. To access the full set of these options:

Click and hold here to access the full range of items available for a category with an arrow here

The full range of default options on the Tools panel is:

The area underneath the tools on the tools panel is for selecting stroke and fill colours for objects. This is looked at in more detail in Chapter Three.

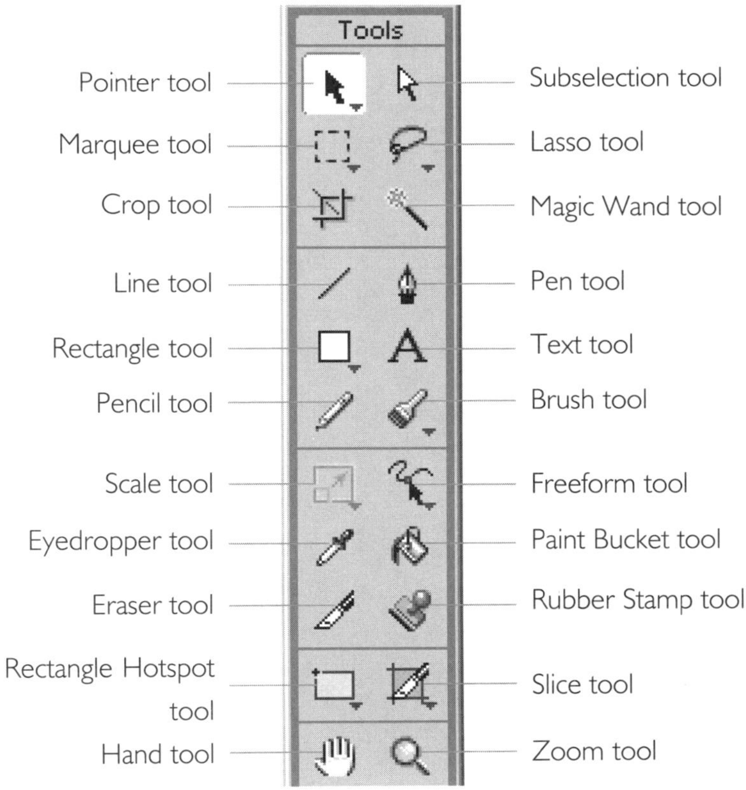

Additional options

The tools that have additional options are:

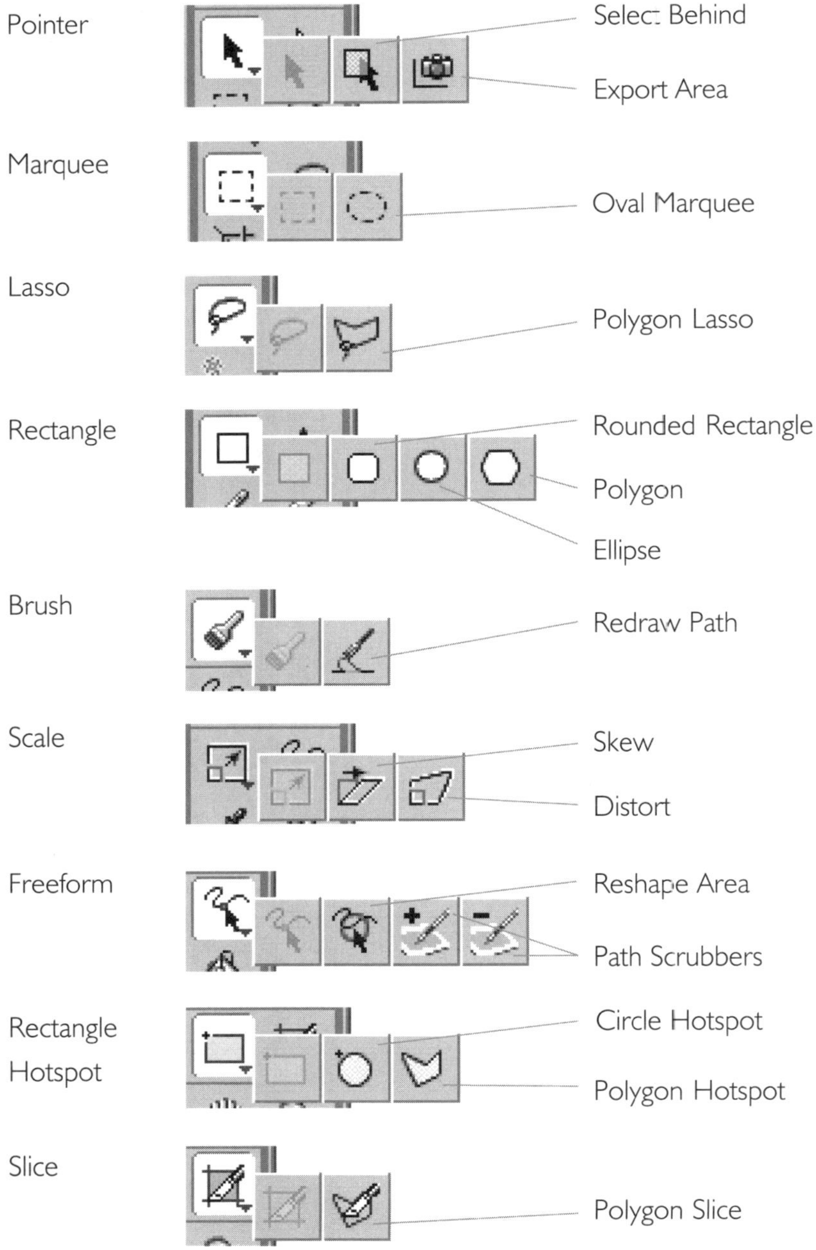

To see what a particular tool does, roll the cursor over it and wait a couple of seconds for a box describing the tool to appear.

Panels

In order to be able to create, edit and manipulate objects, Fireworks provides a number of panels, each containing various devices for working with elements, such as fills, lines, effects, layers, frames and behaviors. Fireworks usually opens with some panels already showing. To view more panels, or hide the ones that are currently visible:

Panels can be hidden by selecting Window from the menu bar and clicking on any item that has a tick next to it. Alternatively, the panel window can be closed down in the same way as you would normally close a window with Windows or a Mac. If a panel is closed down while it is grouped with other panels, all of the panels will be closed. However, if a panel has been separated from its default grouping, this is the only one that will be closed.

Select Window from the menu bar and then click on the panel you want to view. This will open within its default group

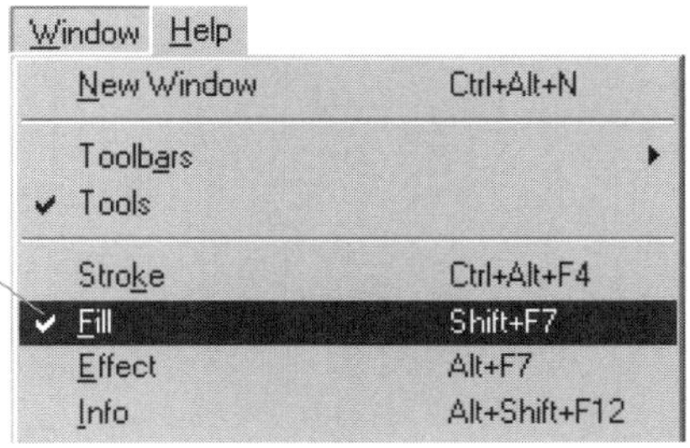

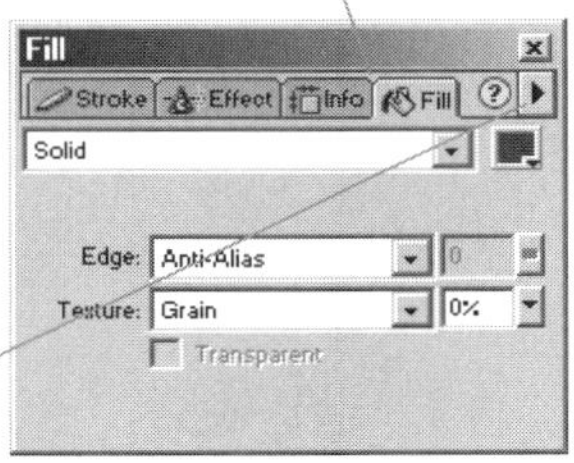

Click here on a panel to view the menu associated with it.

Arranging panels

Panels can be split up from their default groups and viewed individually. To do this:

Click here and drag the panel away from the rest of the group. To return it to the group, drag it back

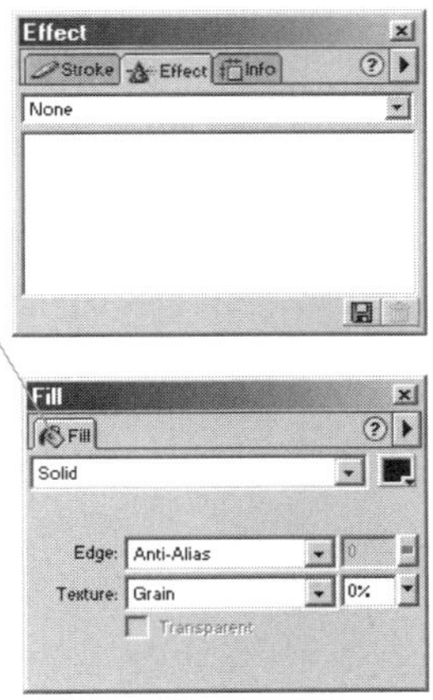

Stroke panel

This contains options for editing the stroke (line) attributes of objects, such as rectangles or ovals.

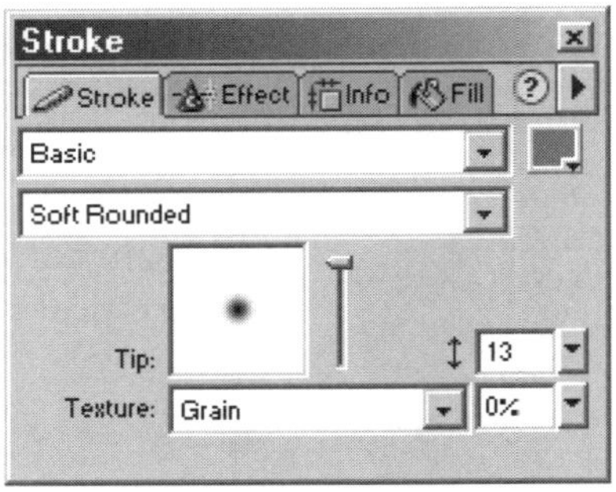

Each panel will be dealt with in greater detail in the chapter to which their functions apply.

Fill panel

This contains options for editing the fill attributes of objects. This can be done with solid colours, or designs.

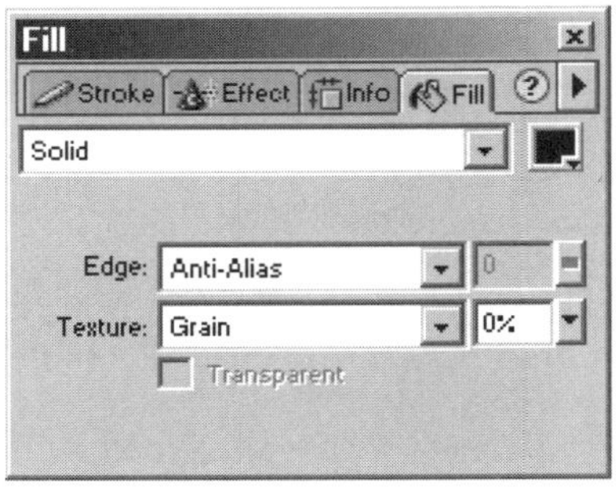

Usually when using panels, an object has to be selected first on the work area. The functions of a particular panel can then be applied to the selected object.

Effect panel

This contains options for editing the colour attributes of an object and adding effects such as embossing and bevelling.

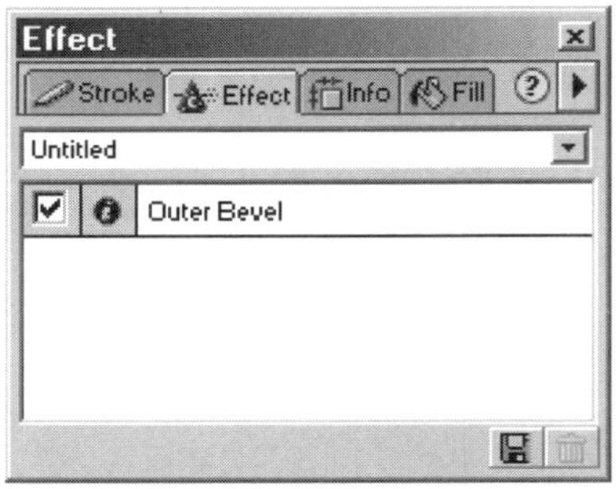

Info panel

This contains information about objects, such as their co-ordinates and their colour attributes.

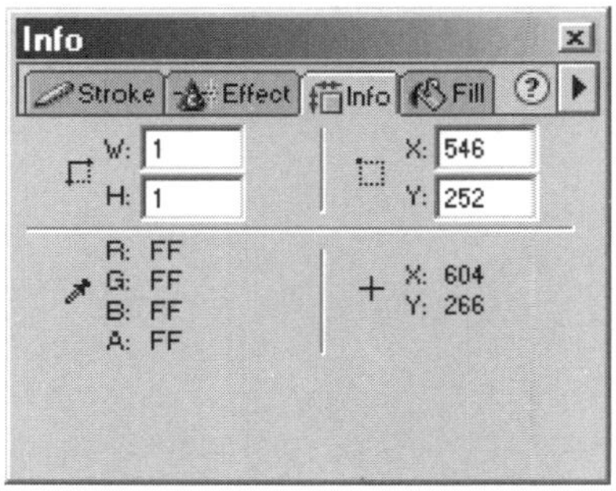

Optimize panel

This is used to convert objects to the most suitable format for use on the Web.

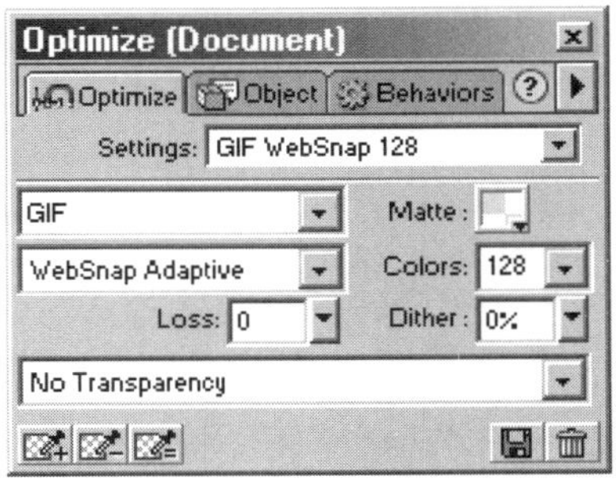

The Optimize panel can be used to create different file formats for publication on the Web. This means that you can choose between different formats, such as GIFs and JPEGs. The quality for each format can be optimised so that you achieve the best available quality while retaining a small file size for fast downloading times.

Object panel

This can be used to set certain attributes for objects, such as rounded corners for rectangles.

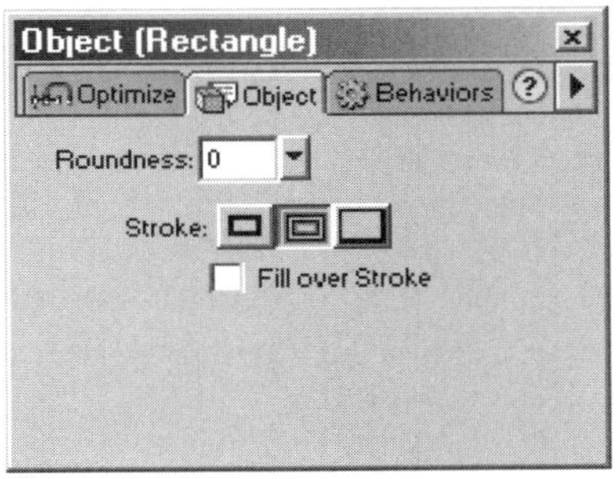

Behaviors panel

This can be used to assign certain behaviors to objects. This allows them to then perform a certain action when they are viewed in a browser.

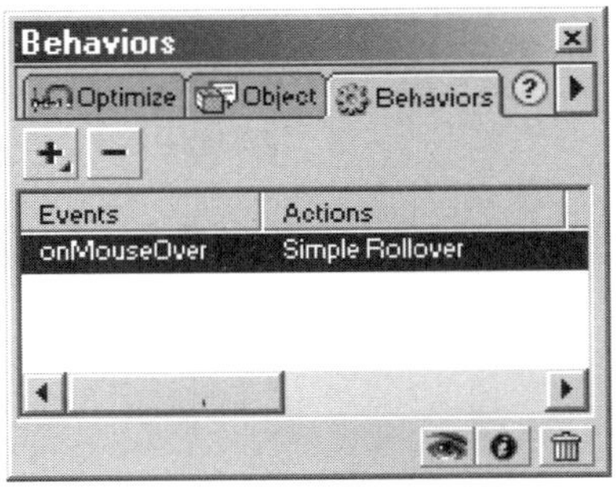

Behaviors are created with Javascript and are activated when the item is viewed in a Web browser that is capable of displaying Javascript.

Color Mixer panel

This enables you to create your own colours.

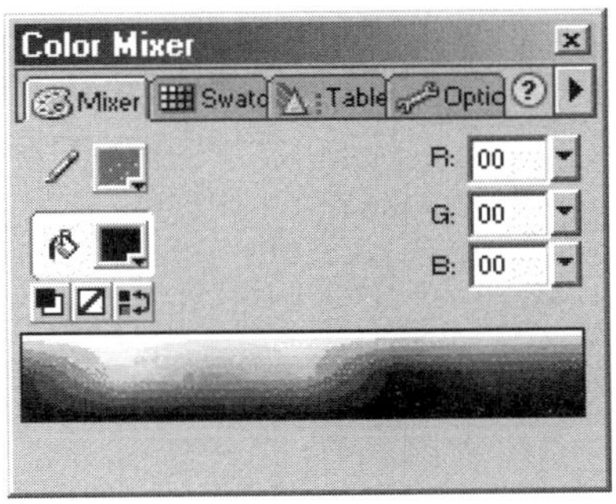

Swatches panel

This can be used to select pre-designed Web-safe colours.

Web-safe colours are a group of colours that will appear the same on the Web regardless of the type of computer or browser on which they are viewed. There are 256 Web-safe colours. If you use colours outside this range i.e. you create your own colours, there is no guarantee they will look the same when viewed on different browsers.

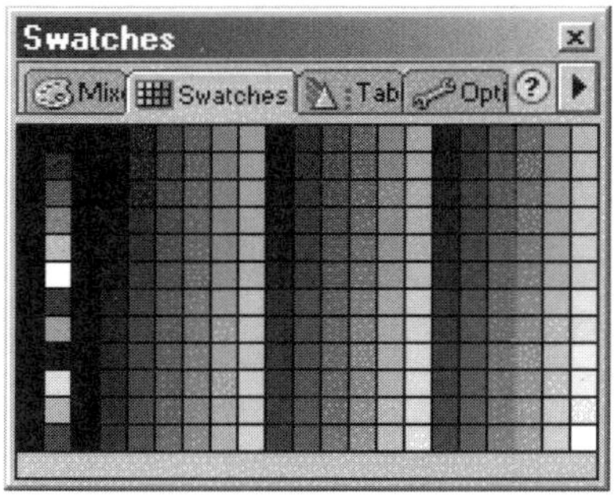

Color Table panel

This can be used to create and store specific colours that you use frequently.

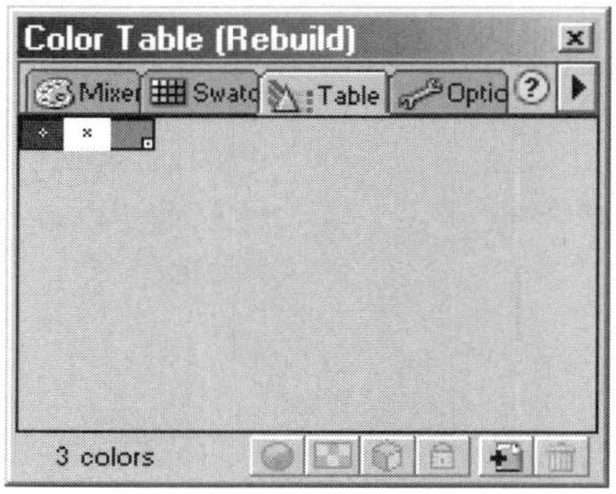

Tool Options panel

This contains options that can be applied to specific tools.

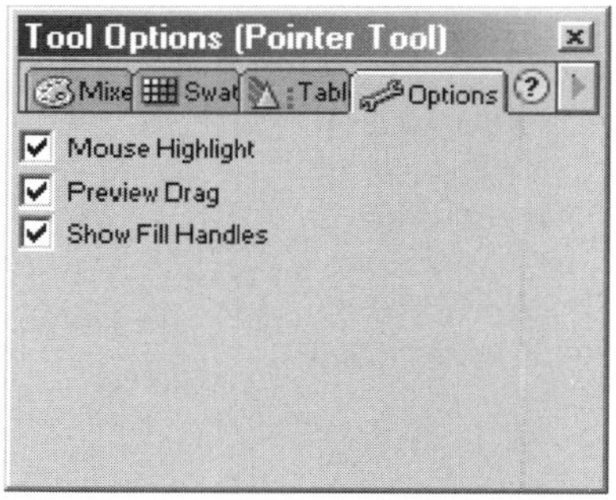

Layers can be used to include several different images within the same document. Each item can be kept separate on its own layer, or the items on different layers can be merged or blended together.

Layers panel

This is used when working with separate layers within a Fireworks document.

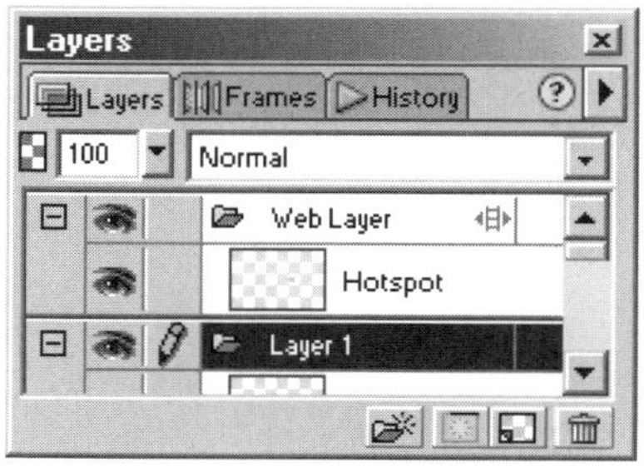

Frames are generally used to create rollover images and animation in Fireworks. This is done by placing different images on separate frames and then playing them back in sequence. For more information on frames, see Chapter Ten.

Frames panel

This is used when you are working with frames. This is usually in relation to animations or rollover images.

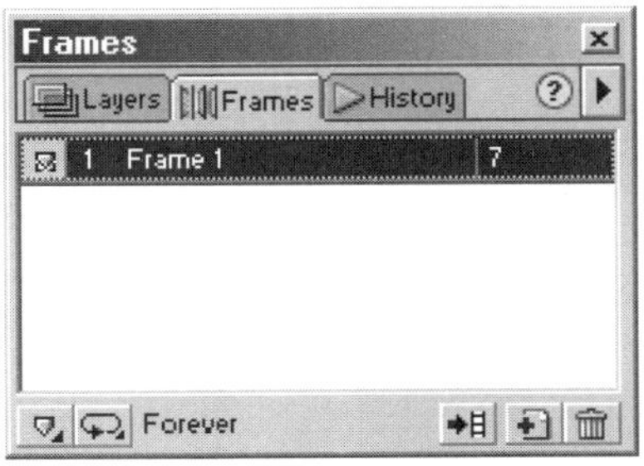

History panel

This contains details of previous editing actions. It can be used to replay sets of commands that have already been applied within a document.

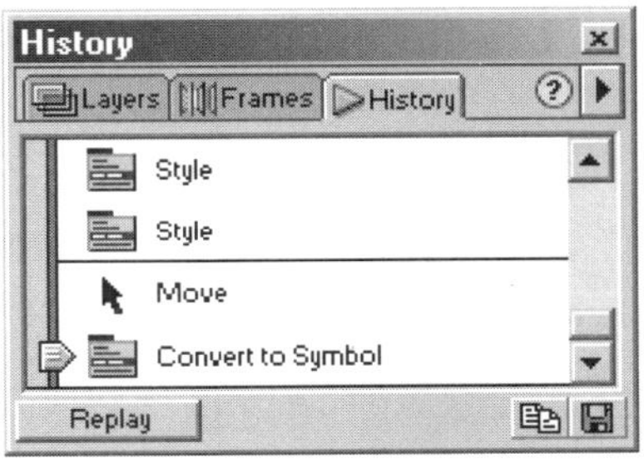

Styles panel

This contains pre-designed styles which can be applied to the fill of objects or to text.

When an item is placed in the Library this is known as a symbol. It can then be inserted into a document, in which case it becomes an instance i.e. not an item in its own right, but a reference back to the symbol in the Library. This means that the file size is kept to a minimum.

Library panel

This can be used to store objects that you are going to use regularly, either within the same document or across several.

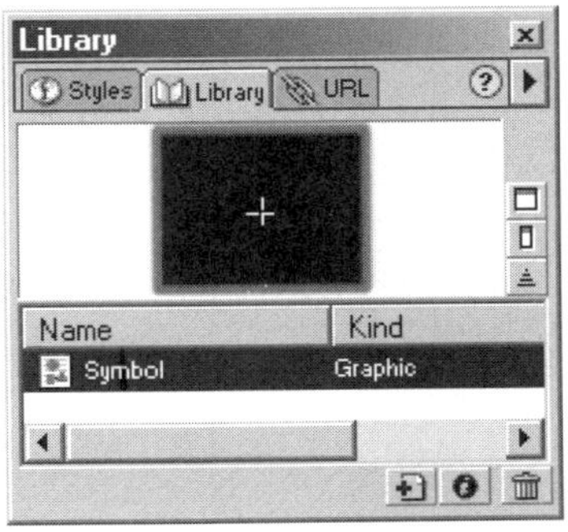

URL panel

This can be used to insert Web addresses (URLs) when you want to add hyperlinks to Fireworks objects.

URL stands for Uniform Resource Locator. It is used to create a unique name for every Web page or site. URLs can be inserted in Fireworks documents. The document can then be imported into a Web authoring program, such as Dreamweaver, and incorporated into a document for use on the Web. When it is displayed in a Web browser the URL link will become active i.e. when the user clicks on it they will be taken to the specified page.

Find and Replace panel

This can be used to find specified items within a Fireworks document and change them to something else. It covers text, fonts, colours and URLs.

The Find and Replace panel functions in a similar way to Find and Replace commands in a word processor such as Word. However, the Fireworks version is more versatile as it can search for text, fonts, colours and URLs.

Project Log panel

This can be used to export files and also select a group of files so that one process can be applied to them all.

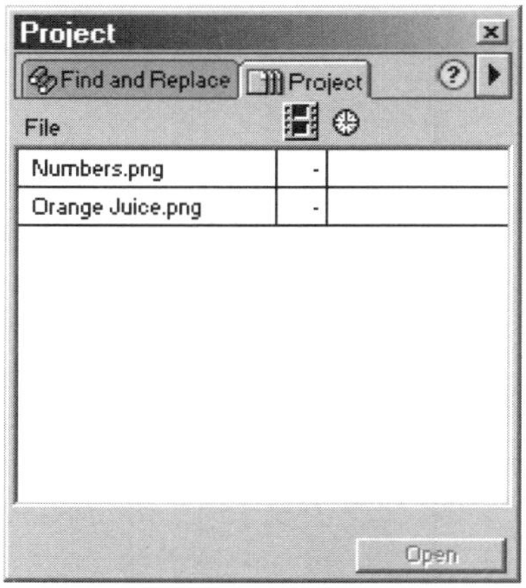

Preferences

The preferences in Fireworks enable users to customise the appearance of the program. There are five preferences panels and these can be accessed from the menu bar by selecting Edit>Preferences. Three of the preferences panels, Launch and Edit, Folders and Import, are associated mainly with importing items into Fireworks from other applications and these will be looked at in greater detail in Chapter Two. The other preferences are:

Make sure the Undo Steps option is set to a reasonably high number. Hopefully you will never have to undo 20–30 steps, but it is useful to have the option available.

General

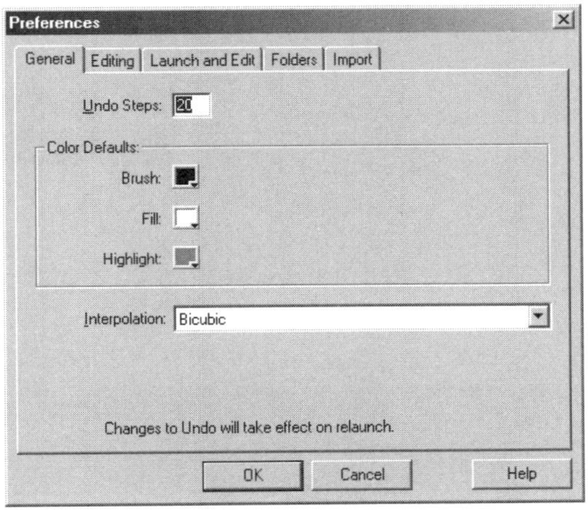

Interpolation is used when bitmap images are increased in size. The program adds pixels next to existing ones by estimating the colour they should be, based on the ones next to them.

Editing

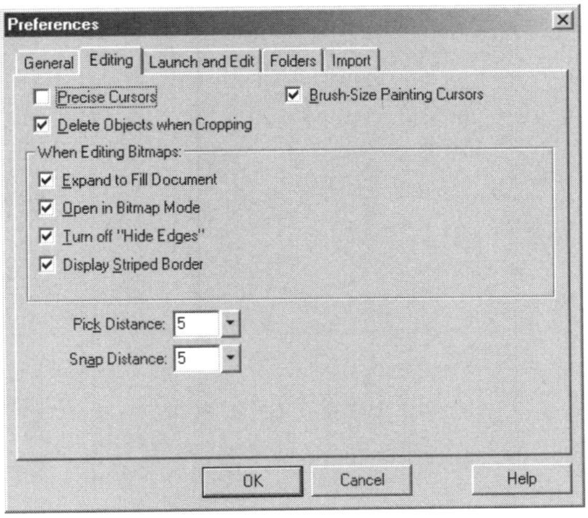

Bitmap images are those that are made up of physical dots of colour, which are known as pixels. The other type of image that can be created or imported into Fireworks is a vector image. This is created from a mathematical formula and means that the image is smaller than a comparable bitmap and it can be resized without losing any image quality.

Creating files

When Fireworks opens, the work area is blank. You then have a choice of creating a new document or opening an existing one. Both new documents and existing ones are opened in PNG format, which is the proprietary file format used by Fireworks. Do not be put off by this: once you have created or opened a document you can then save it in numerous other formats. This is known as exporting a document. Once this has been done, a new file is created in the specified format and the original Fireworks document remains.

PNG stands for Portable Network Graphic, which is a file format that can be used on the Web, although it has not gained such general popularity as GIFs or JPEGs.

If you want to create a new document there are a few options that can be specified first:

1 Select File>New from the menu bar

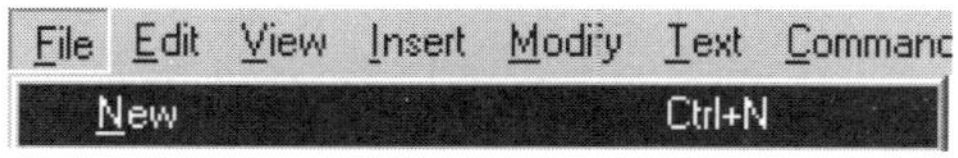

The canvas is the area on which you add content to your Fireworks documents. By default, it is white, but it can be made transparent or specified as a particular colour. If you specify a colour, this will appear behind any part of the canvas that has not had content added to it.

2 Enter values for the width, height and resolution of the new document

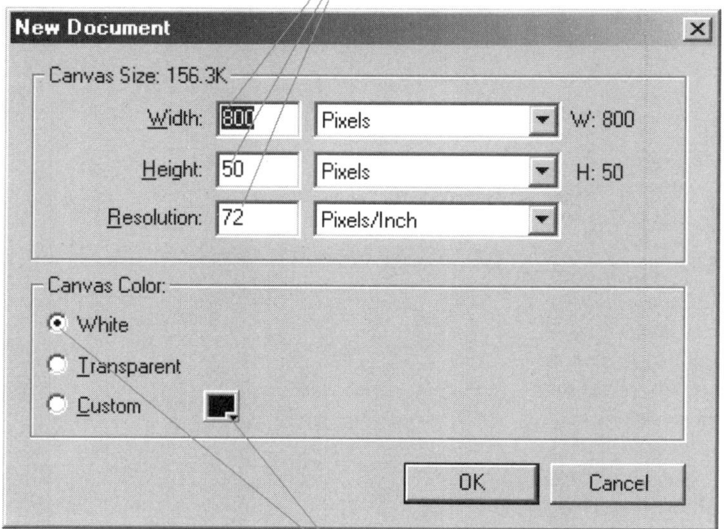

If you want to create a new file with an image you have copied from another application, the size of the canvas is automatically amended to the size of the image to be pasted.

3 Select a colour for the canvas i.e. the background

Opening files

Files created in formats other than PNG can be opened in Fireworks. However, when they are opened, they are done so in PNG format. To open existing files:

When an existing image is opened in Fireworks, the canvas is created at the exact same size as the image that is being opened. If you want to change the canvas size at any point of editing a document, select Modify>Canvas size from the menu bar and enter the required values for the height and width of the canvas.

1 Select File>Open from the menu bar

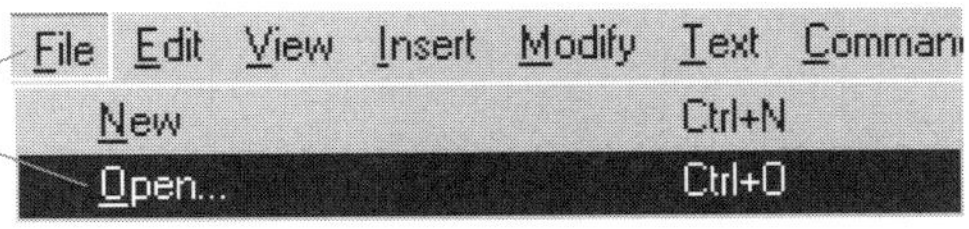

2 Select the file you want to open, from your file structure. Select Open (Windows and Mac)

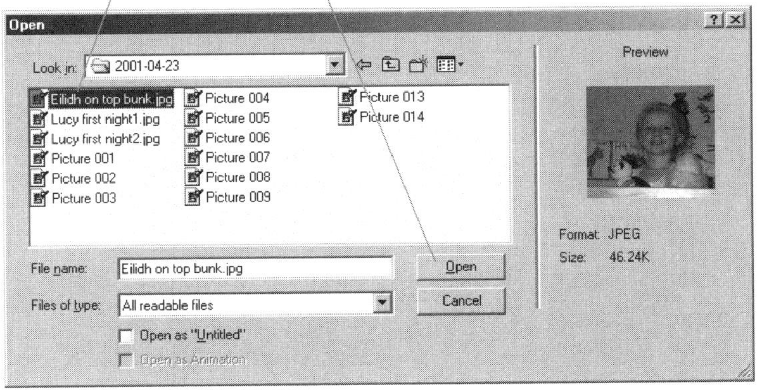

When a file from a format other than PNG is opened, the original file remains the same – the one opened in Fireworks is just a PNG copy of the original.

3 The file opens in the Fireworks work area. This is in PNG format, which is denoted by the icon here

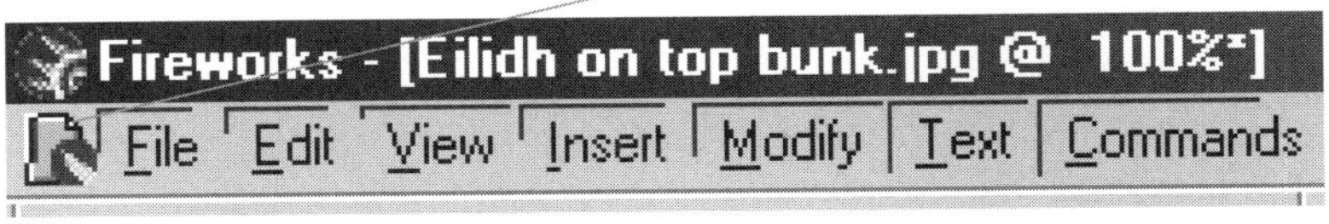

Importing files

The Import function can only be used when another document has already been opened. If there is no opened document, the Import function is greyed out i.e. unavailable.

When you are working with a program such as Fireworks, there will probably be frequent occasions when you want to combine more than one image. This can be done to create montages, or simply to insert an element from one image into another. This is done by importing an image into an existing one. To do this:

1 Make sure an image is already open and select File>Import from the menu bar

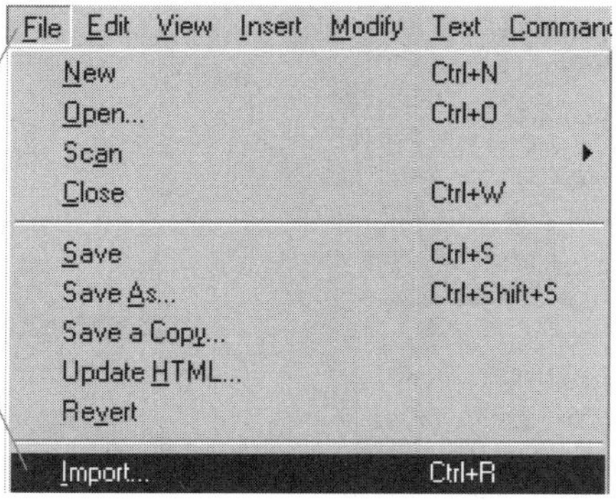

Fireworks supports a wide range of file formats, which can be imported. These include:

- *GIF*
- *JPEG*
- *TIFF*
- *BMP*
- *Targa*
- *EPS*
- *FH or FT (Freehand)*
- *PSD (Photoshop)*
- *AI or ART (Illustrator)*
- *CDR (CorelDraw)*

2 Select a file

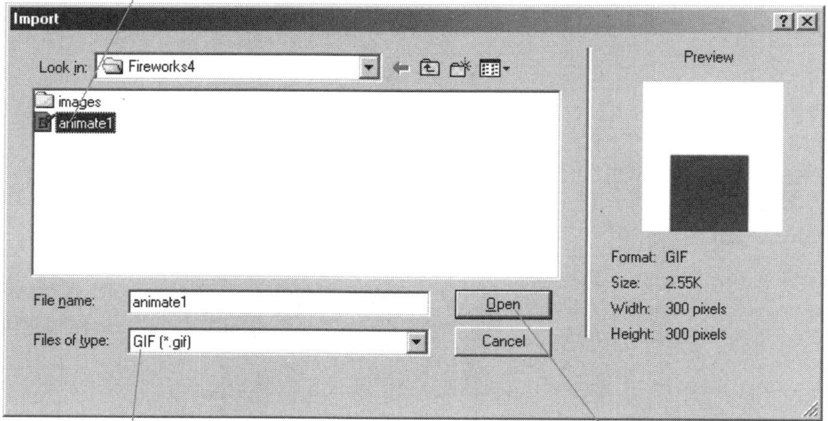

3 Select a file format

4 Select Open (Windows and Mac)

5 Click once with the cursor to insert the image

6 The imported image is placed on a new layer on top of the existing one

It is also possible to import images from scanners and digital cameras, as long as you have the relevant devices and drivers (software). For a scanner, select File>Scan and select the device. For a digital camera, select File>Import and select the device.

When separate layers are used, items on each layer can be edited independently of each other. In addition, layers can also be merged or blended together. For more on working with layers, see Chapter Seven.

For more on importing Photoshop images, see Chapter Six.

Saving files

Since Fireworks uses a variety of different file formats, there are also different choices for saving files, once they have been edited:

Save

The standard Save function can be used to save documents into the Fireworks proprietary file format, '–.png'. To do this:

If you want to save a Fireworks document in a format other than PNG then this cannot be done with the Save or Save As function. The Export function has to be used instead, *see next page.*

1. Select File>Save from the menu bar

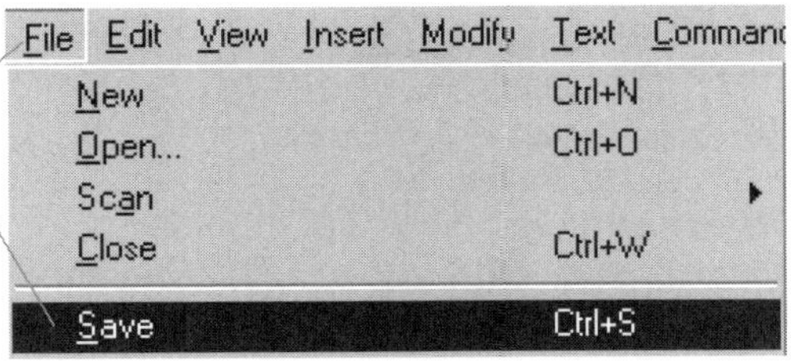

2. Select a location in which to save the file and select Save. The only option available in the Save as type box is PNG

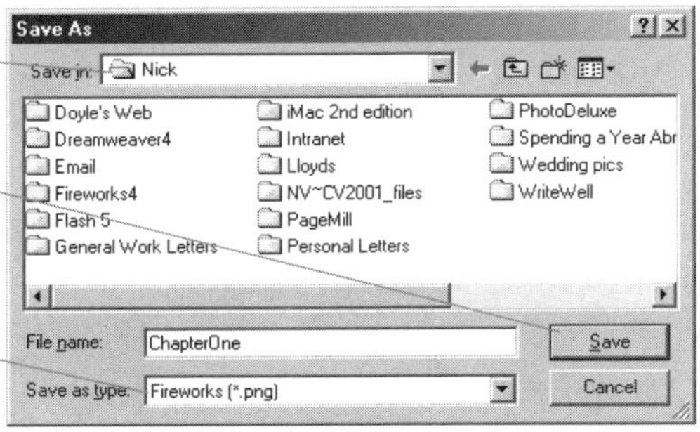

Save As

This is similar to Save, except that it can be used to make a copy of an existing PNG file. This is accessed by selecting File>Save As from the menu bar. By default, the document will be given the same name as the original and a warning dialog box will appear asking if you want to copy over the existing file. If you do, select Yes, if not give the file a different name.

Save As can also be used to save a file for the first time. In this respect it operates in the same way as the Save function.

Save a Copy

This is similar to the Save As function.

Exporting

Both files that are created in Fireworks, and those that have been opened from another file format, can be exported. This means they are saved in a file format other than PNG. This format can be specified before the file is exported. To export a file:

The concept of exporting can seem a little daunting at first but it is a function that is used frequently in Fireworks. Think of it as saving files.

Exporting images is closely associated with optimising them i.e. combining good quality with a small file size so that they can be downloaded quickly on a Web page. For more on this, see Chapter Five.

1 Select File>Export Preview from the menu bar

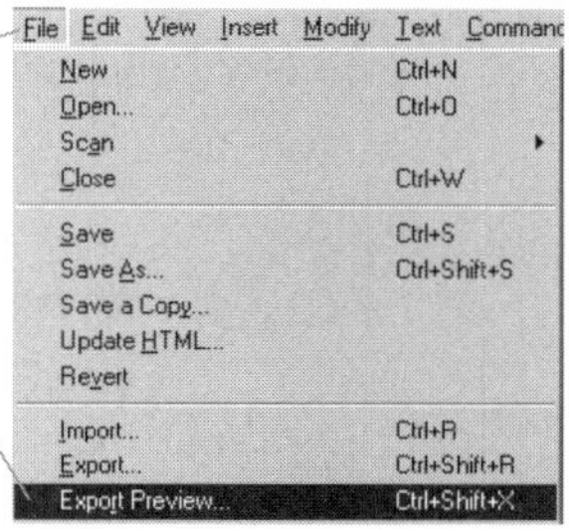

2 Click here to set the default Export format. (This will be used for all other files that are exported, unless specified otherwise)

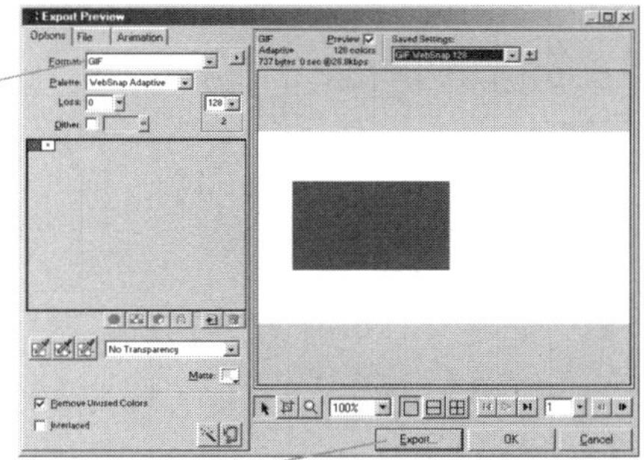

3 Select Export

If you know what the current Export settings are, the Export Preview step can be skipped. Instead, select File>Export from the menu bar and select a location into which to save the file.

4 Give the file a name

5 Select Save

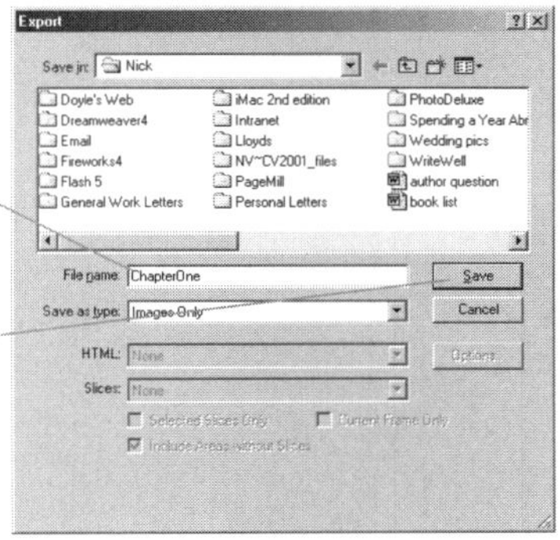

For a standard image the Save as type box in the Export dialog box can be left at Images Only. When using items such as rollovers, slices and hotspots, this requires a different setting and these issues are looked at in Chapters Eight and Nine.

Getting help

As with all Macromedia products, Fireworks has an extensive range of options for getting help:

Fireworks Help

This provides an online guide to all aspects of the program:

Select Help>Using Fireworks from the menu bar

Click here to access the Help contents

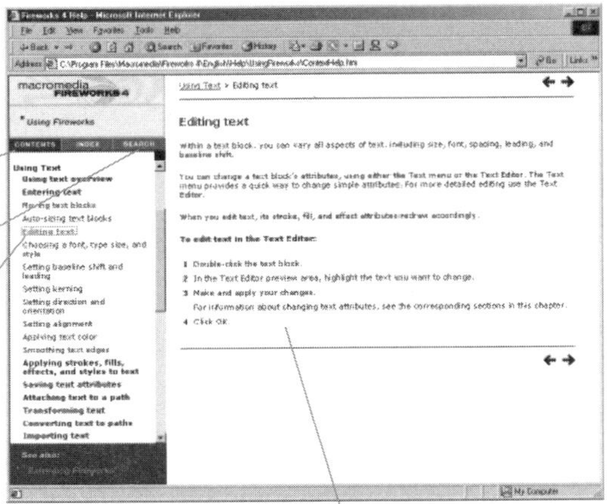

Click here to access topics

The selected topic appears here

Click here to search for specific topics within the online guide. The results appear in a dialog box from which you can select individual headings.

The Help menu also has links to Fireworks resources on the Macromedia Web site at www.macromedia.com/support/fireworks/ (no spaces). This provides help information about the program and also extensions that can be downloaded to expand its functionality.

Lessons

In addition to the online guide there are also six lessons that take you through some of the common tasks that can be performed with Fireworks:

1 Select Help>Lessons from the menu bar

2 Click on one of the topics to be taken through the interactive lessons

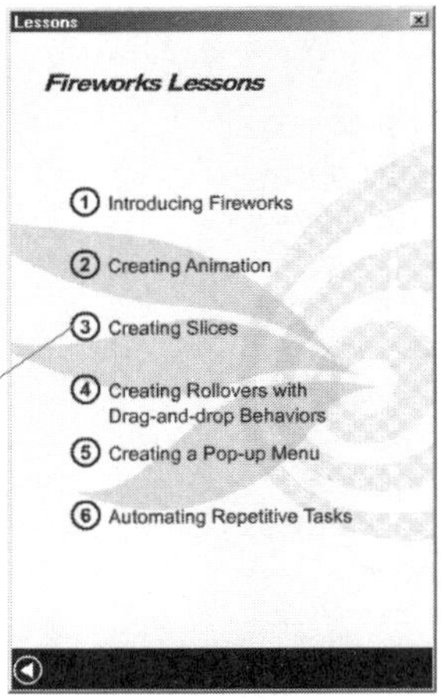

The Help menu also enables you to register your copy of Fireworks online. This entitles you to news about upgrades, technical support and the latest Fireworks news.

Working with images

Either bitmap or vector images can be used in Fireworks. This chapter explains the difference between the two and discusses some of the issues connected with working with both types. It also shows some editing techniques that can be applied to images.

Covers

Chapter Two

Bitmaps

About bitmaps

Fireworks can be used to create and edit two types of image files: bitmaps and vector images. Bitmaps are images that are made up of physical dots of colour, known as pixels. In this respect, bitmaps can be thought of as 'real' images. However, bitmaps have some limitations:

- They tend to result in larger file sizes than their vector counterparts
- They usually suffer from a deterioration in quality when they are resized. This is because each individual pixel has to expand or contract to make an image larger or smaller. This is particularly noticeable when an image is increased in size, since each pixel has to cover a greater area

The overall size of a bitmap depends on the amount of colour information stored within each pixel. This can vary from 8 bits to 24 bits. Bitmaps in 24-bit colour are much bigger in size.

Bitmap images appear most commonly in the form of digital photographs.

A range of editing functions can be applied to bitmaps including recolouring, cloning, cropping and blurring. Some of the tools in the tools panel can only be used on bitmaps, in which case the image mode automatically switches to bitmap mode when the tool is selected.

The two modes in Fireworks are Bitmap mode and Vector mode. You can switch between modes with images of different types, but only some of the tools in the tools panel are available for each mode. For more information on switching modes, see pages 33–34.

Bitmaps appear most commonly as photographic images, which can then have a variety of editing techniques applied to them

Bitmap preferences

The Preferences menu contains options that determine how bitmaps are handled and displayed within Fireworks. To set these preferences:

When you are working in bitmap mode, this is indicated by the words 'Bitmap mode' at the top of the active window, next to the file name.

1. Select Edit> Preferences from the menu bar

2. Select the Editing tab

As well as the striped border indicating that you are in bitmap mode, there is also a Stop icon that appears at the bottom of the window. This is greyed out when you switch to vector mode.

Check this box to enable editing of all of the pixels within the document. If it is deselected, only the pixels within a selected part of the image will be editable

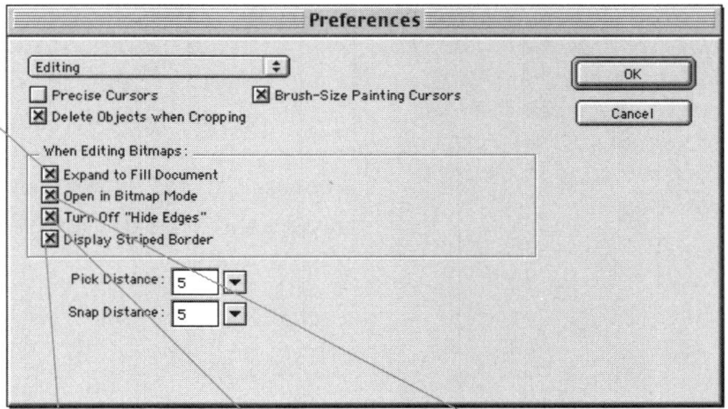

Check this box to display a striped border round the entire bitmap

Check this box to disable the striped border whenever an image is opened in bitmap mode

Check this box to specify that all images that are opened are done so in bitmap mode

Vectors

Vector images can appear the same as bitmap ones, but they are created from mathematical equations rather than physical pixels of colour. However, this does not mean they are limited in what you can do with them and the types of items that can be created. Lines, fills, colours, textures and text can all be created with vectors, as can more complex items such as rollover images, hotspots and sliced images.

Rollover images are ones that change appearance when the cursor is moved over them on a Web page. Hotspots are images that have hyperlinks assigned to particular parts of them. Slices are images that are broken (or sliced) into smaller parts. The whole image can then be recreated on a Web page by re-assembling the slices of the image.

The two main advantages of vector images are:

- Since they are based on a mathematical equation rather than a physical object, they create files that are much smaller in size than their bitmap counterparts. This is an important consideration when designing items for use on a Web site
- It is possible to resize vector images without losing any image quality. This is because the resized image relies on a newly created mathematical equation rather than stretching pixels. This gives much greater flexibility to designers

Vectors can be used to design entire Web sites or for items such as navigation bars or buttons.

Vector images can be created using items such as fills, lines and text

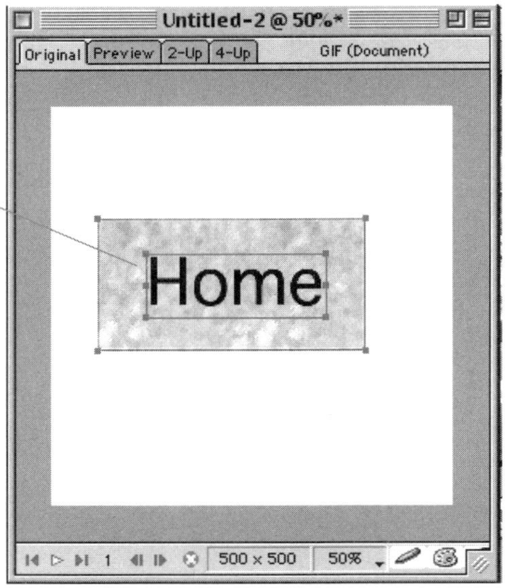

Switching modes

Depending on the bitmap preferences that have been selected (see page 31) a thick border will appear around an image when it is in bitmap mode.

Vector images cannot have areas selected in the same way as bitmaps, because there are no physical pixels to select. If you want to use tools like the Marquee, Lasso, Eraser, Magic Wand and Rubber Stamp the mode has to be switched to bitmap. See tip below for details about converting a vector image into a bitmap one.

If you want to use a bitmap tool on a vector image, that image has to first be converted into a bitmap. To do this, select the vector image and select Modify>Convert to Bitmap from the menu bar.

It is possible to switch between bitmap and vector mode for any image that is a bitmap i.e. one that contains pixels rather than vectors.

Switching to bitmap mode

There are several ways to access bitmap mode:

Select the bitmap with any of these tools

Marquee

Magic Wand

Eraser

Rubber Stamp

Lasso

Double-click on the image with the Pointer tool

Select Modify> Edit Bitmap from the menu bar

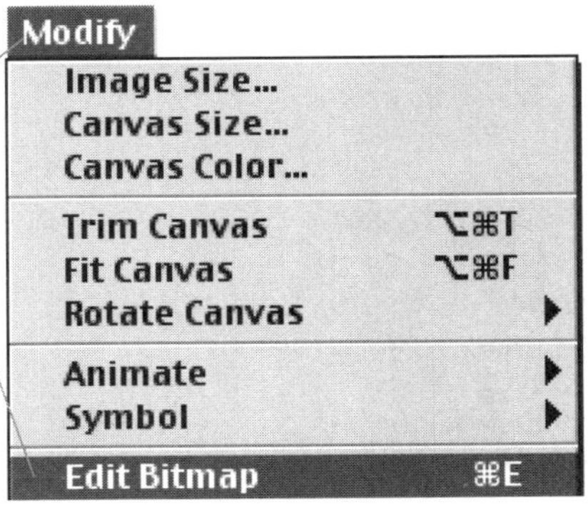

Switching to vector mode

To switch from bitmap mode to vector mode:

Double-click outside the bitmap border, using any tool

Bitmap and vector images can be included within the same document. However, you will have to switch modes to perform certain editing tasks on each item.

Click the Stop button that appears at the bottom of the window when in bitmap mode

When vectors and bitmaps are added to the same document, they are placed on different layers within the image. This makes it easier to edit them independently from each other. It is also possible to switch between modes using these layers – click on the layer which contains a bitmap or a vector image to switch to that mode. Once you have finished editing the items in your image it can be saved so that all of the layers are combined. For more information about working with layers, see Chapter Seven.

Select Modify>Exit Bitmap Mode from the menu bar

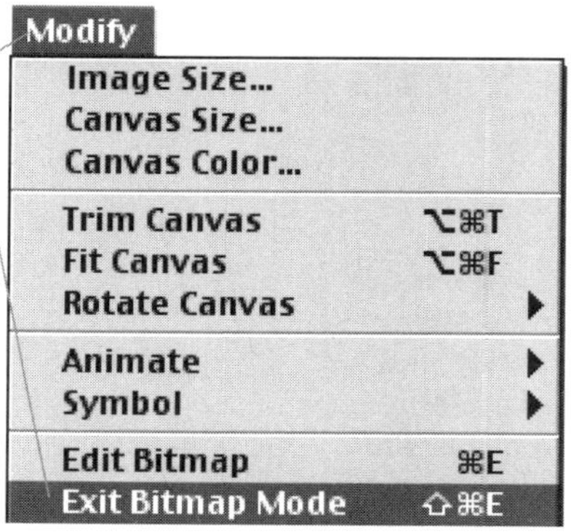

Press the Esc key on the keyboard

Identifying selected items

When working with both vectors and bitmaps it is important to know when particular items are selected. As shown on page 30, bitmaps are identified, by default, by a thick green border around them.

Identifying vector selections

Vector items can be identified by thin lines around their border. When an object is selected this is light-blue. When you pass the cursor over a vector object that is not selected, the border appears red, to show the boundaries of the object even though it is not selected.

The blue border around a vector object denotes its path and points. For more information on this, see the next page.

To select a vector object, click on it once with the Pointer tool. A light-blue border will appear around the object, with small rectangles at the points where a border changes direction

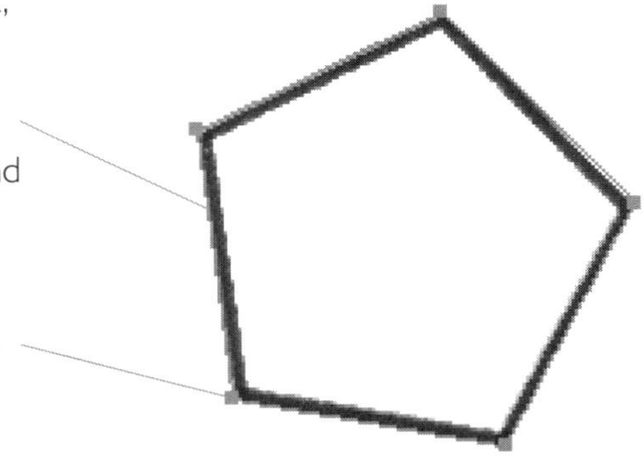

Bitmaps can be selected when in vector mode, in which case they also display a blue border. It is possible to identify whether an object is a bitmap or a vector by selecting it with the Subselection tool. For a vector, the small rectangular points will be hollow, while for a bitmap they will be solid.

To select numerous vector objects, hold down the Shift key and click on each item in turn

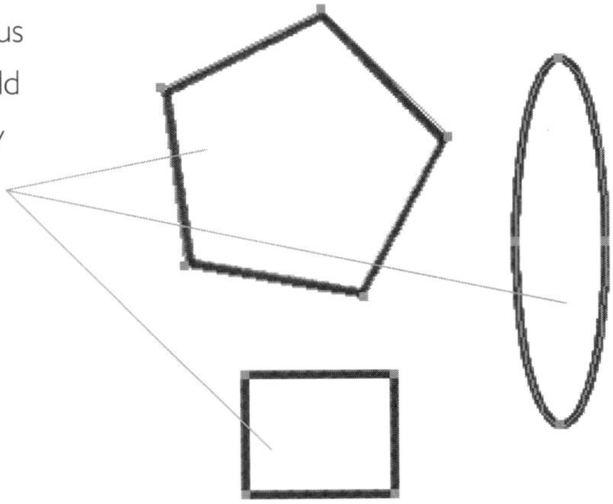

Points and paths

Since vectors are based on mathematical calculations, they have clearly defined paths and points as items of reference. A path is a line, which may be straight or curved, made up of straight line segments and points when the path changes direction. Points are denoted by small rectangles on an object's path. A path can be as simple or as complicated as you want:

A simple path: a straight line between two points

A more complex path, with points occurring whenever there is a change in direction of the path

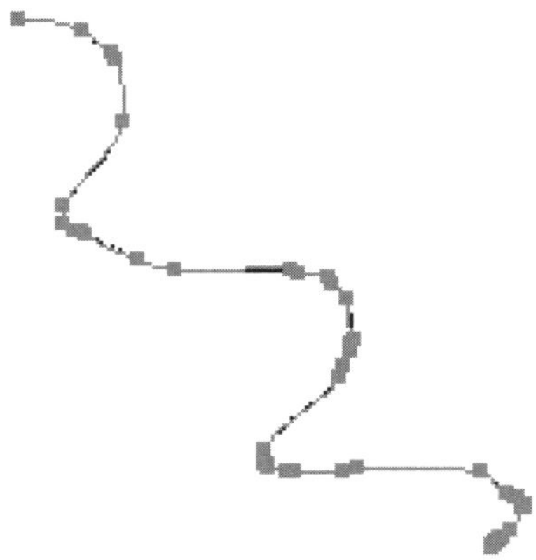

When separate paths are created, they are done so on different layers. However, it is possible to combine different paths. To do this, select the paths you want to combine by holding down Shift and clicking on each path (even when they are on separate layers this should select them all). Select Modify>Join from the menu bar to create a composite path. Paths can be overlapping to do this, but they do not have to be.

Vector paths can be converted into bitmaps by selecting the object and selecting Modify>Convert to Bitmap from the menu bar. This then places a rectangular border around the object, regardless of its vector appearance

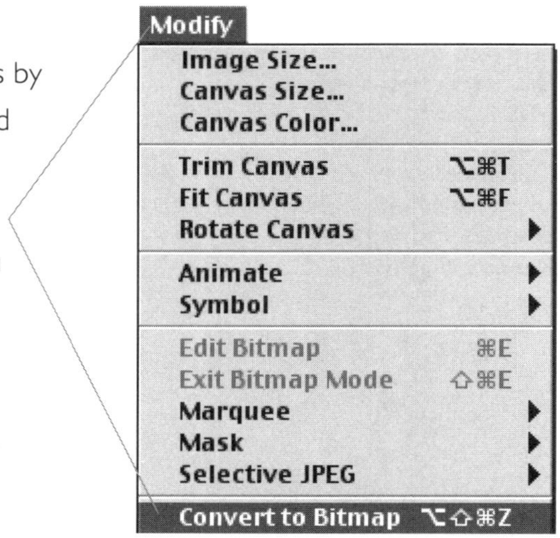

Once a vector has been converted into a bitmap, some of the tools, such as the Freeform tool, cannot be used on the vector object. If the tool is unavailable, a warning dialog box will appear alerting you to this.

Working with paths

In vector mode there is a great deal of flexibility for working with objects created with paths. It is possible to reshape them, resize them and move them, using the Pointer and the Subselection tools.

When reshaping vectors, the Subselection tool works in a similar way to the Pen tool. For more information about this, see Chapter Four.

Reshaping vectors

1 Select the Subselection tool and select a vector object by clicking on it once

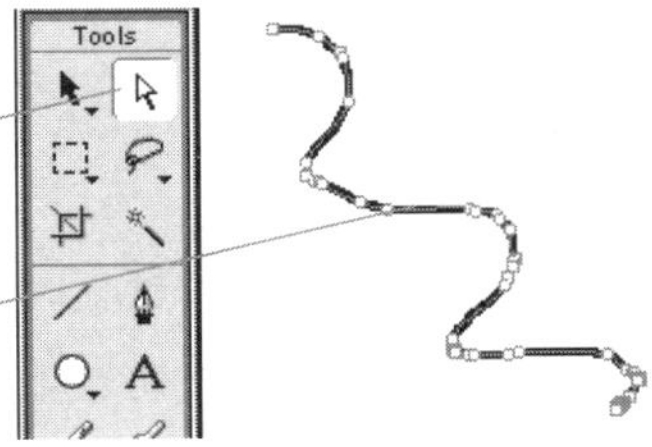

2 Click and drag a point to reshape the object

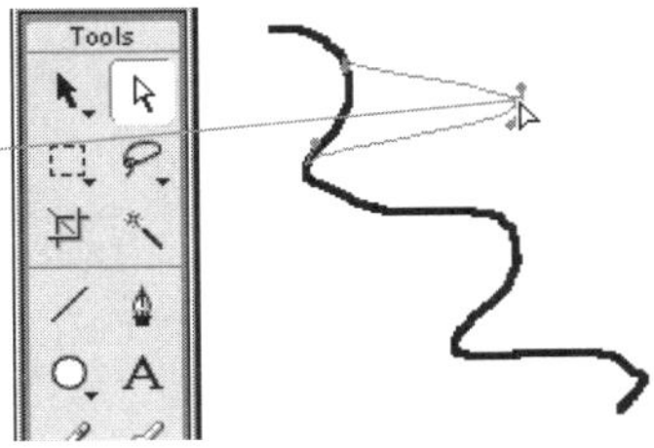

The Freeform tool can also be used to reshape vector objects. This can be used to create a more curved appearance.

Moving vectors

For more information about resizing objects, see Chapter Four.

With the Subselection tool, click and drag on a path

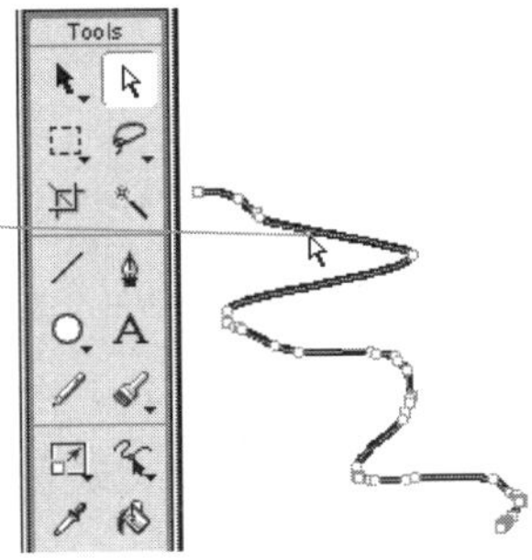

With the Pointer tool, click and drag anywhere on the vector object

Resizing images

Resizing an entire image is not the same as resizing individual elements within it. It is best to resize the whole image once you have finished all of the editing tasks that you need to perform on it.

You do not have to use the Trim Canvas option, but if you do not, you may find that you have some unwanted space around your image. This could be a problem on a Web page, since the space will be treated as part of the image and you will not be able to add any more content to this area. This could then start to impact on the overall design of the page.

Even vector images are calculated in pixels when it comes to the overall image size.

Check the Resample Image box if you want pixels to be added when you increase the size of the image. This is educated guesswork that tries to ensure that image quality is maintained.

When working with images in Fireworks there will be plenty of occasions when you will want to edit the overall size of an image. This may be to ensure it fits properly on a Web page, or for printing a hard copy. This may be particularly useful if you are printing photographs. To do this:

1. Select Modify> Trim Canvas from the menu bar. This reduces the background to the widest points of the image

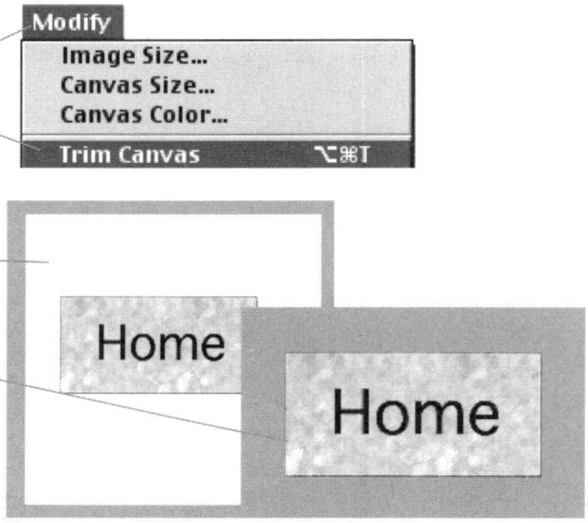

2. Select Modify> Image Size from the menu bar

3. Enter values here to change the size of the image

4. Enter values here for a specific print size

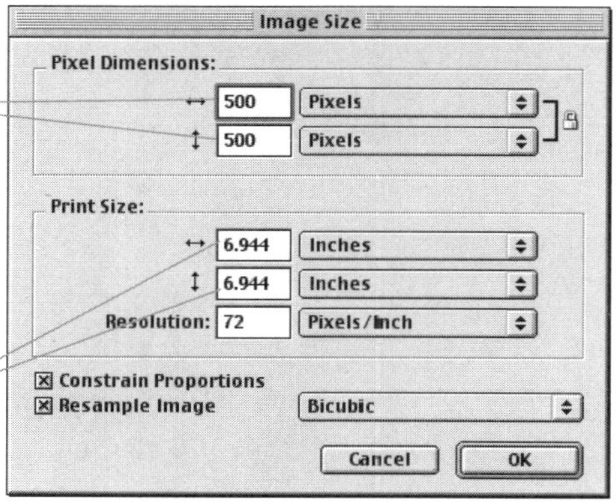

Image editing

Fireworks has some functions for enhancing photographic images. However, they are generally not as sophisticated or extensive as those in a program such as Photoshop. They are useful for quick editing techniques, but nothing too complex.

The Auto Levels option can be used to instruct Fireworks to automatically adjust a range of colour options, such as brightness and contrast, colour levels and hue and saturation. However, this can be a bit hit and miss so be prepared to use the Undo button if you do not like the end result.

Adjusting colour

Select Xtras>Adjust Color from the menu bar and select the effect you want to apply. Some simple effects can be achieved and also some more surreal ones

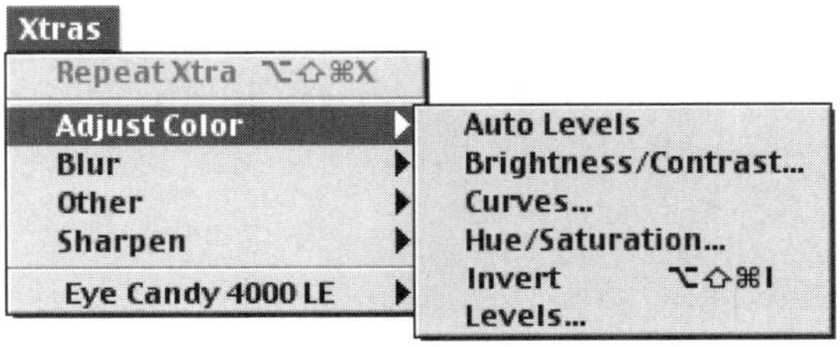

Original

Brightness and Contrast

Hue and Saturation

Invert

Experiment with different combinations of brightness and contrast and hue and saturation to see what kind of effects can be achieved. When you are working with images you may not always want to use realistic ones.

Blurring and sharpening

Blurring can be used to give an image a soft focus effect, while sharpening can be used to give a crisper appearance to an image that appears slightly out of focus. Both of these have different options that can be selected, which vary the amount of the effect that is applied. To use blurring and sharpening:

Specific areas of an image can have blurring or sharpening applied to them, while leaving the rest of the image untouched. To do this, select an area with the Marquee or the Lasso tools and then apply the required effect to the selected area. This is a useful way to convey the impression of speed for a vehicle such as a car or a motorbike. Select the background behind a vehicle (you could select the vehicle itself and then invert the selection by clicking on Modify>Marquee>Select Inverse from the menu bar) and apply blur to the background. Experiment with different levels until you achieve the right effect.

Select Xtras>Blur (or Sharpen) from the menu bar and then select the amount of the effect that you want to apply

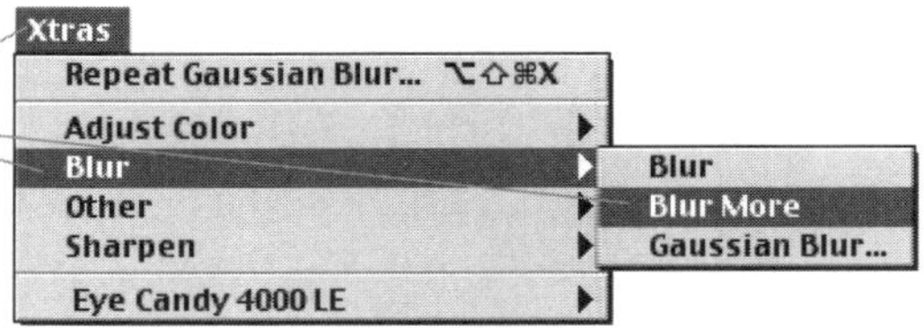

Eye Candy

This can be used to add weird and wonderful special effects to an image. It can be previewed in Fireworks, but the effects themselves have to be bought separately:

Select Xtras>Eye Candy from the menu bar. Preview the effect here and click here to buy it

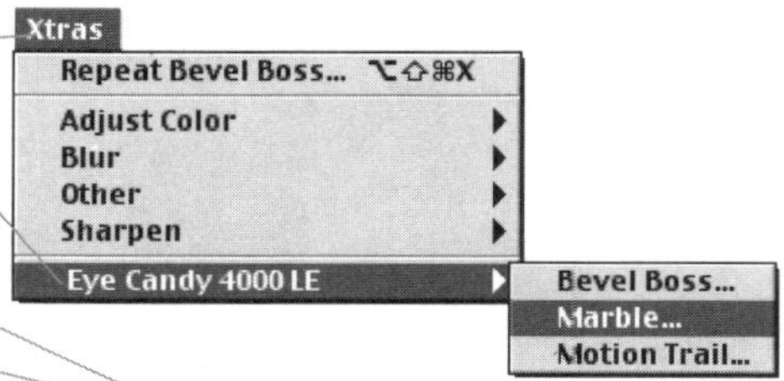

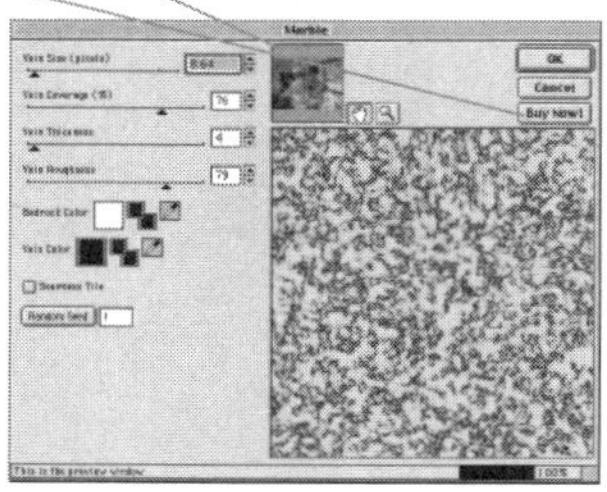

Creating objects

Fireworks has an extensive array of options available for creating graphical objects. This chapter shows how to use some of the drawing tools and it also details the panels that can be used to edit and enhance objects.

Covers

Chapter Three

Drawing modifiers

Objects are created in Fireworks by using the drawing tools in the Tools panel. This chapter will look specifically at the tools that are used for creating objects, while the next chapter will cover those that are used to edit existing objects.

For all of the tools used to create objects, modifiers can be accessed to specify fill and stroke colours. This can either be done before the object is created or it can be used to edit the stroke and fill colour of an existing object. The modifiers are located underneath the tools on the Tools panel:

If the Tools panel is not visible, select Window>Tools from the menu bar.

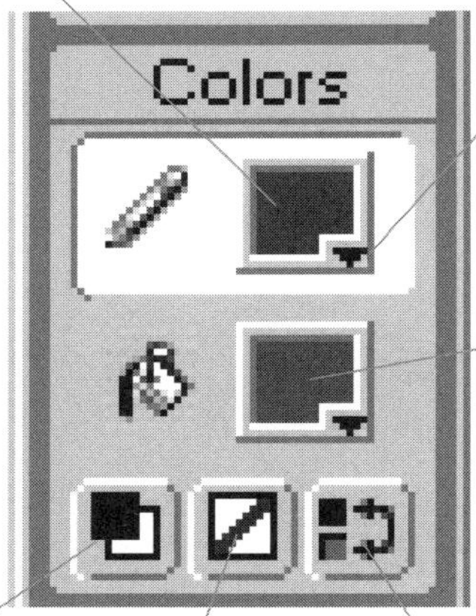

Stroke and fill colours can also be selected and mixed in the Swatches and Mixer panels.

The default colours are black for stroke and white for fill. These can be amended by selecting Edit>Preferences from the menu bar and changing the required settings under the General tab.

Drawing tools

Rectangle set

The tools that appear with the Rectangle tool as the default are the ones to use if you want to create geometric shapes such as squares and circles. Each tool is used to create objects by selecting it from the Tools panel and then clicking and dragging on the work area. Objects will be created with the currently selected stroke and fill attributes. These tools are:

To draw a perfect circle or square select the Ellipse (or Rectangle) tool and hold down the Shift key while drawing the object.

Rectangle tool

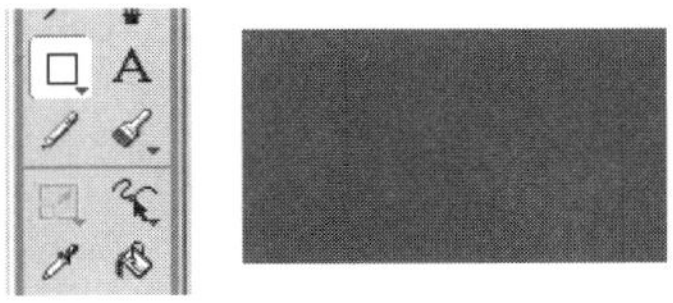

Rounded Rectangle tool

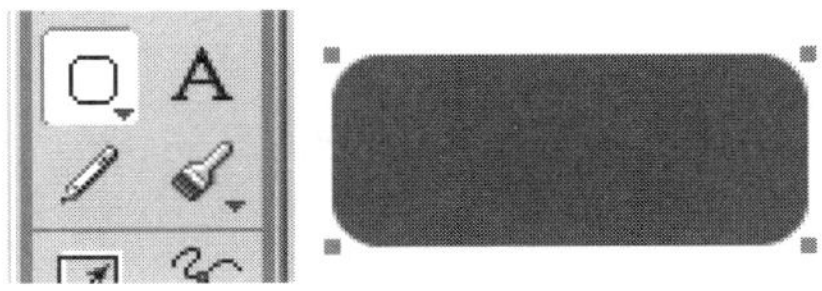

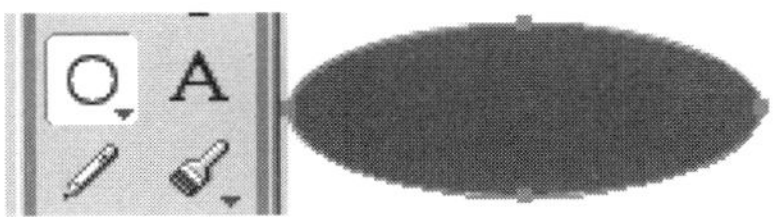

Ellipse tool

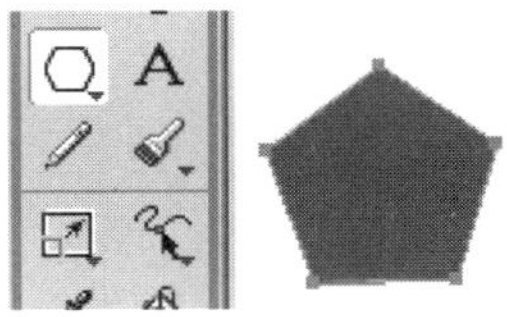

Polygon tool

When using the Rounded Rectangle tool the degree of roundness can be altered in the Object panel. To access the Object panel, select Window>Object from the menu bar.

Click here and drag the slider to change the amount of roundness for the corners of a rectangle

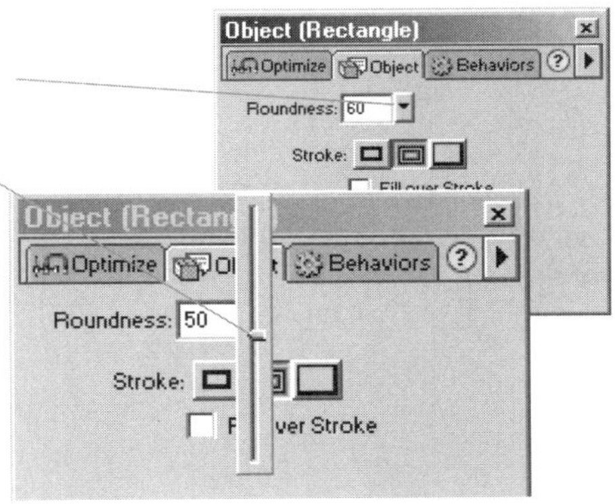

Pen tool

This is used to create lines and items called Bezier curves, which are shapes created based on mathematical formulae. It can also be used to create shapes in a similar way to producing a dot-to-dot picture. To create straight-lined objects with the Pen tool:

1. Select the Pen tool and click once on the work area. This is the start point of the object

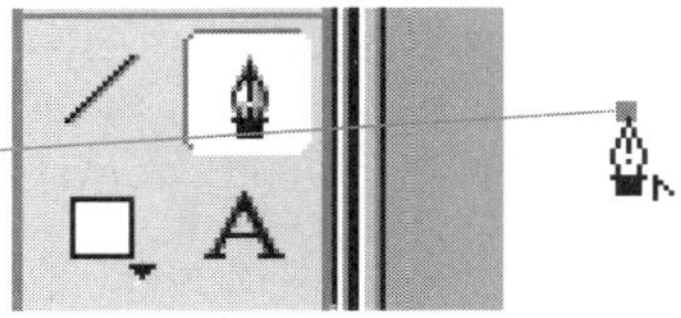

Objects created with the Pen tool can be edited with the Subselection tool.

2. Click on another point to create a straight line

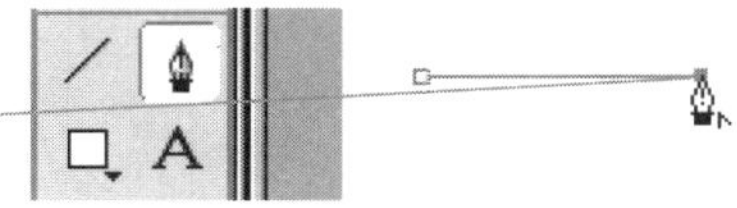

It can take a bit of practice to get exactly the right shapes with the Pen tool. But it is worth persevering with as it can be a flexible and powerful tool when used to its full potential.

3. Continue with this technique and click back on the start point to create an enclosed object

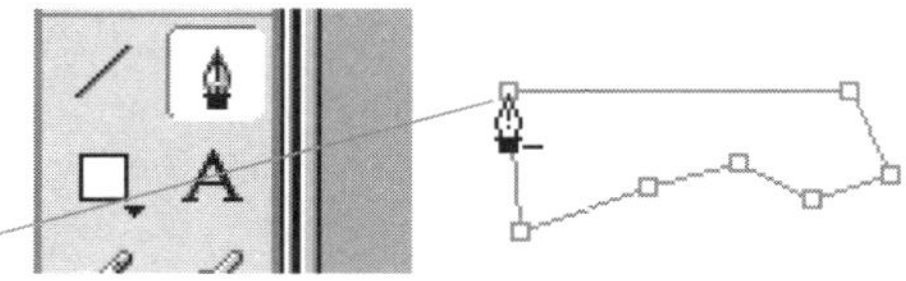

To create a curved object:

You can add new points to an existing path by using the Pen tool. To do this, click once anywhere on a path where there is not already a point.

1. Select the Pen tool and click and drag to create a line

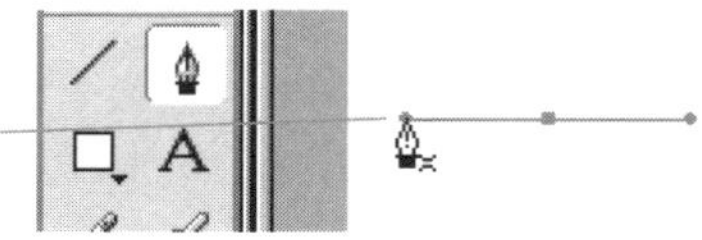

2. Click and drag to continue adding curves or click once for straight lines

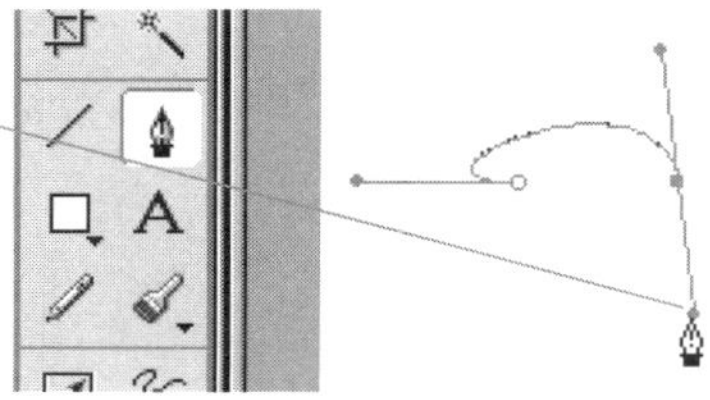

Line tool

This is used to draw straight lines.

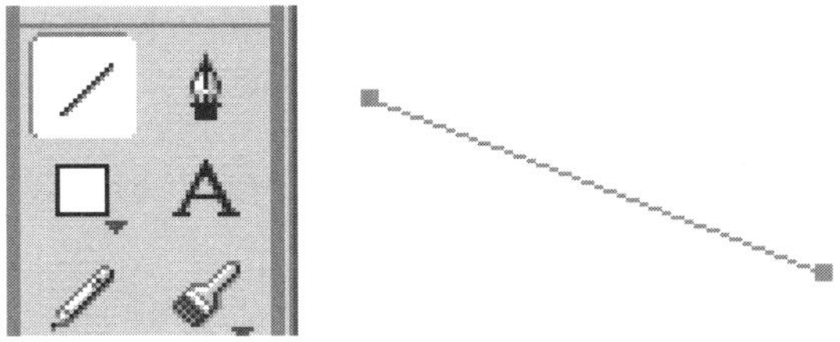

Objects created with the Line, Pencil and Brush tools are vector items and can be edited accordingly.

Pencil tool

This is used to draw freehand lines.

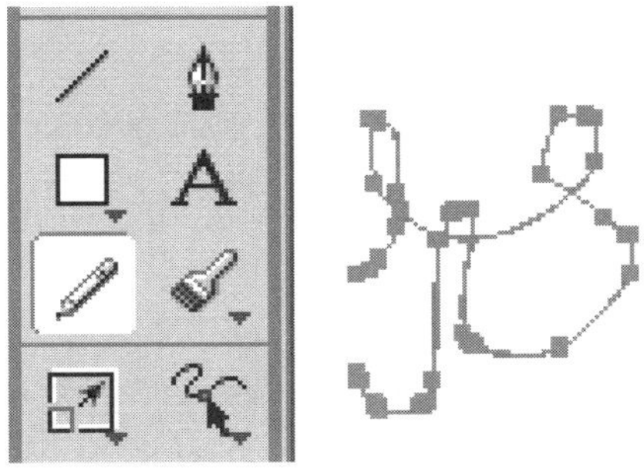

The attributes of the Line, Pencil and Brush tools can all be edited with the Stroke panel. This is looked at on page 50.

Brush tool

This is used to create the effect of lines drawn with a large paintbrush.

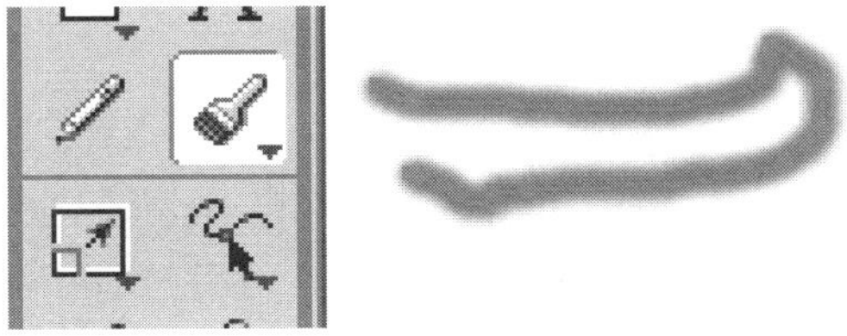

To use the Paint Bucket tool, click once on it on the Tools panel, select a fill colour and then click once inside the object whose fill you want to edit. The whole area will then be filled with the specified fill colour.

Paint Bucket tool

This is used to add or change the fill colour of an object.

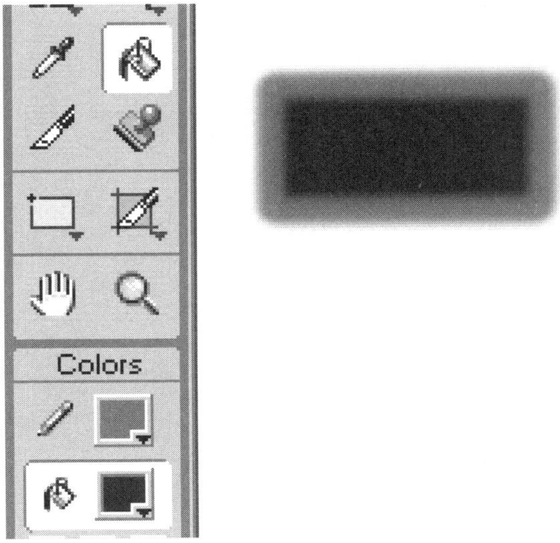

Adding text

When creating objects, text can be as important an element as colour or shape. Text can be used with images for items such as headings, captions and labels for buttons on a Web page. To add text to an image:

When you click on the canvas a text box is inserted at that point. As the text is typed into the text dialog box it appears at this point on the canvas too. Do not worry if it is not in the right position at this point; it is easy to drag and drop it into position when you have finished entering your text.

1 Select the Text tool from the Tools panel

2 Click once on the canvas. This will activate the text dialog box and insert a text box on the canvas

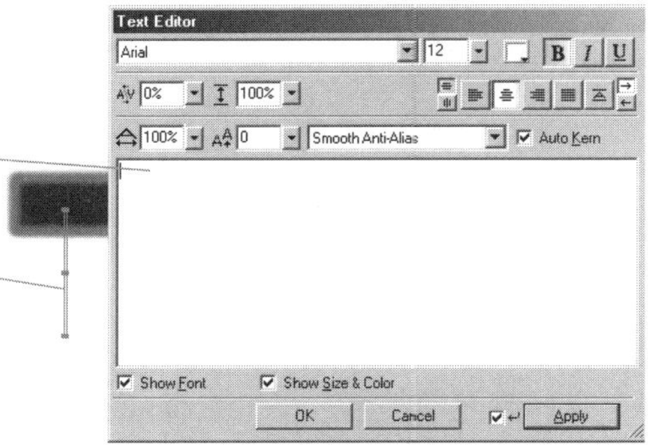

Positioning text is one function where it is useful to zoom in on the element being positioned. This will allow for greater accuracy. If you are having trouble positioning it exactly where you want, select View>Grid from the menu bar and make sure that Snap to Grid is deselected.

3 Select formatting options and enter text

Click here to select font, size, colour and formatting

Click here to select alignment

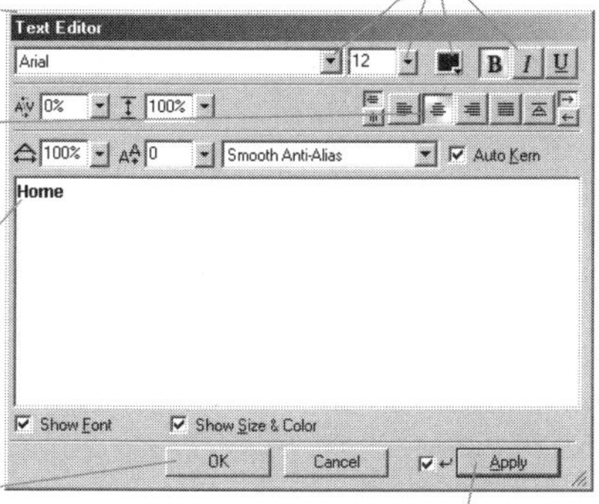

Enter text here

Select OK to apply the changes and exit the text dialog box

Select Apply to preview the changes without leaving the text dialog box

Once an image has been saved it is not then possible to edit text boxes independently from the rest of the image.

Text can be edited by double-clicking on the text box on the canvas.

Viewing objects

When creating and editing objects, it is useful to be able to view them at different magnifications. For instance, you may want to zoom in to edit a small part of an object and then view the whole of the object within one screen. There are several ways to do this:

Zoom tool

Select the Zoom tool and click once to increase the magnification. This goes as high as 6400%

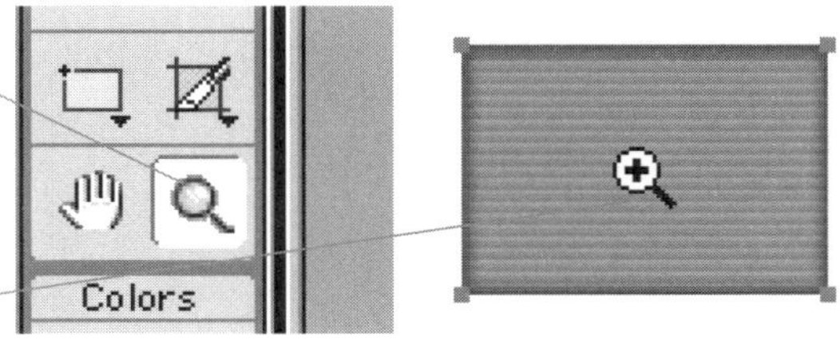

Magnification can be decreased by selecting the Zoom tool, holding down the Alt key and clicking within the work area.

Menu bar

Select View and then the required viewing option. Select Magnification to access a sub-menu of options

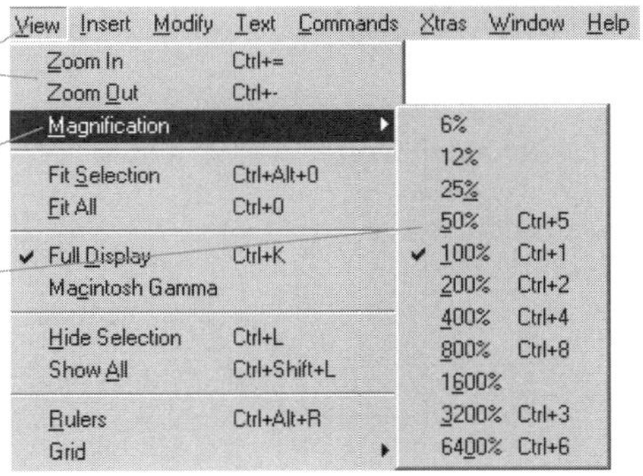

When working with images it is always a good idea to zoom in to certain areas to make sure it is exactly as intended. This is particularly important for items such as straight lines that have to join exactly.

Document window

Click here next to the Mini Launcher to access the magnification menu

Fill panel

When working with objects the Fill panel provides a wide range of options for adding content within them. This gives greater flexibility than the standard fill colours that can be selected from the Tools panel. The Fill panel can be used to add patterns and textures to an object and it can be used as a powerful design tool. To use the Fill panel:

It is perfectly acceptable to use solid colours for the fill of objects, and there will be times when this is preferable to more artistic designs.

1. Select Window>Fill from the menu bar to access the Fill panel

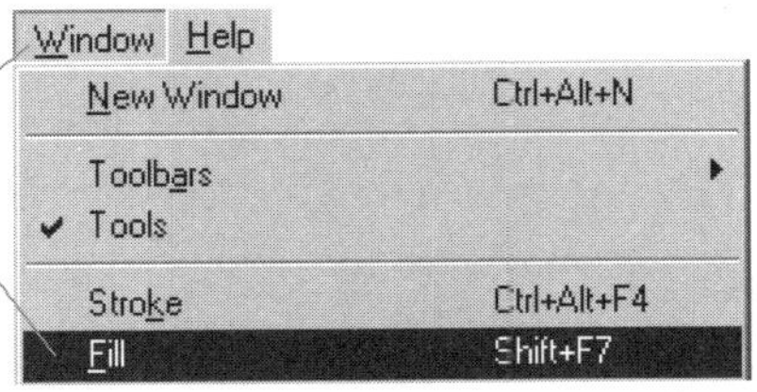

2. The currently selected solid fill colour on the Tools panel is displayed here

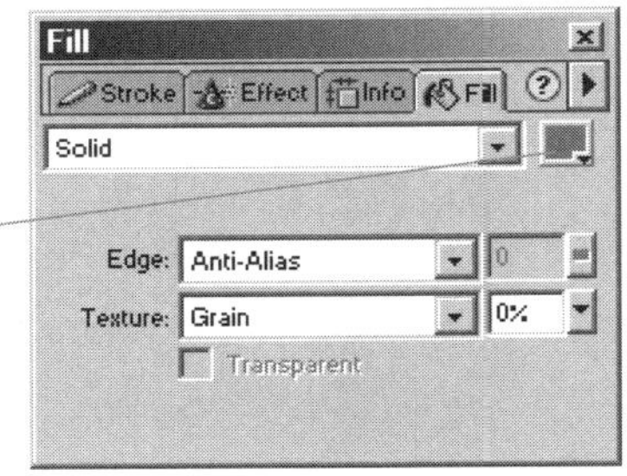

You can change the solid colour selection in the Fill panel by clicking on the colour box. The new colour will then also be the one in the fill box on the Tools panel.

3. Click here to access the menu for fill patterns

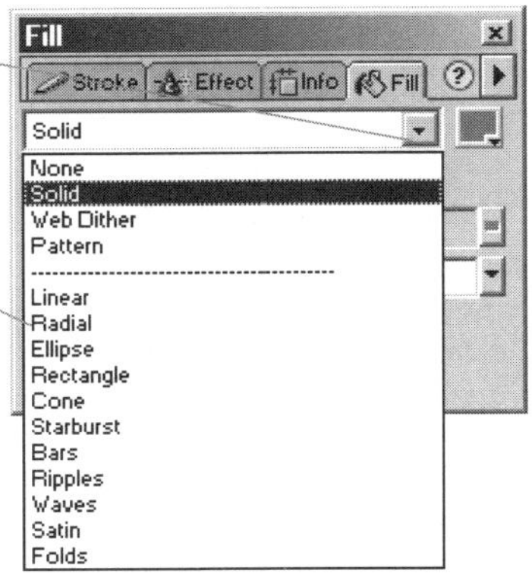

The Edit button next to the colour gradient scheme can be used to edit the currently selected scheme. It accesses a dialog box in which you can drag markers which increase or decrease the amounts of the colours in the scheme. This way, you can create your own custom designs.

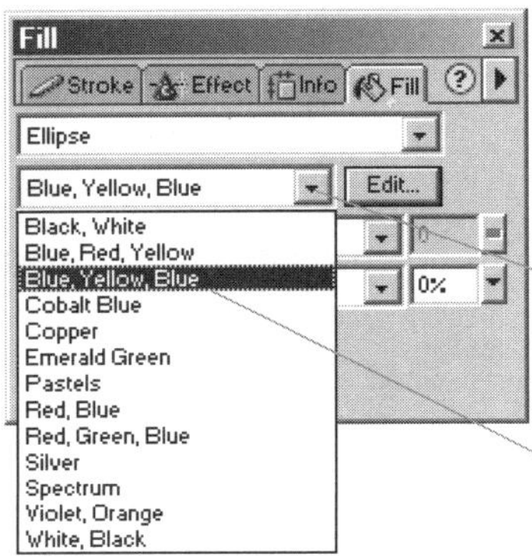

4. Click here to select a colour gradient scheme

Anti-alias edges give a smoother appearance to the edges of objects. This is particularly effective for items such as circles or ovals. The Hard option creates a straighter, but less forgiving, edge and is better suited to items such as rectangles and squares. The feather option creates a blurred effect around the edges. The level of this can be altered (i.e. more or less of the edge area can be blurred) and it is a good option if you want to blend the object into the background.

5 Click here to select a style for the edges of the fill

6 Click here to select texture

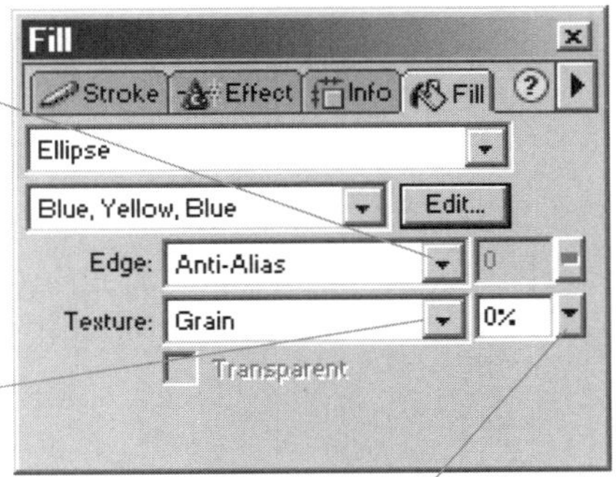

7 Click here to select the amount of texture that is to be applied

Some examples of how the Fill panel can be used on objects:

Ellipse fill, copper gradient, anti-alias edges and Chiffon texture at 50%

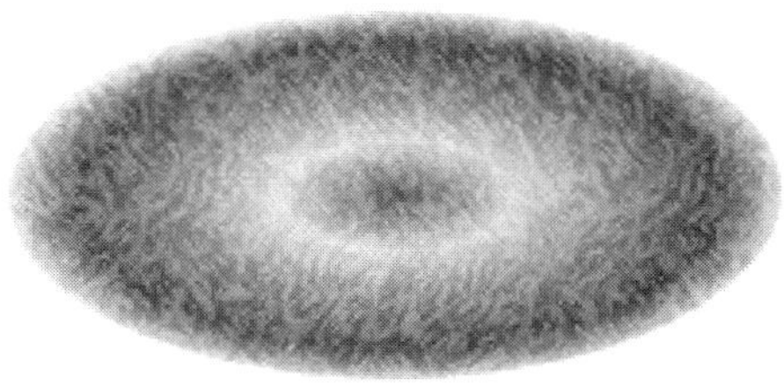

The Fill panel is an excellent way to create buttons for Web pages. However, do not get too carried away with surreal designs. This may look striking initially, but the effect can become tiresome when viewed frequently. Tailor the design to the type of site you are creating.

Starburst fill, pastels gradient, feather edges and Confetti texture at 80%

Stroke panel

The Stroke panel is similar to the Fill panel in that it can be used to specify and change attributes of the stroke of an object. This can be a straight line, or the border around an object. To use the Stroke panel:

1 Select Window>Stroke from the menu bar to access the Stroke panel

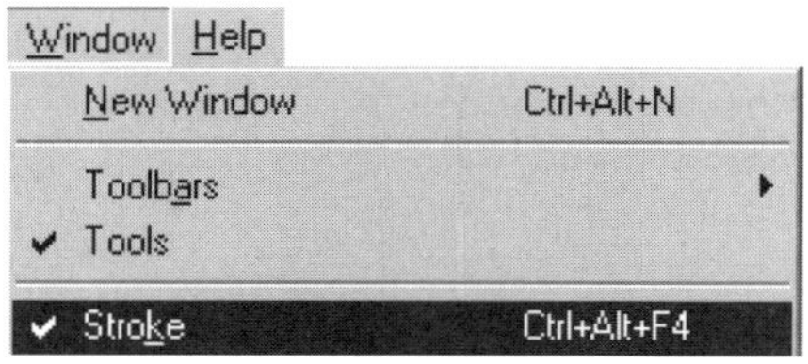

An object has to be selected for the attributes in the Stroke panel to be visible.

2 The currently selected stroke attributes are displayed here

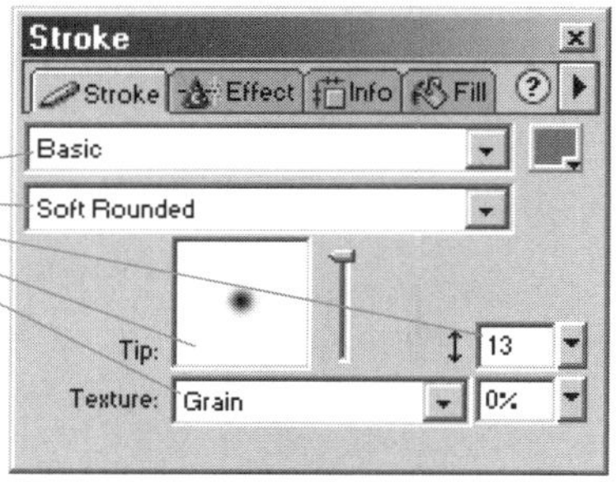

Once attributes have been specified in the Fill or Stroke panels, these become the default ones for any new objects that are created and override the solid colours selected in the Fill and Stroke colour panels on the Tools panel. These will then be used until the settings are changed in the Fill or Stroke panels.

3 Click here to select the type of stroke and colour

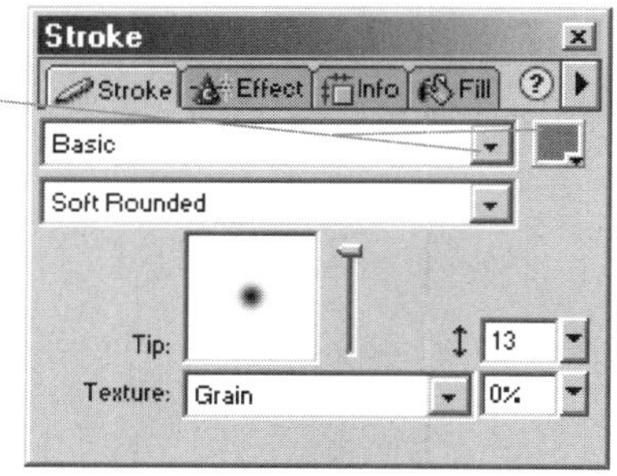

4 Click here to select the line style of the stroke

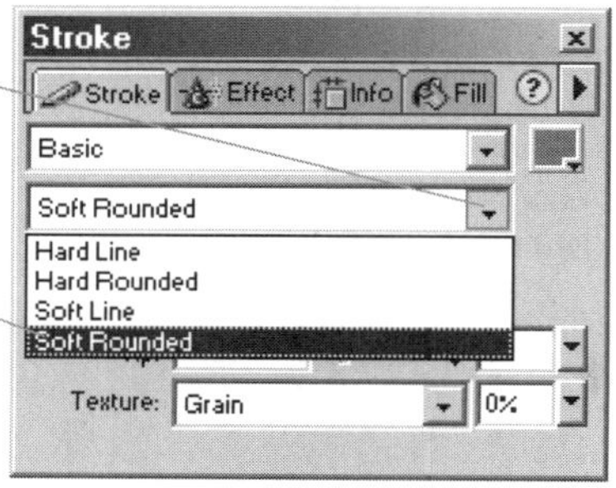

5 Click here to set the softness or hardness of the edges of the stroke

6 Click here to select the width of the stroke

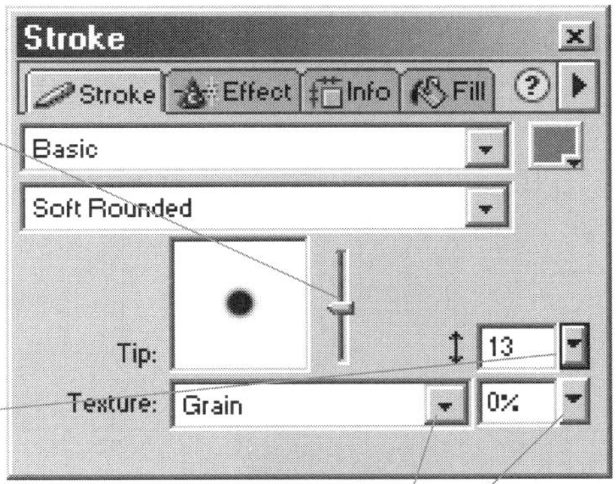

7 Click here to select the texture of the stroke and the amount to be applied

The stroke width is set by dragging the button on a slider. This technique is used throughout Fireworks for increasing or decreasing the size of items. In some cases, such as text size, the new size is previewed on the canvas as you drag the slider. However, with the stroke width you have to click away from the slider for the effect to be applied.

Some examples of how the Stroke panel can be used on objects:

Watercolour type, heavy effect, medium edge softness, 13 width, Grain texture at 20%

Depending on the width of the stroke, the object could look smaller than the stroke. This is okay if it is the intended effect, but it could detract from the object itself.

Airbrush type, textured effect, hard edge, 10 width, Fiber texture at 80%

Effect panel

The Effect panel can be used to further refine the appearance of objects:

Default effect settings

1 Select Window>Effect from the menu bar to access the Effect panel

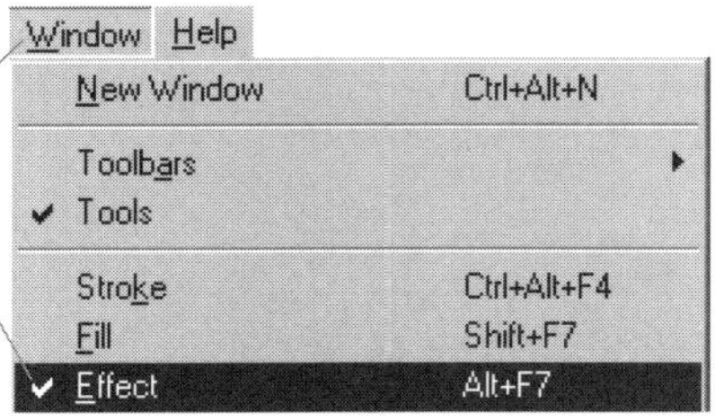

The subtle use of effects such as embossing and bevelling can produce stylish buttons and graphics for use on Web pages.

2 Click here to select the effect options

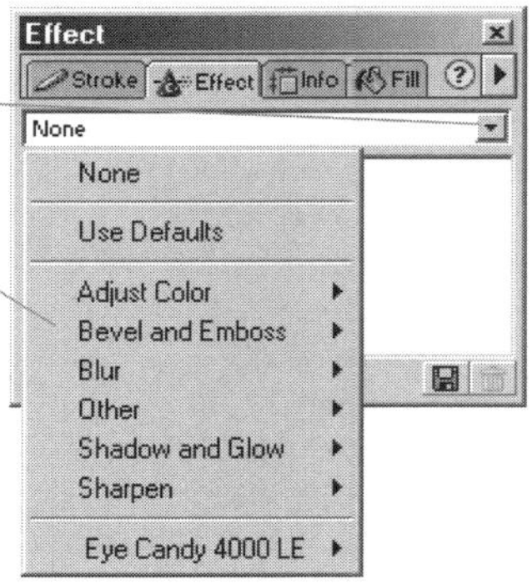

Several effects can be applied to the same item.

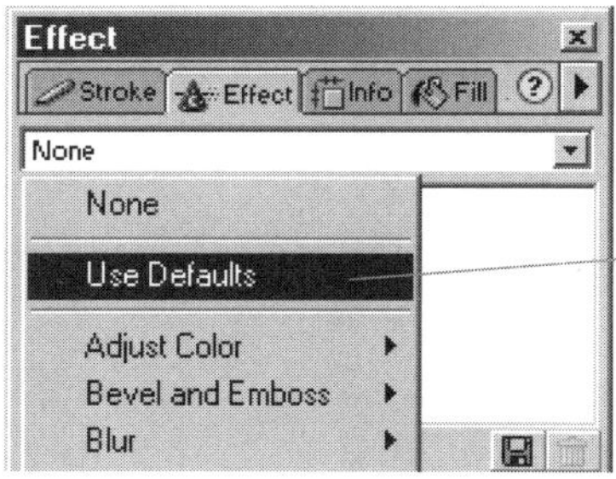

3 Click here to use the default settings for each option

Effects are only applied to the currently selected item. If you then create a new object, this will just have the currently selected stroke and fill attributes applied to it, not any effects.

4 Check the required boxes to apply the effect

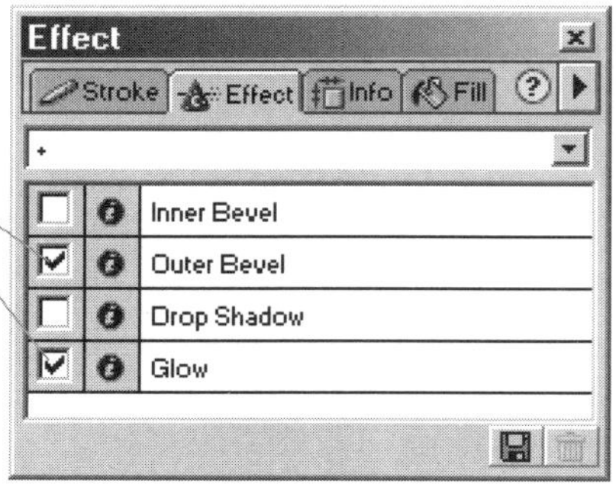

Manual effect settings

As with many things connected with design, particularly Web design, a less-is-more approach is a sensible one when dealing with effects.

1. Access the Effect panel as shown on the previous page. Select one of the options from the effects menu

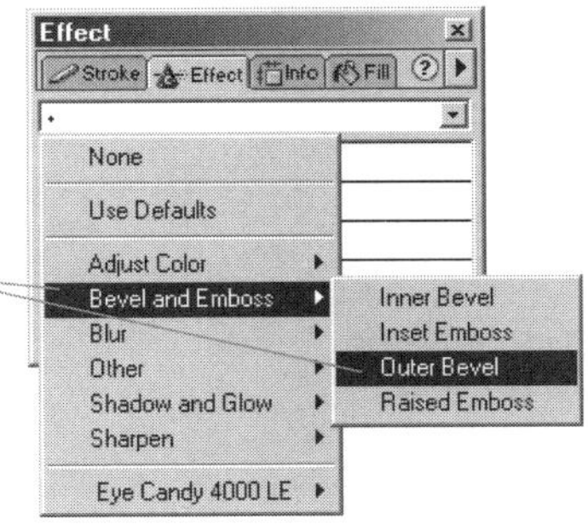

To remove an effect, select it in the Effect panel so that its name is highlighted with a black band and then click on the wastebasket icon at the bottom right of the panel.

2. Each effect has a menu for setting its attributes. Select the required options and then click outside the box to apply the effect

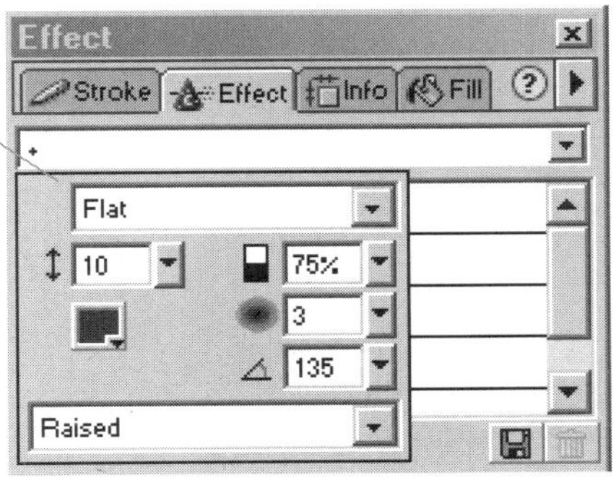

Saving and reapplying effects is similar to creating styles in a word processor. They can be applied to numerous items to create an overall consistency of design.

3. If you create an effect you think you will want to use again, select it in the Effect panel and click here

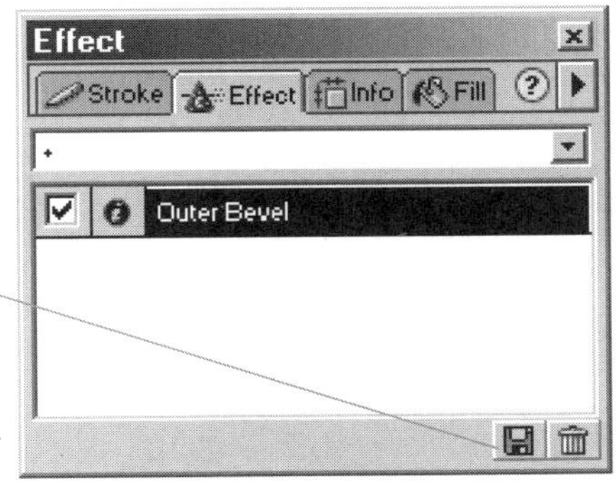

4. Give the effect a name and select OK. This will now appear in the effects menu

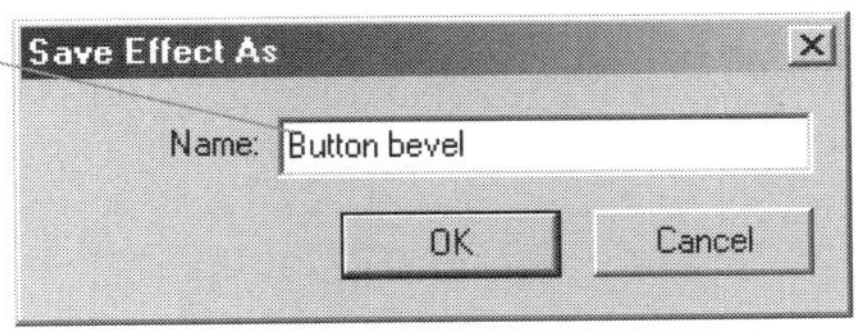

Styles panel

For the designer who does not want to have to go to the trouble of creating his or her own designs, there is a useful Styles panel of pre-designed fills and strokes. These can be applied to objects and also text:

A style from the Styles panel will over-write any previously selected fill or stroke attributes, even if they have been selected in the Fill and Stroke panels.

1 Select Window>Styles from the menu bar to access the Styles panel

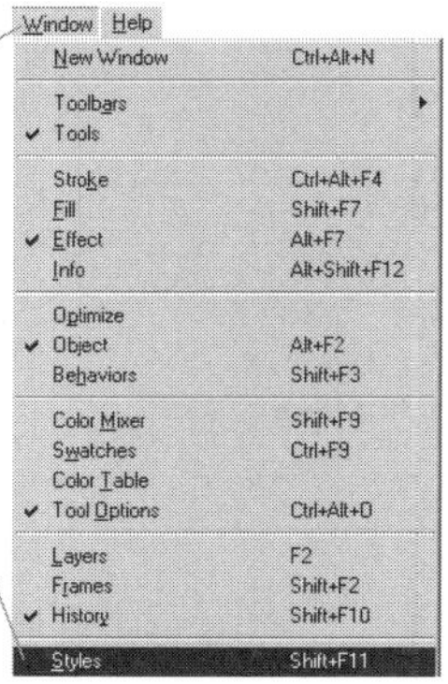

Existing styles can be edited by double-clicking on them in the Styles panel and then changing their attributes in the Edit Style dialog box.

2 Select an object and click here to apply a pre-set style

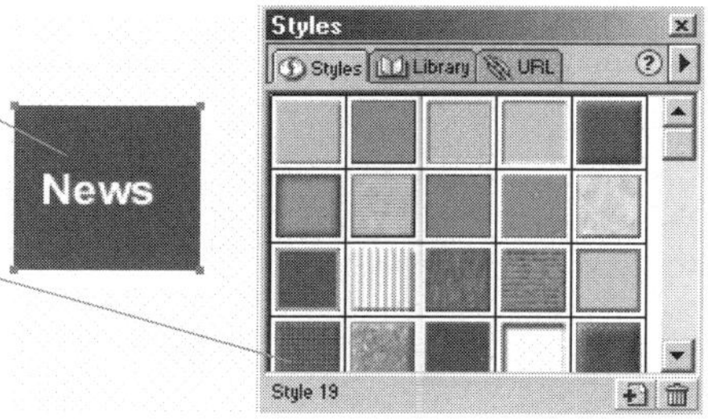

Text styles can be used to dramatic effect for items such as headings or sub-headings.

3 Select a text box and click here to apply a pre-set text style

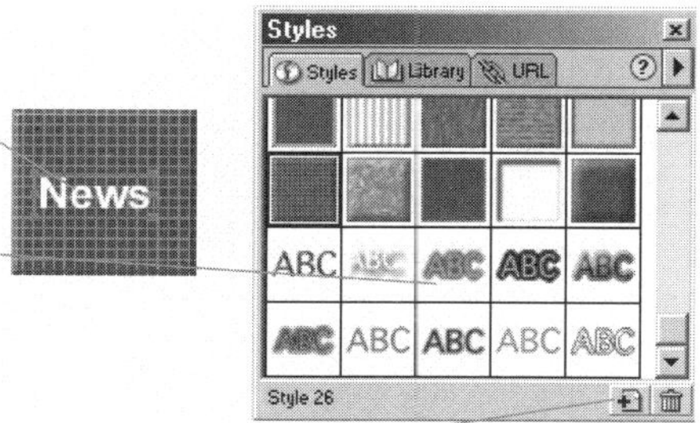

4 Click here to create your own custom styles

Color Mixer panel

The Color Mixer panel can be used to create your own custom colours, in addition to the ones in the standard colour palette. To use the Color Mixer panel:

1 Select Window> Color Mixer from the menu bar to access the Color Mixer panel

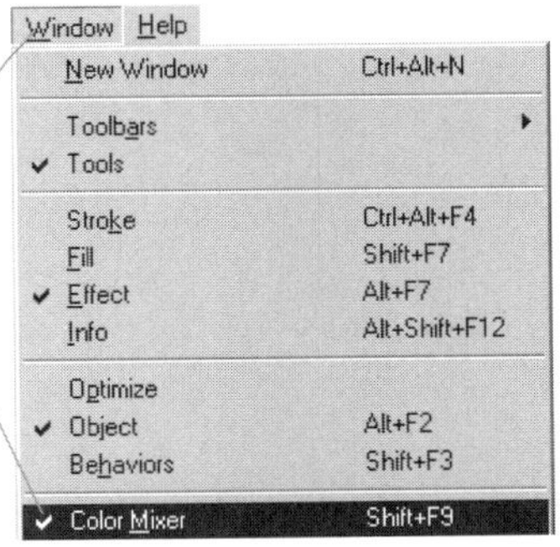

If you create your own colour it may not be one of the 256 Web-safe colours that appear the same on all Web browsers. This may mean that the colour you have specified will not appear consistently across different browsers.

2 Select either the stroke or the fill option

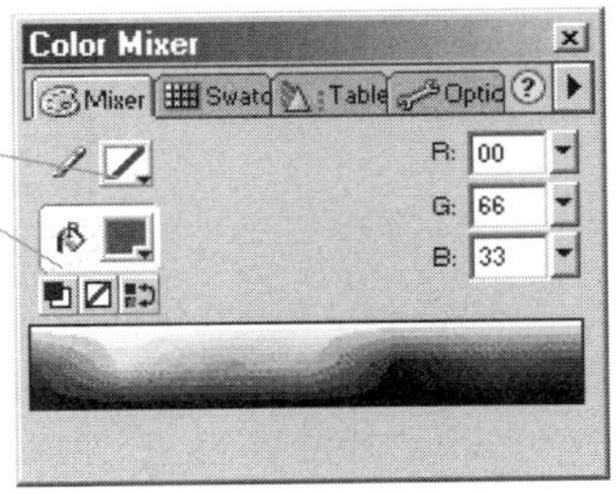

3 Click here to select a colour from the colour palette

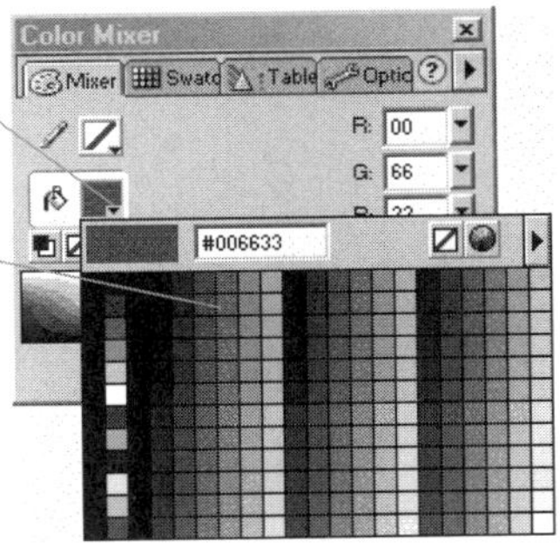

A hexadecimal colour is one where the levels of red, green and blue are determined by a two-digit code.

4 Click here to select a custom colour

5 Enter values here to specify a colour through a hexadecimal code

Swatches panel

The Swatches panel can be used to select colours for the stroke and fill of objects. It is possible to add colours to the Swatches panel, and also import whole new panels. To use the Swatches panel:

1 Select Window> Swatches from the menu bar to access the Swatches panel

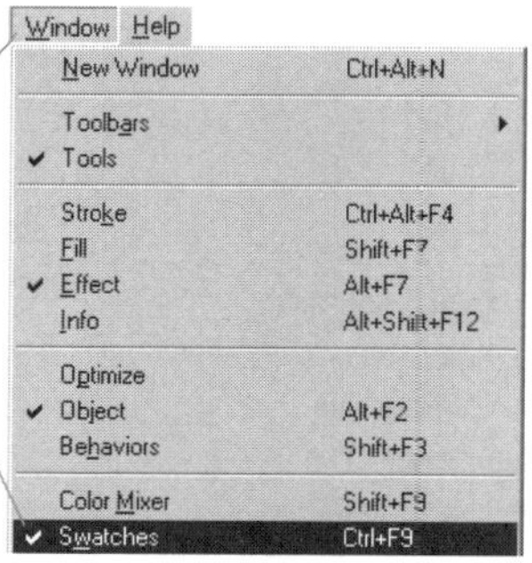

Don't forget: If you want to add more swatches to Fireworks, these have to be already installed on your computer. Use the Add Swatches menu option and then select a colour table. This will have an 'act' file extension.

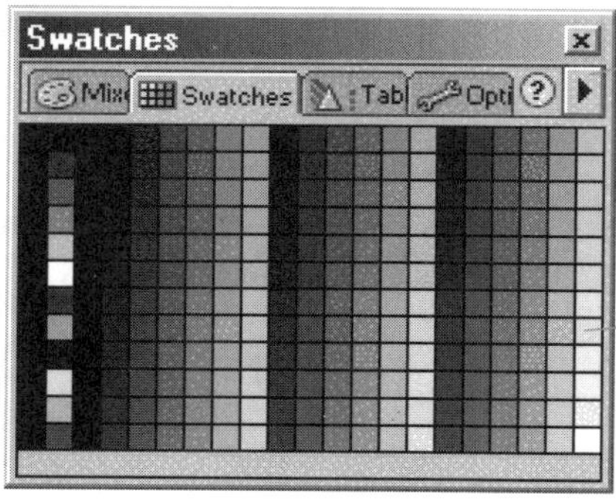

3 Click here to access the Swatches menu

2 Click here to select a colour

Select one of these options to add or remove swatches

Select one of these to change the appearance of the swatches e.g. for use with Windows

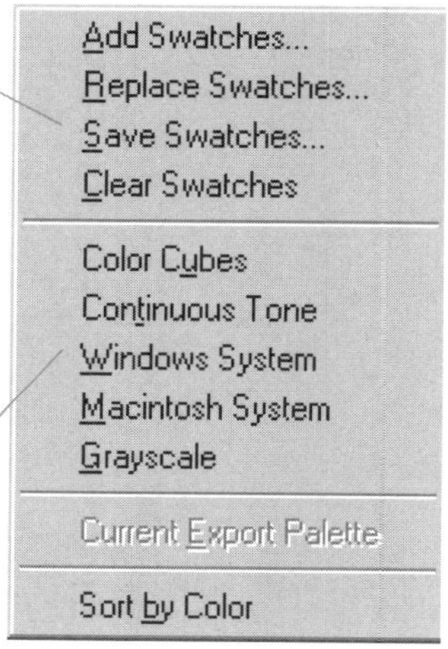

Editing objects

Once objects have been created it is possible to apply a variety of editing techniques to them. This provides enormous flexibility for creative design. This chapter looks at some of the tools that can be used for editing objects and some of the effects that can be achieved.

Covers

Chapter Four

Reshaping

One of the most powerful object editing functions in Fireworks is the ability to reshape vector objects. This is done through the use of several tools:

Subselection tool

Select the Subselection tool and click and drag on a point to stretch the object at that point

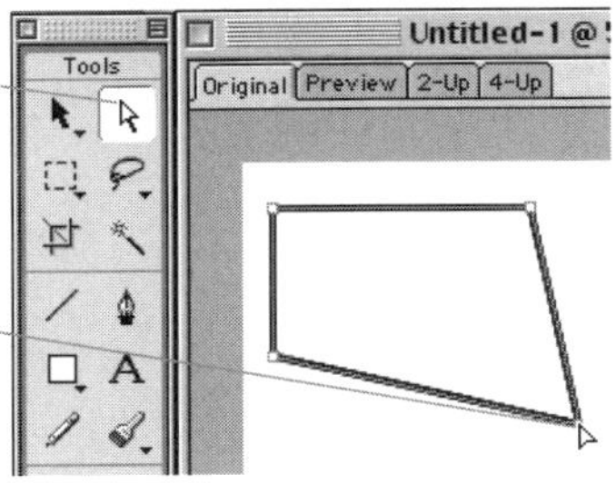

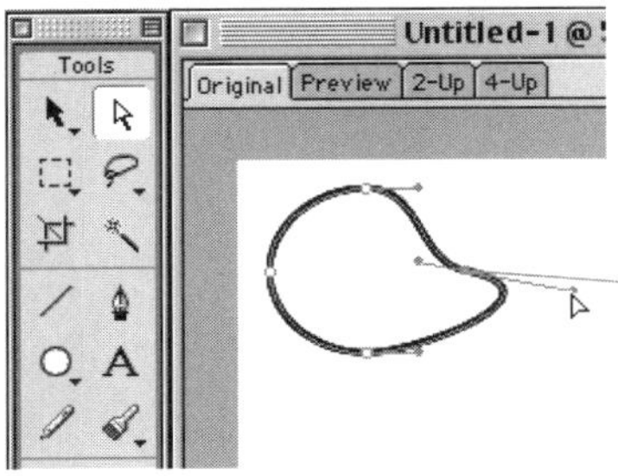

Click on a point and click and drag on a handle to distort the object

When a path is selected with the Subselection tool a hollow square indicates a point. When this is selected, solid squares appear along a line that goes through the point. These are known as point handles and can be used to edit an object.

Freeform tool

Select the Freeform tool. Move it over a point until a small S shape appears next to it. Use this to drag and distort the object around this point

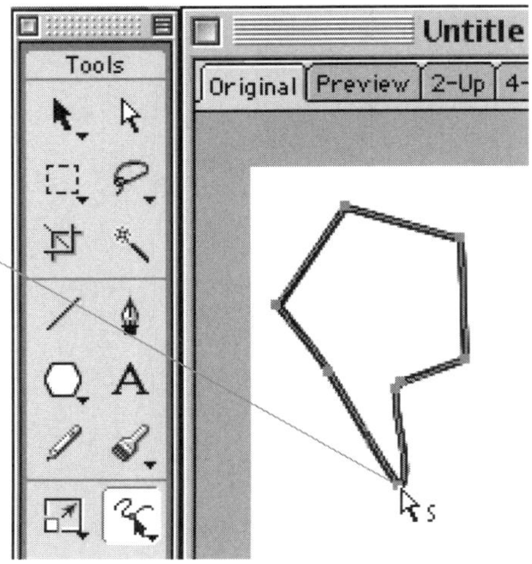

If the Freeform tool is clicked within an object and then dragged outwards, this will expand the fill in the direction the tool is moved.

Move the Freeform tool towards a path, until a small circle appears next to the cursor. Click and push to distort the object inwards

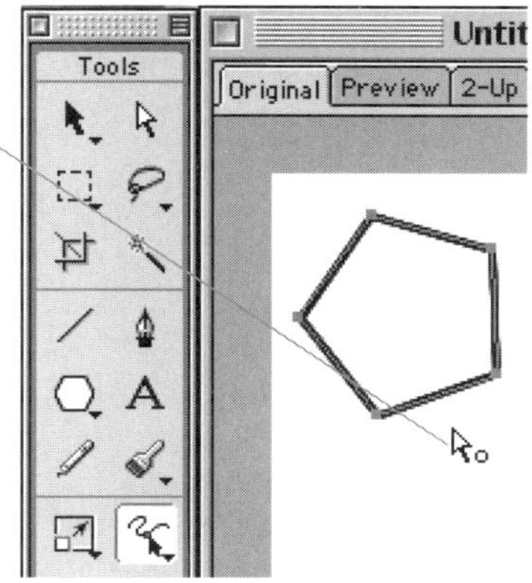

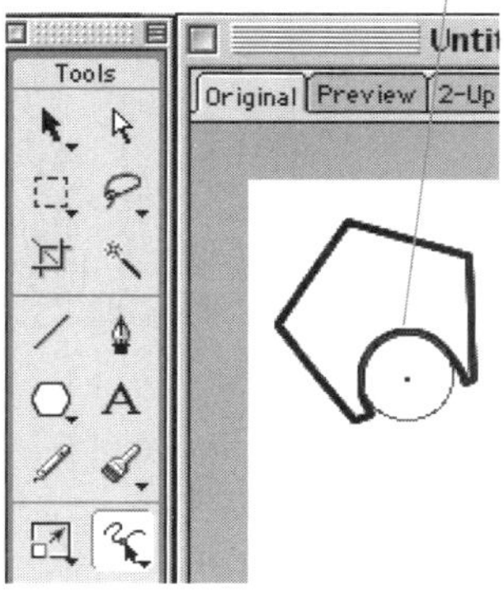

By default, the Reshape Area tool is not selected. If this is the case, click on the black triangle next to the Freeform tool and then select the Reshape Area tool that appears.

Reshape Area tool

Select the Reshape Area tool. Click and push to reshape an object, in a similar way to pushing sand with a cup

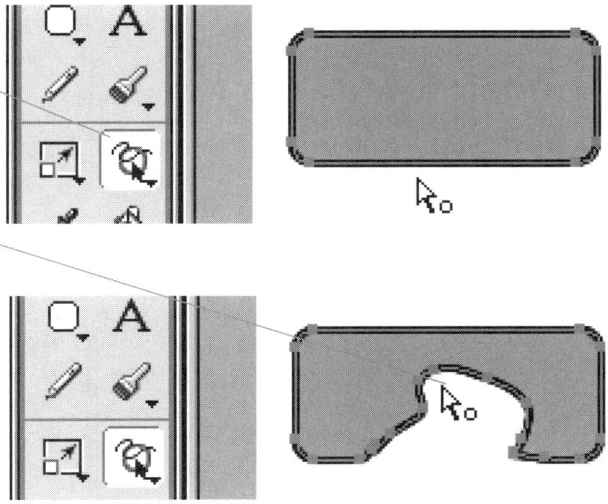

The size of the Reshape Area tool and the pressure with which it pushes the fill are determined in the Tool Options panel, in the Size and Strength boxes.

Orientation

Once an object has been created it is useful to be able to change its orientation i.e. rotate it by varying degrees on the canvas. There are several options for doing this:

Scale tool

This can be used to rotate an object manually:

1 Select an object and select the Scale tool from the Tools panel

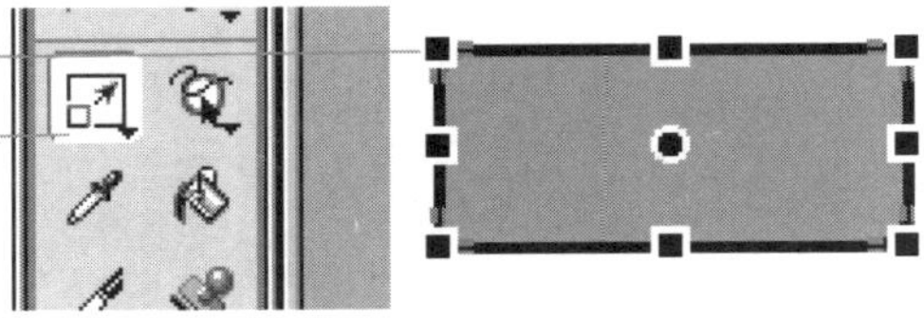

Although the Scale tool's primary function is to change the size of an object it also performs rotating perfectly well. Use this if you want to scale and rotate an object simultaneously.

2 Click anywhere on the canvas until the circular arrowhead appears

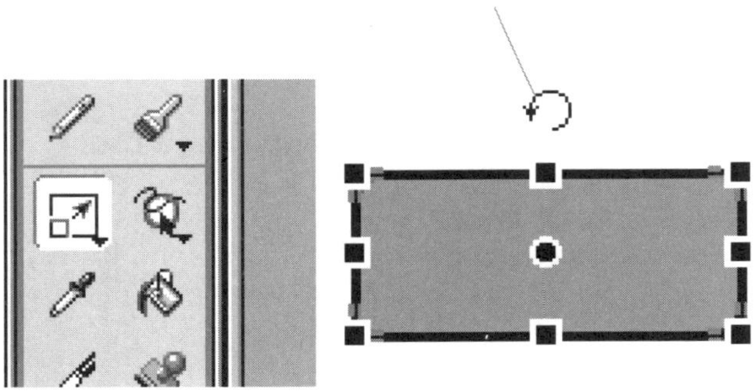

The other tools grouped with the Scale tool, i.e. the Distort and the Skew tools can also be used to rotate an object.

3 Drag to rotate the object

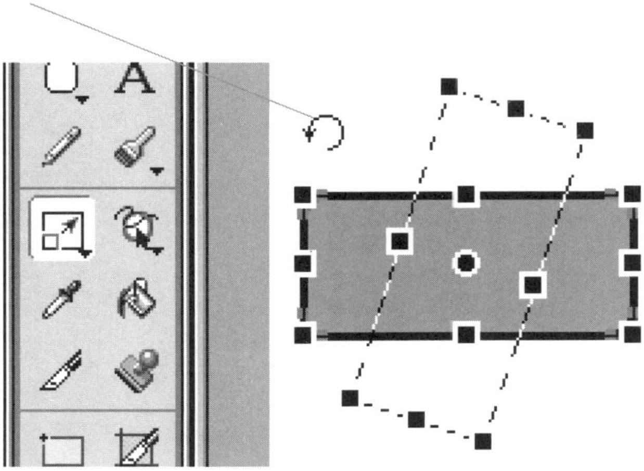

To rotate the whole canvas, select Modify> Rotate Canvas from the menu bar and then apply the required amount of rotation. This can be used for items such as photographs that appear on their sides or upside down.

Numeric Transform

The Free Transform option on the Transform menu works in the same way as rotating an object with the tools on the previous page.

1 Select an object and select Modify>Transform>Numeric Transform from the menu bar

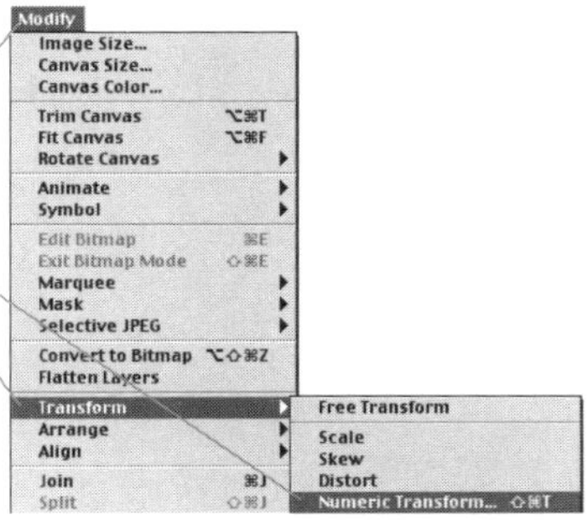

Numeric Transform is a useful option if you want to achieve an exact amount of rotation e.g. to set an object at an exact 45 degree angle so that it bisects the corner of a square.

2 In the Numeric Transform dialog box, select Rotate here and enter the amount you want the object to rotate here

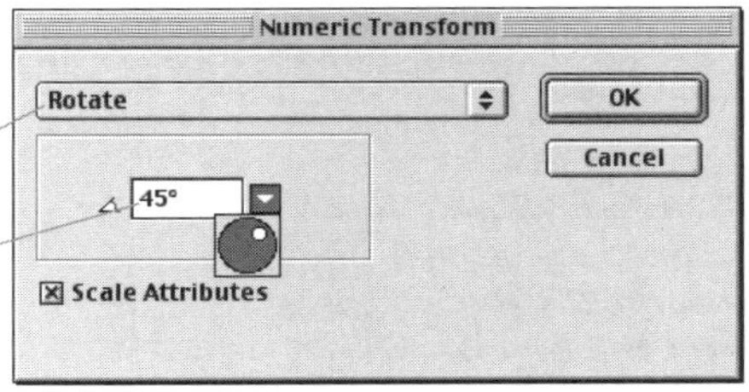

The Flip Horizontal and Flip Vertical options are useful if you want to create a mirror image of an object. It is also useful if you want to make an object face the opposite direction. This can be effective on a Web page, where it is better to have objects facing into the page rather than away from it.

Preset Transform

The options on the Transform menu can also be used to rotate an object by a specific angle:

Select an object and select one of these options from the Transform menu

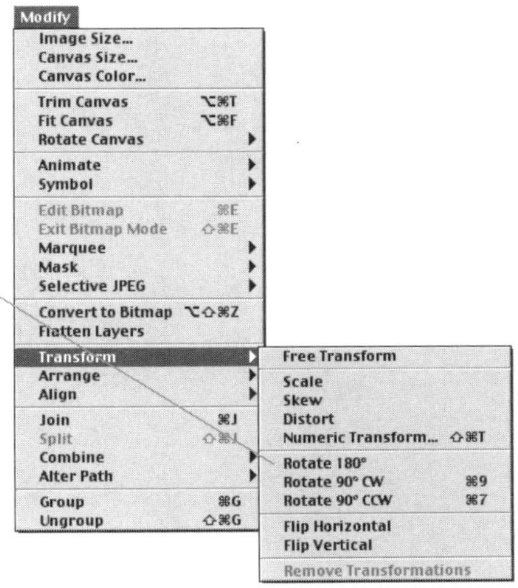

The Flip Horizontal and Flip Vertical options can also be accessed from the Modify toolbar. If this is not showing select Window>Toolbars>Modify from the menu bar.

Scaling

When working with objects designers frequently need to change the size of them. This can be done with the Scale tool:

1 Select an object and select the Scale tool on the Tools panel

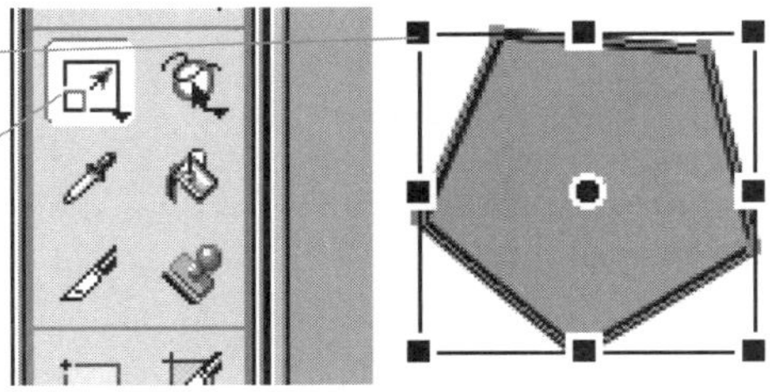

The Scale option can also be accessed from the menu bar, by selecting Modify> Transform>Scale. This is also the case for the Skew and the Distort options (see next two pages).

2 Click and drag here to change the horizontal size of the object

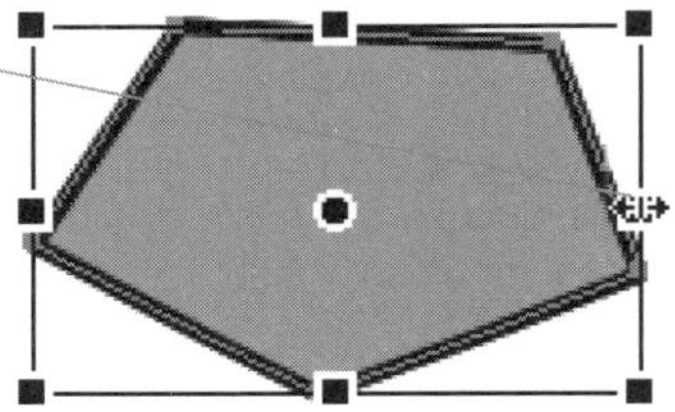

3 Click and drag here to change the vertical size of the object

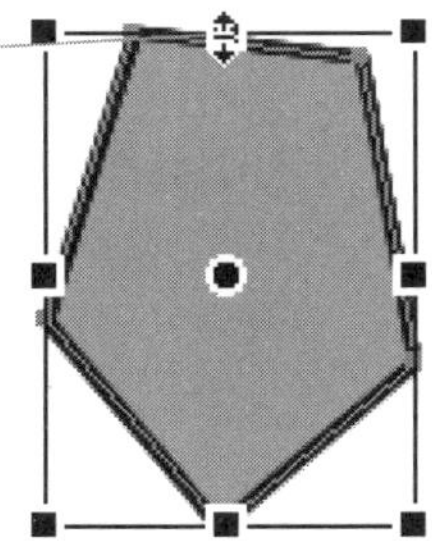

To scale an object to a specific value, select Modify> Transform> Numeric Transform from the menu bar. Make sure Scale is selected in the top box and then enter values in the boxes below for the new scale size.

4 Click and drag here to change the horizontal and vertical size of the object. This is done in proportion

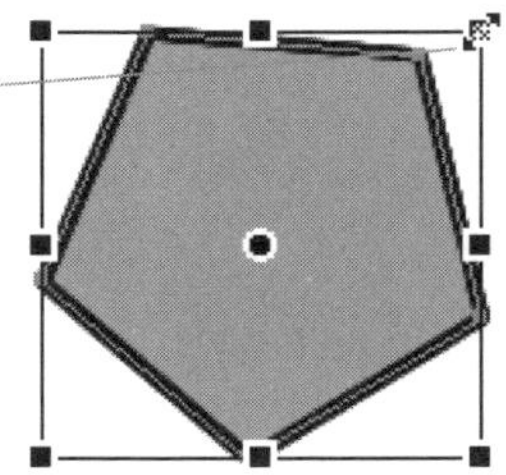

Skewing

Skewing can be used to change the shape of an object. It is particularly effective for creating a sense of perspective.

1 Select an object and select the Skew tool on the Tools panel

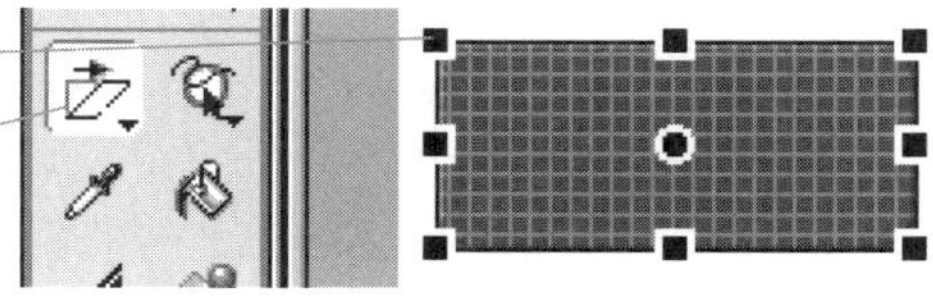

Skewing can be used to achieve creative effects with photographic images. However, do not overapply this effect, otherwise the photograph may become unrecognisable.

2 Click and drag here to skew the horizontal axis of the object

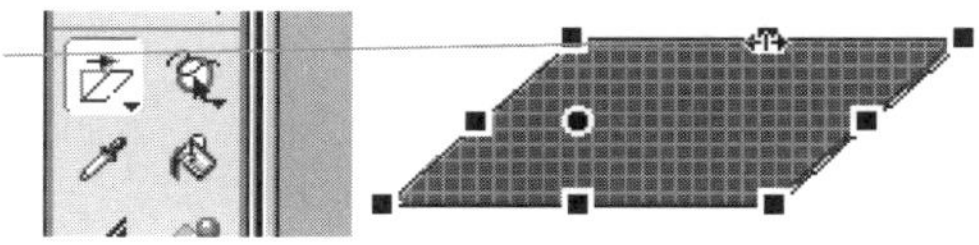

3 Click and drag here to skew the vertical axis of the object

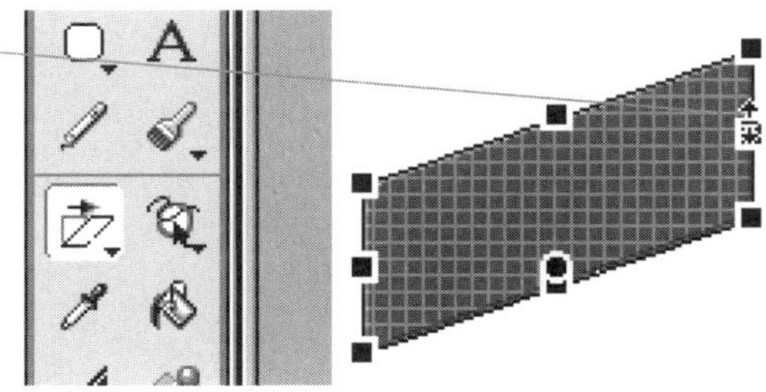

To achieve a sense of distance with an object, skew the top horizontal axis inwards. This will make the object the widest at the bottom, giving the effect that it is disappearing into the distance.

4 Click and drag here to skew one side of the object

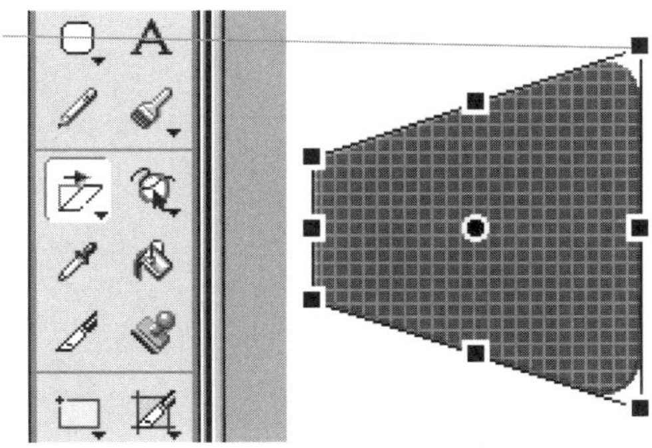

Distorting

1 Select an object and select the Distort tool on the Tools panel

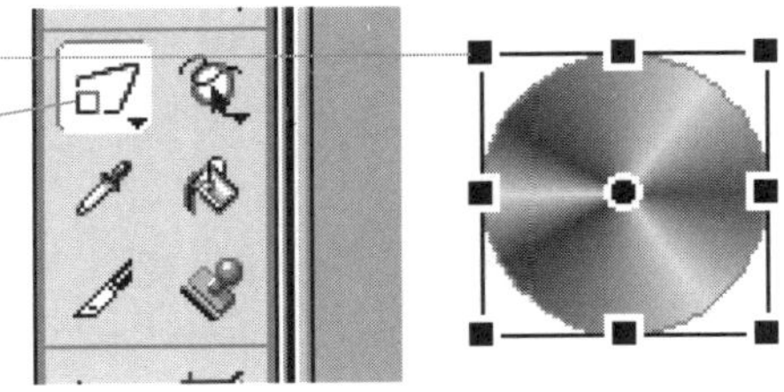

If you try and distort an object by dragging a corner handle over and beyond its opposite side, you will not be able to do so.

2 Click and drag here to distort the horizontal axis of the object

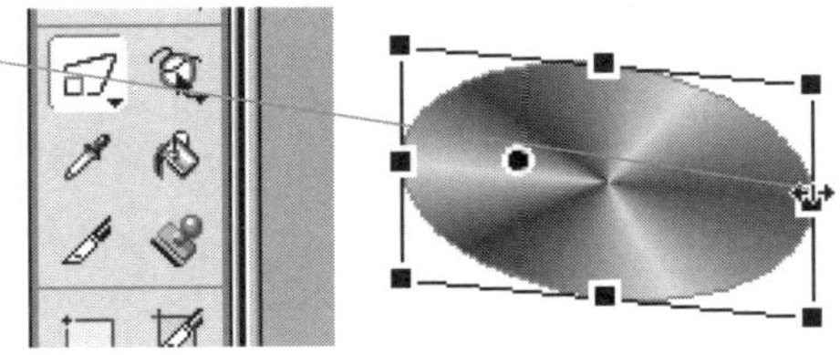

By default, all of the attributes of an object, i.e. stroke, fill and text, are scaled in proportion. To turn this off, select Window>Tool Options from the menu bar. In the Tool Options panel, uncheck the Scale Attributes box. This will result in the distortion being even more pronounced, as individual attributes become distorted independently of each other.

3 Click and drag here to distort the vertical axis of the object

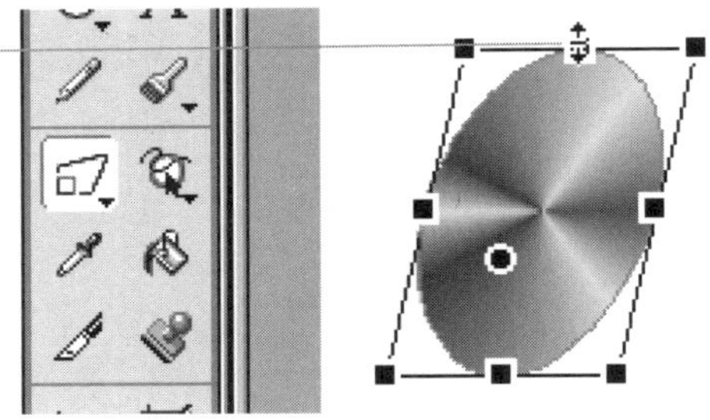

4 Click and drag here to distort the two sides next to this point

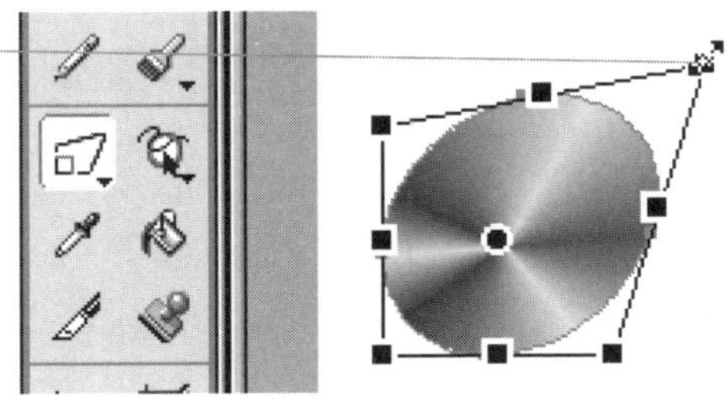

Arranging

If you are working with several objects on the same layer you will soon find that you want to place certain objects, or parts of objects, above or below others. This is known as the stacking order. For instance, you may want to create an image of a person sitting behind a table, in which case the table will be above the person in the stacking order. To arrange objects:

Another way to arrange objects within an image is through the use of layers. This places objects on separate layers. This means that they can have editing effects applied to them without altering other elements of the image. However, it also means that their interaction with other objects is more limited. For more information about layers, see Chapter Seven.

1 Create three objects and overlap them all. Select the bottom object

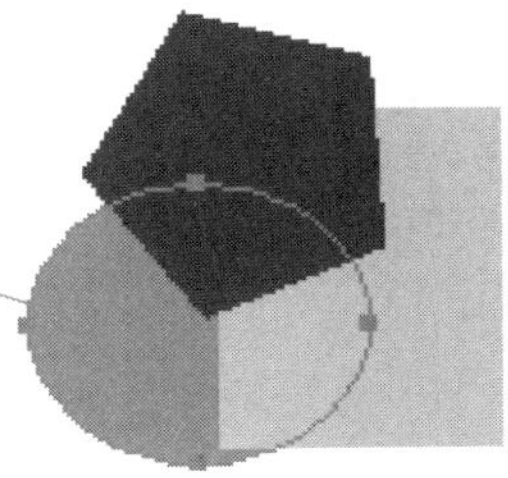

2 Select Modify> Arrange>Bring Forward. This brings the object in front of the item immediately above it

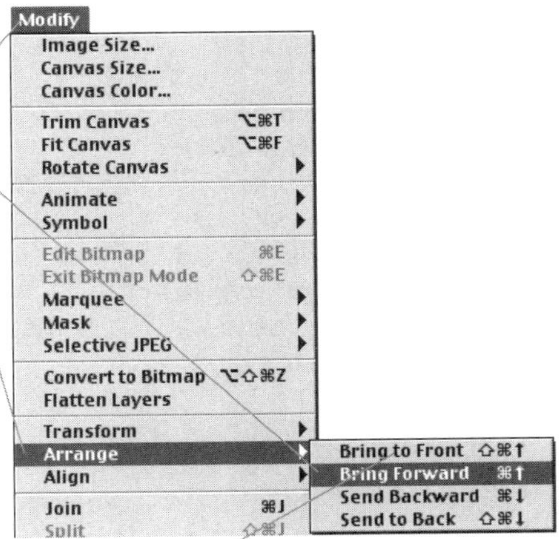

If you want to send an item behind other objects the commands are the same in reverse: Send Backward sends an object behind the item immediately behind it; Send to Back sends it behind all of the items below it i.e. it goes to the bottom of the stacking order.

3 Select Modify> Arrange>Bring to Front. This brings the object above all of the items above it

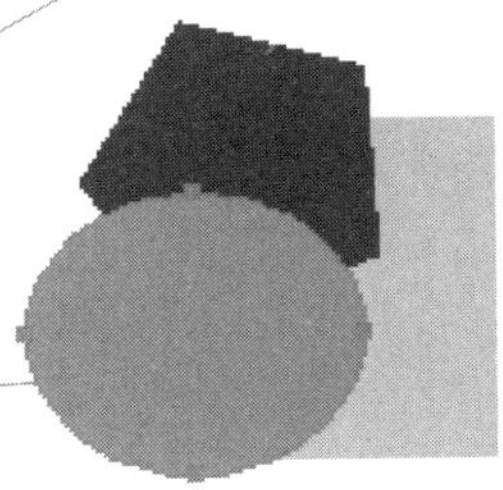

The Arrange options are also available as icons on the Modify toolbar.

Aligning

When working with elements such as buttons for a Web page it is necessary to be able to align them either horizontally or vertically. This can be done manually by using the Fireworks grid and dragging them into place. However a much more efficient way is to use the Align options:

The grid is a non-printing element that lies on the work area. This can then be used to position elements on the canvas. To view the grid, select View>Grid>Show Grid from the menu bar.

1 Select two or more objects

2 Select Modify>Align from the menu bar and select one of the options

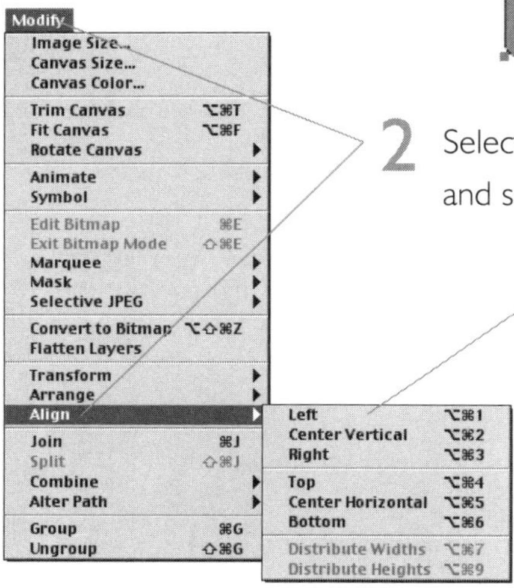

If you are designing a series of buttons for a navigation bar on a Web page, align them according to where you are going to place the navigation bar i.e. left if it is going to be on the left of the page, top if it is going to be at the top and so on.

Left

Center Vertical

Right

Top

Center Horizontal

Bottom

Items on different layers can still be aligned together within the same image.

Selecting parts of objects

There are two tools that can be used to select parts of objects, rather than entire objects. These are the Marquee tool and the Lasso tool.

DON'T FORGET

Hold down the Shift key when using the Marquee tools to create an exactly square or circular selection.

Marquee tool

There are two choices of Marquee tool, the rectangular Marquee tool, (which is just known as the Marquee tool) and the Oval Marquee tool. Both operate in the same way:

1. Select one of the Marquee tools

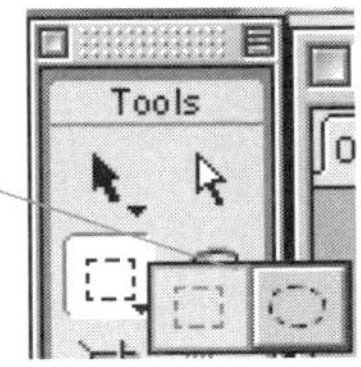

DON'T FORGET

To change a vector object into a bitmap one, select the object and select Modify>Convert to Bitmap from the menu bar.

2. Select an area on an object by clicking and dragging. This has to be a bitmap object rather than a vector one

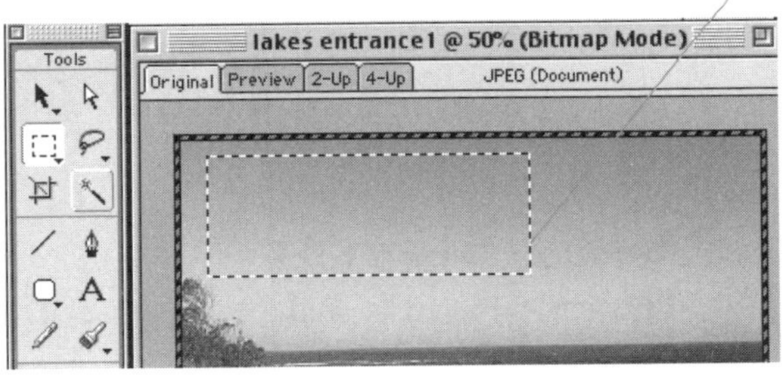

BEWARE

Even when a selection has been dragged away from the original object, it is still part of that object, even though it looks like it is detached from it.

3. Once an area has been selected it can then be edited independently. This can include dragging the selection away from the original object, or editing its fill and stroke attributes

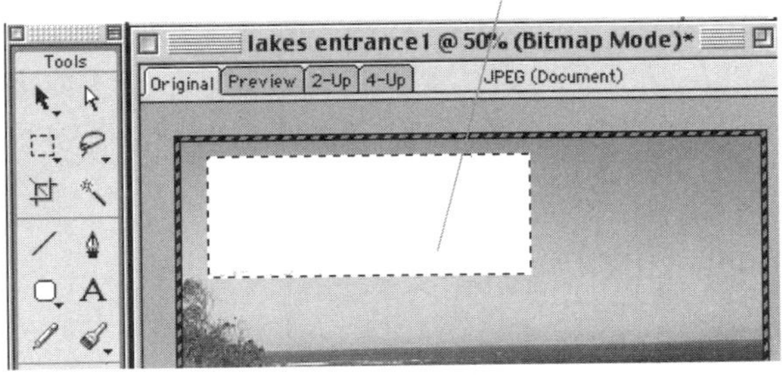

HOT TIP

Once you have selected an area of an object it is then possible to feather it i.e. give it blurred edges. This can be put to good effect for softening the edges around items such as photographs. To do this, make a selection and select Modify>Marquee>Feather from the menu bar and enter a value for the amount of feathering you want to apply.

Lasso tool

The Lasso tool, and its grouped tools, can be used to make irregular selections, rather than symmetrical ones:

One effective use for the Lasso tool is for selecting red eyes in photographic images. These can then be edited by applying a more appropriate colour.

1. Select the Lasso tool

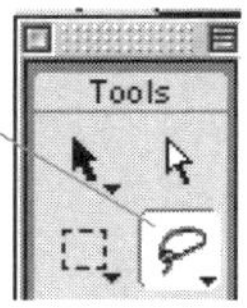

2. Make a freehand selection on an object

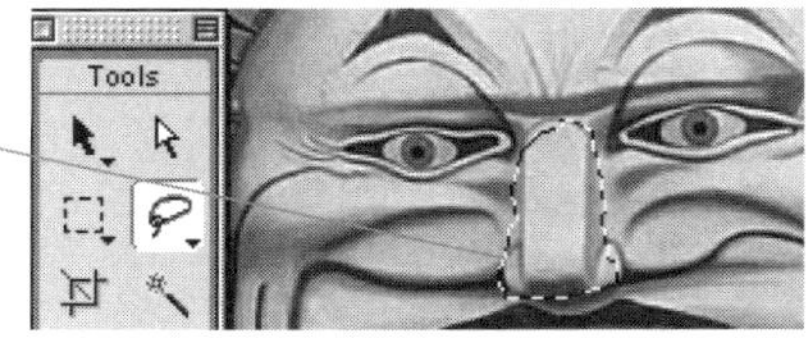

As with the Marquee tools, Lasso selections can only be made on bitmap images.

3. Edit the selection as appropriate

Polygon Lasso tool

This can be used to make a 'dot-to-dot' selection:

1. Select the Polygon Lasso tool

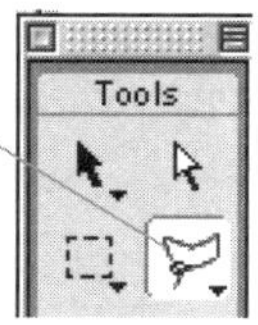

2. Make the selection by clicking once at each point around the object you want included

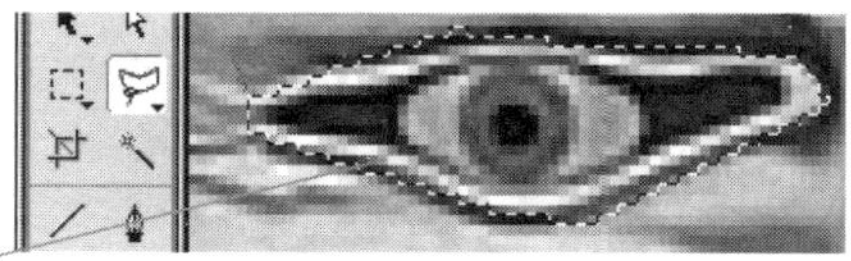

Magic Wand tool

The Magic Wand tool can be used to select areas of the same, or similar, colour. Its attributes can be set to vary the range of colours that are selected. To select an area with the Magic Wand tool:

The Magic Wand tool is a good option if you want to select an irregular area of a particular colour, without having to use the Lasso tools.

1 Select the Magic Wand tool

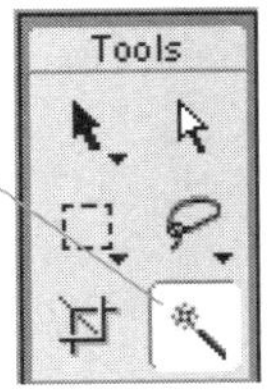

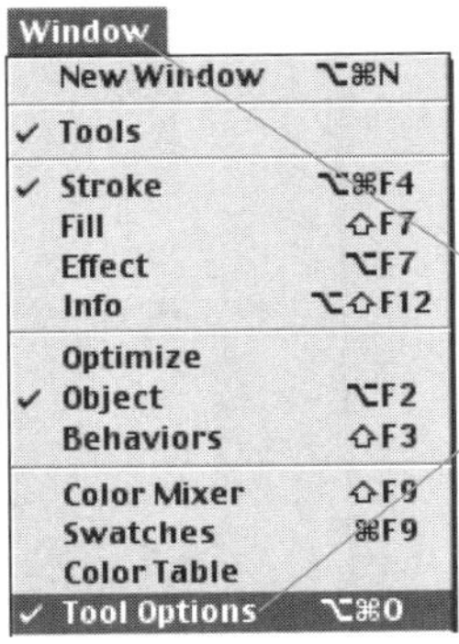

2 Select Window> Tool Options from the menu bar

The Magic Wand tool works by selecting similarly coloured pixels to the one that is first selected. The level of tolerance dictates the divergence in colour that is allowed between pixels. So if the tolerance is set to a low value, e.g. 10, only very similarly coloured pixels will be selected. At a high tolerance, such as 80, a much wider range of pixels will be selected and so the overall selection will be bigger.

3 Enter a value for the Tolerance and the type of edge you want for your selection

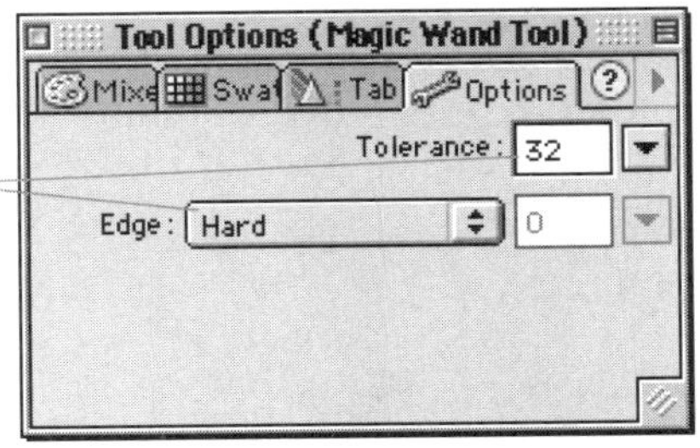

4 Click once on an area to select it

To deselect an area that has been selected with the Magic Wand tool, click on it again with the same tool.

Tolerance at 10

Tolerance at 80

Cropping

Cropping is a technique that is most frequently used in connection with photographic images. Even the best photographers do not always capture images exactly as they want them and cropping can be used to remove the unwanted area behind the main subject of an image. To crop an image:

1 Select the Crop tool

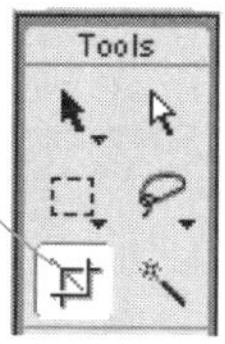

Cropping should always be considered in connection with images of people, since these often contain background areas that are unnecessary and distracting. Try to remove as much of this as possible so that there is as little as possible to detract from the main subject of the image.

2 Click and drag around the area of the image that you want to keep

3 If necessary, edit the selection by dragging the resizing handles

Cropping not only improves the visual appearance of images, it also reduces the file size, which decreases their downloading time over the Web.

4 Press Return or Enter to crop the image so that only the selected area is visible

Cloning

Cloning is one of the reasons why digital images should never be fully trusted. This technique enables you to copy or remove elements of a photograph, or graphic, to a standard that makes it look like an original. For instance, it is possible to remove individuals or unwanted objects from a photograph, or copy existing ones so that they are perfectly duplicated. In Fireworks, this is done with the Rubber Stamp tool.

Cloning is a good option if you have text on an object that you want to change (this is once an image has been saved and the text has become part of the image rather than an individual text block.) Use the Rubber Stamp tool to cover over the text, then add a new text block and save the image.

If you are removing an item in a photographic image, you will need to move the cloning point several times in order to create a seamless finished product.

Removing elements

1 Select the Rubber Stamp tool

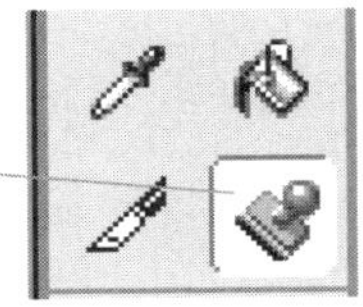

2 Hold down Alt and click on a part of the image that you want to use as the starting point for cloning. A circle with a blue outline will appear

3 Drag the cursor over the item to be removed. As the blue circle moves over the image in tandem with the cursor, the area in the circle will be copied at the point where the cursor is

Duplicating elements

1 Select the Rubber Stamp tool

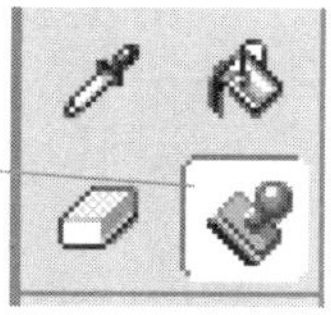

There is also a menu bar function for duplicating objects. This is accessed by selecting an object, or part of an object, and selecting Edit>Duplicate from the menu bar. This can be used to duplicate whole images or selected areas. However, for tasks such as duplicating a person in a photograph, the Rubber Stamp tool is a better option.

2 Hold down Alt and click once at the point where you want to start duplicating an object

When duplicating an object with the Rubber Stamp tool, make sure you keep the mouse button pressed continuously throughout the operation. This will ensure that the object is copied in one smooth operation.

3 Move to the point where you want to copy the object and click and drag. As the blue circle moves over the image in tandem with the cursor, the area in the circle will be copied at the point where the cursor is. Make sure the blue circle only moves over the element you want to copy

Erasing

The Eraser tool can be used to remove areas of a bitmap object, or replace them with a different colour. To do this:

1 Select a bitmap object and select the Eraser tool

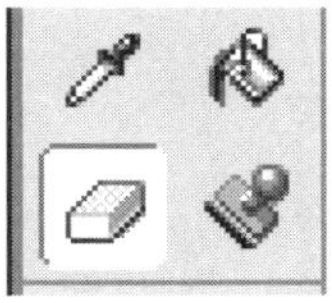

If you try to select the Eraser tool when a vector object is selected, it will be the Knife tool instead. This can be used to break up existing paths by clicking on the path to add another point, or dragging points across a path.

2 Select Window>Tool Options from the menu bar to view the options for the Eraser tool

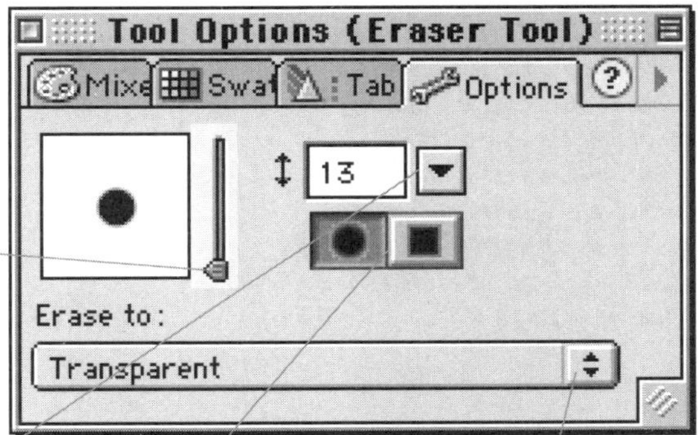

Click and drag here to select the softness of the edges

Click here to select the size of the tip

Click here to select the shape of the tip

Click here to select the Eraser colour

The options for the eraser colour are: Transparent, which removes the element and leaves the canvas showing underneath; Fill colour, which covers the erased area with the currently selected fill colour; Stroke colour, which covers the selection with the currently selected stroke colour; and Canvas colour, which covers the selection with the currently selected canvas colour.

3 Click and drag to remove elements from an image

Selecting colours

If you want to reuse a particular colour that appears in an existing object, but you are unsure about making an exact match, the Eyedropper tool can be used to copy it into one of the colour palettes. To do this:

If you want to copy something like skin-tone colours, the Eyedropper tool is not the best option to choose. This is because it only picks up a singe colour and when this is reapplied it is done so as a continuous tone. If this is then used to recolour someone's face, they will end up looking very two-dimensional. A better option in this instance is to clone one area to another, as shown on page 72.

1. Select the Eyedropper tool

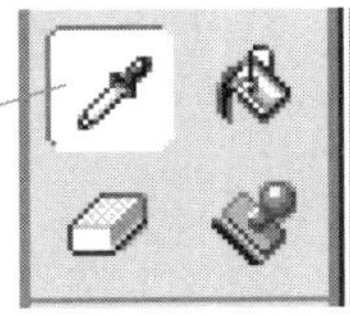

2. On a bitmap image, click once on the colour that you want to copy. This will then appear as the default for either the stroke or the fill colour

3. Click on the colour box for the colour you have selected. Click here to access the Color dialog box

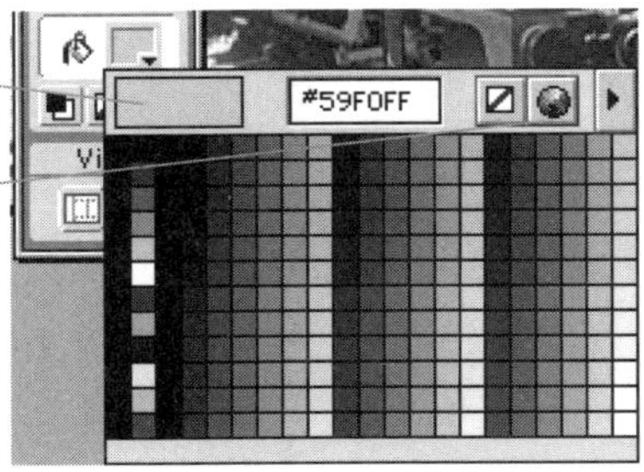

In Windows when a colour has been added as a Custom Color it will not be available in the standard colour palettes. To access it you have to access the Color dialog box as in Step 3 and then select the colour from the Custom colors list.

4. The colour's details appear here

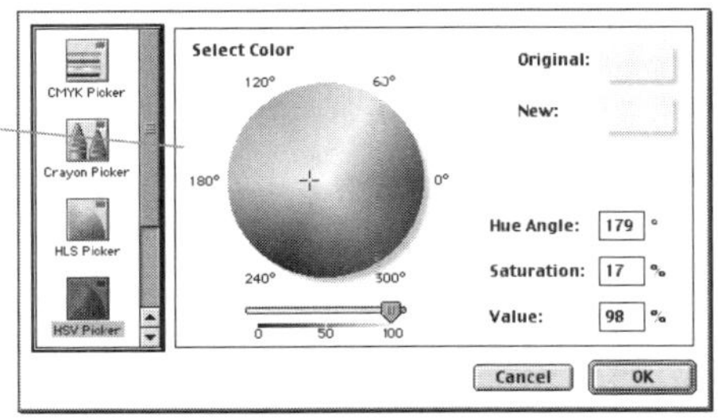

Optimising images

The combination of good quality images and small file sizes is known as optimisation. This is an important aspect of using images on the Internet as the file sizes have to be as small as possible to speed up downloading time while still retaining a suitable image quality. This chapter explains the basics behind optimising images and shows the ways in which it can be achieved in Fireworks.

Covers

Chapter Five

Why optimise images?

If images on the Internet have been optimised effectively, it is sometimes hard to tell any difference in quality between one of a large file size and a much smaller one.

The issue of optimising images is essentially one that concerns images that are going to be used on the Internet, either as part of a Web page or as an email attachment. What optimising is concerned with is creating the best quality image, with the smallest file size. The issue of file size is paramount because this effects the way it is downloaded over the Internet: the bigger the file size, the longer it takes to download. As Internet users become more sophisticated, so the issue of downloading time takes centre stage: if people are not prepared to wait for your images to download, they will quickly move on to something else.

The fireworks proprietary image format, PNG (Portable Network Group), can also be used on the Internet, but it has not been as widely accepted as GIFs and JPEGs.

As far as optimising images is concerned, viewing them on computers has one big advantage: a computer monitor can only display a certain amount of colour (usually 72–96 pixels, or coloured dots, for every inch of monitor space). This means that a lot of colour information can be discarded without any noticeable loss of quality on a monitor. There is an entire industry devoted to the issue of optimising images for use on the Internet and it has come up with some dramatic developments over the years.

GIFs or JPEGs

The two main image formats used on the Internet are GIFs (Graphical Interchange Format) and JPEGs (Joint Photographic Experts Group). Both use systems of image compression to ensure that the images are as compact as possible. JPEGs use up to 16 million colours and are best for displaying photographic images, while GIFs only use 256 colours and are better suited for continuous tone images. However, both formats can be used for all types of images and there is not as big a difference between 256 and 16 million as you might think.

When using images on Web pages, try and keep them below 50 KB in size, if possible.

With terms like compression and image resolution being frequently used in relation to optimising images, it can seem like a complicated business and, behind the scenes, it is. However, Fireworks provides step-by-step guidance to make the process as simple as possible.

Previewing images

In the work area it is possible to preview the download time of the image you are currently working on. This will give you an idea of whether you need to optimise it or not.

1 Click here to preview the current image. This is how it will appear when published on a Web page

2 The image size, downloading time and image type are shown here

In the Preview panel, the downloading time is estimated using a modem that downloads at 28 kbps. Obviously, if a quicker modem is being used, or cable, the downloading time will be faster.

Images can also be previewed with two or four options on screen:

Click here to preview two versions of the image

Click here to preview four versions of the image

When the 2-Up or 4-Up preview options are selected, all of the images retain the attributes of the original. However, it is possible to use these panels to optimise the image and view the different results.

Optimize panel

The main tool for optimising images is the Optimize panel. This displays the attributes for the currently selected image. The Optimize panel works with GIF or JPEG images. To use the Optimize panel:

1 Select Window>Optimize from the menu bar

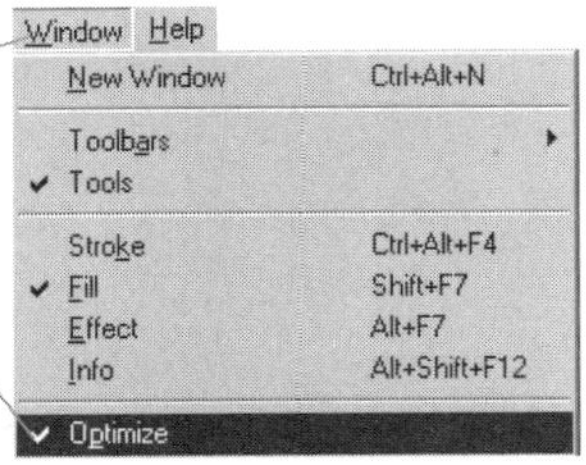

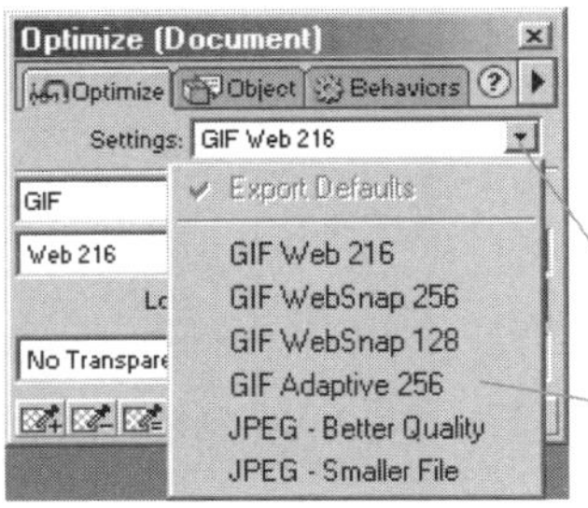

2 Click here to select GIF or JPEG settings

There are various colour palettes that can be used within the GIF settings. Most of these ensure that all colours used are, or are converted to, Web-safe colours i.e. ones that will appear the same on all Web browsers.

GIF settings

The palette from which the colours are taken

The type of image compression used

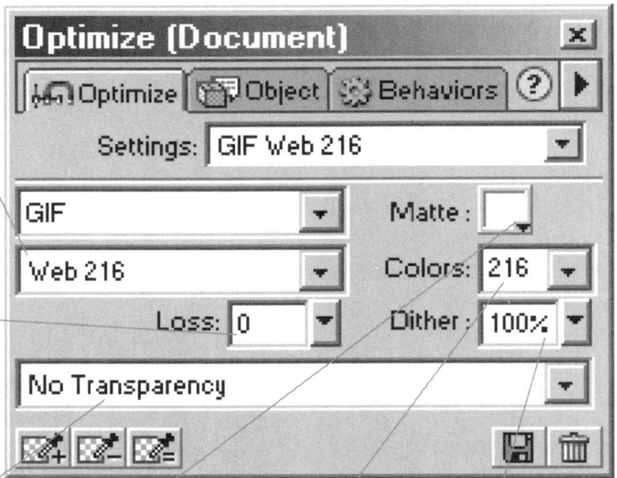

The type of transparency used

Background colour

Number of colours used

Colour blending amount

Dithering is a technique that is used to compensate for the fact that GIFs only use 256 colours.

JPEG settings

The Quality setting can be used to increase or decrease the file size of an image. A higher setting e.g. 80 will produce a larger file size, while a lower setting e.g. 40 will produce a smaller file size. Experiment with different settings to see at which levels the image quality is acceptable and at which it deteriorates too much.

Background colour

Quality setting

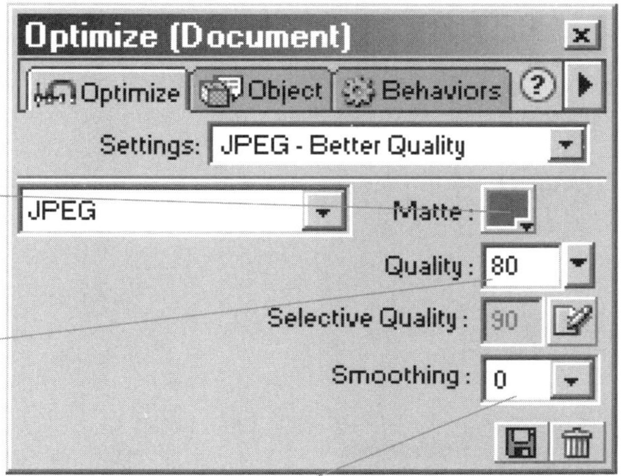

Smoothing setting. If this is increased it gives the image a blurry effect

If you have created your own custom optimise settings these will appear in the Settings box of the Optimize panel, with the names that they were given when they were created.

Saving settings

Once you have set optimise attributes for an image you may want to keep these so that they can be reapplied to another image. To do this:

1 Click here on the Optimize panel

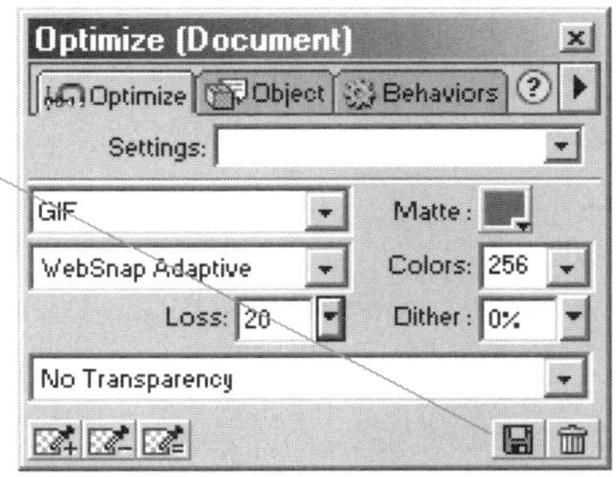

To delete a custom setting, select it in the Settings box and click on the wastebasket icon. A warning message will appear asking if you are sure you want to delete this setting. Select OK.

2 Enter a name for the settings and select OK

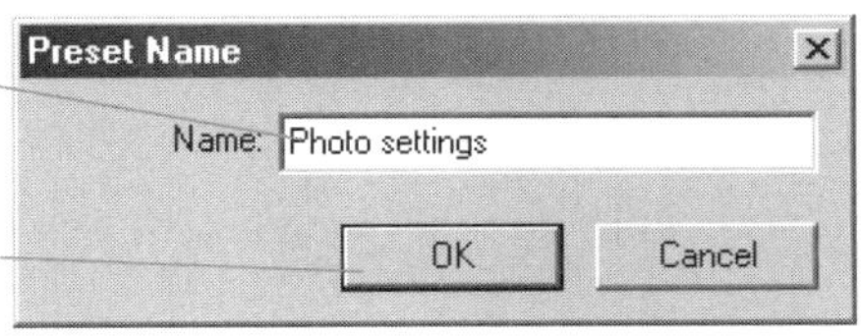

Applying optimisation

To optimise an image and then save it:

Images can also be optimised in other file formats including PNG, TIFF, WBMP and BMP.

1. Select either the Preview, 2-Up or 4-Up panel

2. Click on one of the image windows

File formats such as TIFF and BMP should be used if you want to print out hard copies of images. Images in these formats can be optimised in just the same way as GIFs and JPEGs.

3. Apply optimisation settings from the Optimize panel

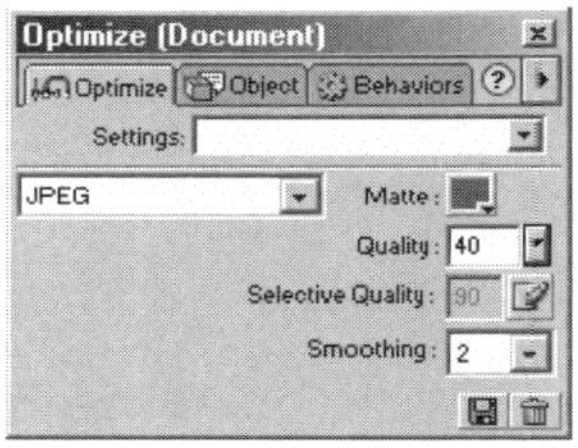

4. When you have the best optimise settings, select File>Export from the menu bar

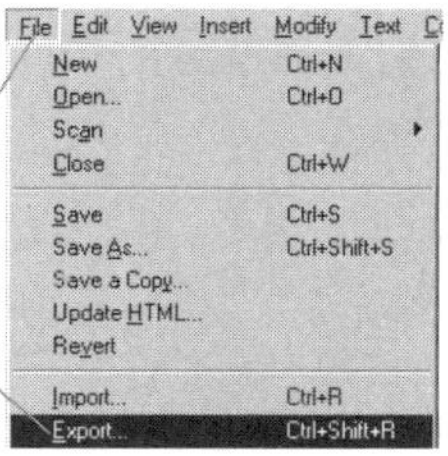

Once you have optimised an image, always save it using the Export function. If you use the Save function it will automatically be saved as a PNG file.

5. Save the image as you would any other file. Check in the file's directory to make sure it has been saved as the correct type of file

Export Preview

If you want to get a clearer look at the way an image will appear with a certain set of optimise settings, you can do so with the Export Preview function:

The magnification for the preview image in Export Preview can be increased or decreased. If it is viewed at 100% this should be the size it will appear when viewed on a Web page.

1 Select an image and apply optimisation settings

2 Select File>Export Preview from the menu bar

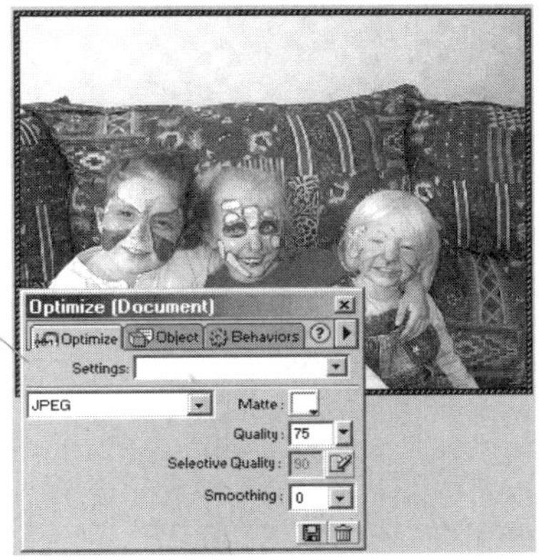

If you select OK in the Export Preview dialog box, this saves the current settings and exits the dialog box: it does not export and save the image. To do this, you have to select the Export button.

3 The Export Preview window is an enlarged version of the image preview windows, and it also includes the settings from the Optimize panel. These can be edited before exporting

In the Export Preview window there is a tab for File. This contains options for changing the scale and dimensions of the currently selected image.

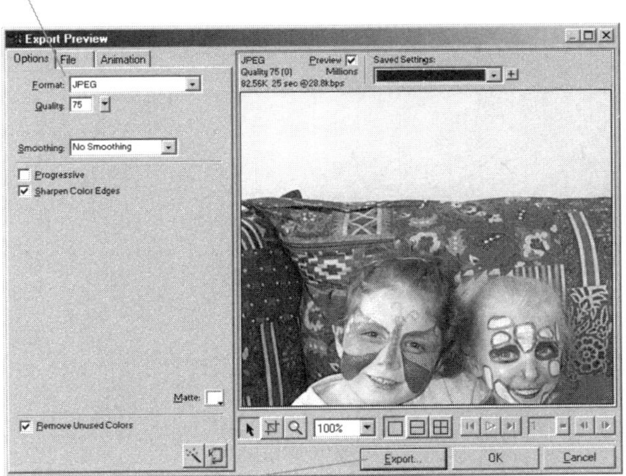

4 Select Export to save the image with the current settings

Export Wizard

For anyone who does not feel completely confident about optimising and exporting images, there is a wizard that guides you through all of the required steps. To use the Export Wizard:

If you select File>Export in Original mode, without the use of Export Preview, Export Wizard or the Optimize panel, the image will be exported in the same format as it was opened in. So if it was opened as a GIF, this is the format in which it will be exported. If you want to export it to another format then the optimise settings have to be changed in either the Optimize panel or during the export process with Export Preview or Export Wizard.

1. Select the image you want to export, from either the Original, Preview, 2-Up or 4-Up panels

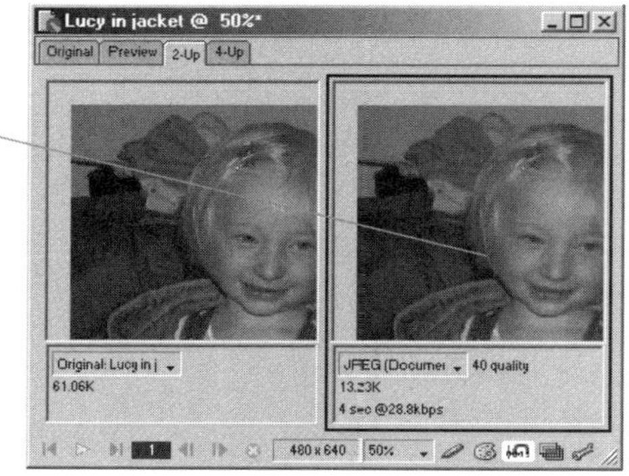

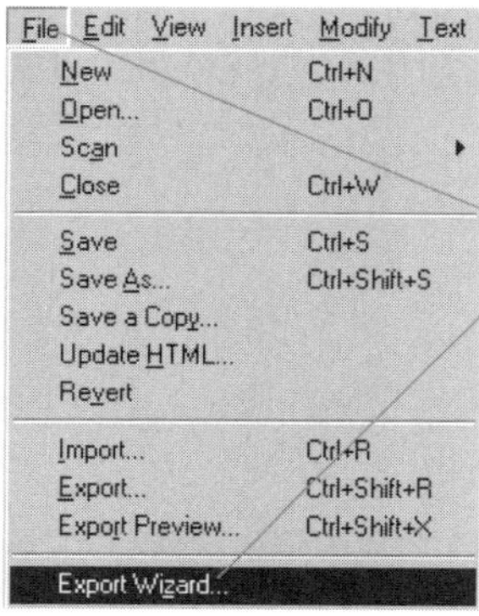

2. Select File>Export Wizard from the menu bar

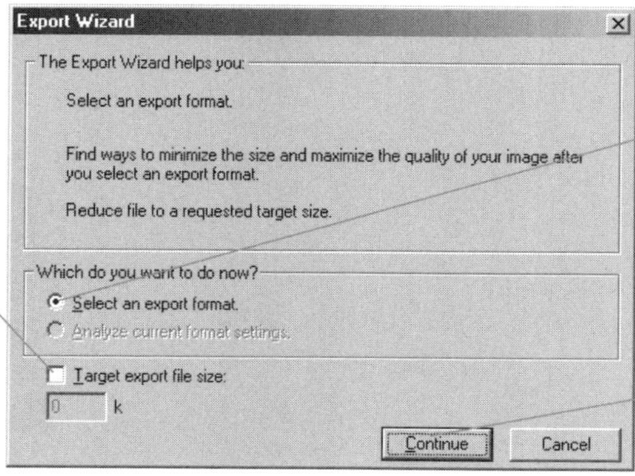

3. Click here to enable the Wizard to select an appropriate file format. Select Continue

If you want an image to be optimised to a certain size, click here and enter the target size that you want the image to be. The Wizard will automatically set the image's attributes to meet this file size.

By default, the settings chosen by the Export Wizard for images to be used on the Web or with Dreamweaver are GIF or JPEG format. For image editing and desktop publishing applications, the default format is TIFF.

If you want to export an image with a transparent background, it has to be in a GIF format. For more on creating transparent images, see the next page.

4 Specify how you intend to use the image. The Wizard will then select the most appropriate file format. Select Continue

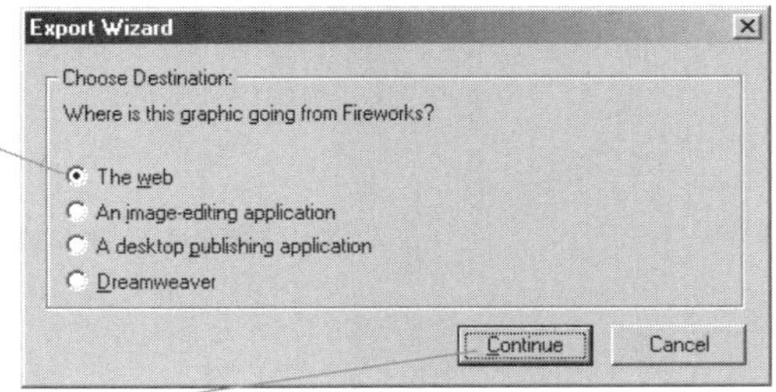

5 A dialog box will detail the selected file format and explain any issues connected with it. Select Exit to continue

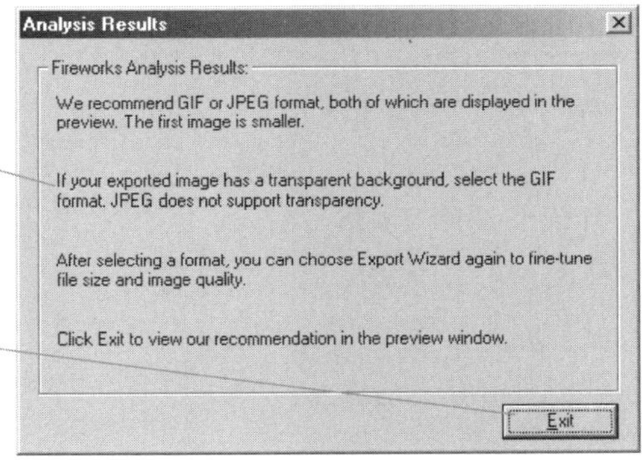

6 The Export Preview dialog will appear. This is the same as on page 81. Edit any settings as required and select Export to export and save the file

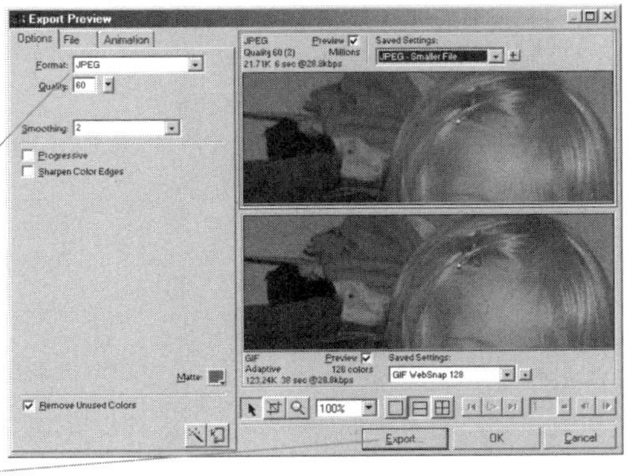

Transparency

One of the most effective techniques for displaying images on Web pages is to make their background transparent, or part of the images themselves.

Index transparency

This is used to make specific colour transparent:

Images have to be in GIF format in order to be able to apply transparency to them.

When applying transparency, the effect can only be seen in Preview, 2-Up or 4-Up mode. It cannot be seen if the image is being viewed in Original mode.

One of the best uses of transparency is for an item where you want to make the whole background transparent, such as with a company logo. This means that the image will blend into a Web page background rather than appear to sit on top of it.

1. Select a GIF image and click here on the Optimize panel. Select Index Transparency

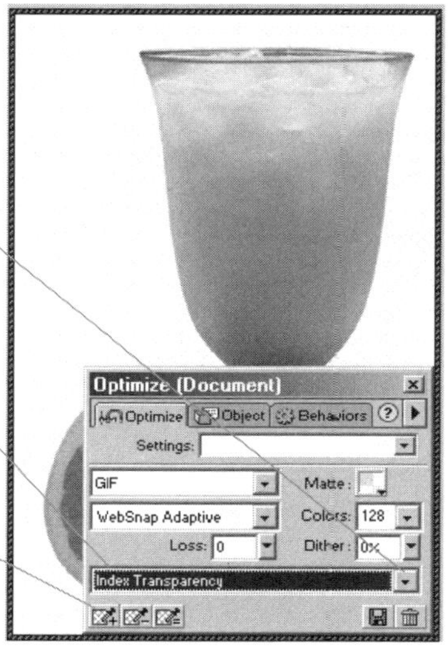

2. Click here to select a colour to make transparent

3. Click on the image. The colour at this point will then become transparent wherever it occurs in the image. So when the image is viewed on a Web page, the page background will be visible through the transparent area

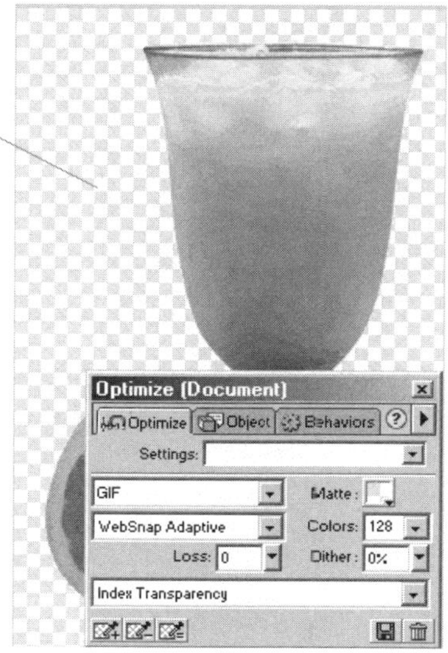

Dreamweaver and more

Fireworks is closely integrated with the Web authoring program, Dreamweaver. This chapter shows how the two programs can be used together to speed up workflow when working with images and Web pages. It also gives an overview of creating HTML elements in Fireworks. Finally, it shows how to import images created in another popular image editing program, Adobe Photoshop.

Covers

Chapter Six

Fireworks and Dreamweaver

For a detailed view of Dreamweaver, take a look at Dreamweaver 4 in easy steps.

A studio version of Fireworks and Dreamweaver can be bought for approximately £350–£420.

For more information about slices and hotspots, see Chapter Seven. For more information on rollovers and pop-up menus, see Chapter Nine.

If you are going to be using a Web authoring program then it should definitely be Dreamweaver if you use Fireworks.

Since images are an integral part of Web sites, it makes sense for companies to closely integrate their Web authoring tools with their image editing ones. That is exactly what Macromedia have done with Fireworks and Dreamweaver. Dreamweaver is the Macromedia Web authoring program and it is widely regarded as one of the best tools for the job on the market, particularly by professional designers. It has a powerful array of features to satisfy even the most demanding of designers and it has an interface that can enable people to get up and running with the program quickly.

With the latest versions of Fireworks and Dreamweaver it is possible to move seamlessly between the two to edit images and create elements for Web pages. In addition, the user interfaces are designed in the same way, so when you move from one to another you will still be in a familiar working environment. Some of the functions that can be performed with Fireworks and Dreamweaver are:

- Rountrip image editing. This means you can open a page in Dreamweaver and then edit images directly in Fireworks: you do not have to open the image separately, edit it and then place it back into Dreamweaver. When you have finished editing the image in Fireworks, the changes are automatically applied to the Dreamweaver document
- Importing HTML files used to create more complex items such as slices, hotspots, rollovers and pop-up menus. Since Fireworks is not just an image editor it can also create HTML documents. The designer specifies which images to use in a document and the functions they are going to perform, e.g. two different images that are going to be combined as a rollover button, and then Fireworks creates all of the necessary files and code to create the effect. It is then a case of importing the images and HTML into Dreamweaver. This gives designers a great deal of power and flexibility

Roundtrip image editing

Before images are added to a page in Dreamweaver they will probably already have been edited and optimised in Fireworks. However, if further work is required, this can be done by accessing Fireworks directly from Dreamweaver. To do this:

A contextual menu is one that contains options that apply to the currently selected item. These are always accessed by right-clicking (Windows) or Ctrl+click (Mac) on an item on the page.

1 Right-click (Windows) or Ctrl+click (Mac) the image you want to edit in Dreamweaver

2 Select Edit with Fireworks 4 from the contextual menu

You can also select Optimize in Fireworks from the contextual menu, in which case you will be taken to a dialog box in Fireworks which is the same as the Export Preview one.

3 In the Find Source dialog box. select No, unless you want to edit any existing PNG file

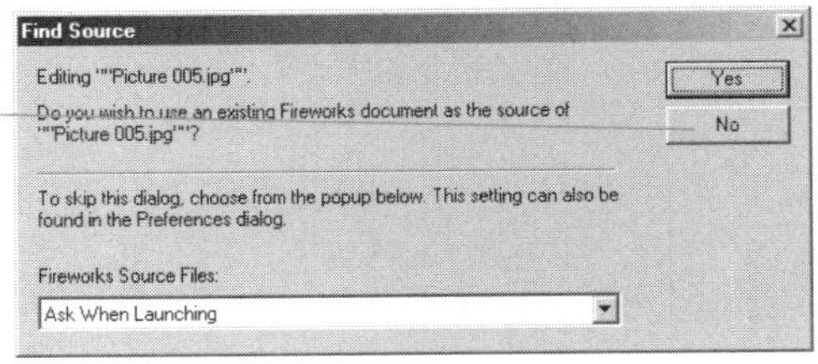

To make sure the Find Source dialog box does not appear everytime you want to edit an image from Dreamweaver, select Never Use Source PNG in the Fireworks Source Files box.

4 The image is opened in the normal Fireworks environment, except that it indicates here that the document is one that is being edited from Dreamweaver

Roundtrip editing can also be accessed by selecting an image in Dreamweaver and clicking on the Edit button on the Properties Inspector.

5 Apply editing changes as you normally would within Fireworks (in this case the image has been cropped)

6 Select Done

7 You will be taken back to Dreamweaver and the original image will have had the editing changes applied to it

If you select File>Update while editing the image in Fireworks, the changes will be applied within the Dreamweaver document but you will remain in Fireworks. To apply the changes and return to Dreamweaver, the Done button has to be selected.

If you have edited the size of an image in Fireworks, you will need to reset the size when you return to Dreamweaver. See the next two pages for details on how to do this.

Once an image has been updated with roundtrip editing, the original will also have been changed, not just the version in Dreamweaver. Make sure that any editing changes you make are ones you want to apply permanently before selecting Done in Fireworks.

Resizing images

It is possible to resize images in a Dreamweaver document by applying the changes in a similar way to the editing changes shown on the previous two pages. However, there is one extra step that needs to be applied:

It is possible to resize an image within the Dreamweaver environment by selecting it and dragging the resizing handles. However this results in poorer image quality than if it is resized in Fireworks.

1 Right-click (Windows) or Ctrl+click (Mac) on a Dreamweaver document and select Edit in Fireworks 4 from the contextual menu

2 In Fireworks, select Modify> Image Size from the menu bar

When entering values for editing the image size, check the Constrain Proportions box to ensure that the image is resized proportionally, i.e. when the height value is changed the width value is updated automatically to keep the image in the correct proportion, and vice versa.

3 Enter the new image size values here. Select OK

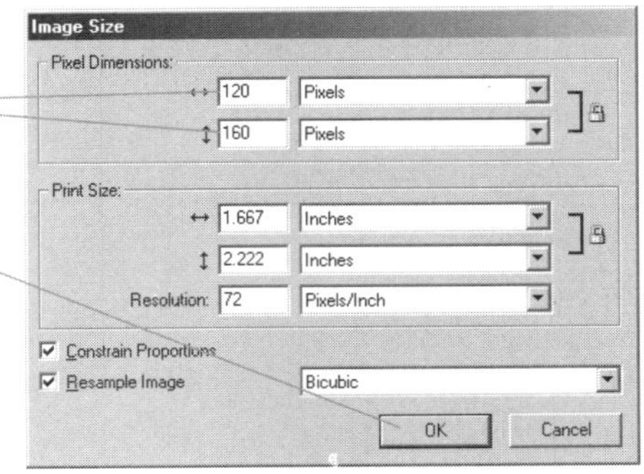

If other image editing changes have been applied to an image, these will appear when the image is viewed again in Dreamweaver. However, any resizing changes have to be applied by using the Reset command.

4 In Dreamweaver the image initially appears the same size as the original

5 Right-click (Windows) or Ctrl+click (Mac) on the image and select Reset Size from the contextual menu

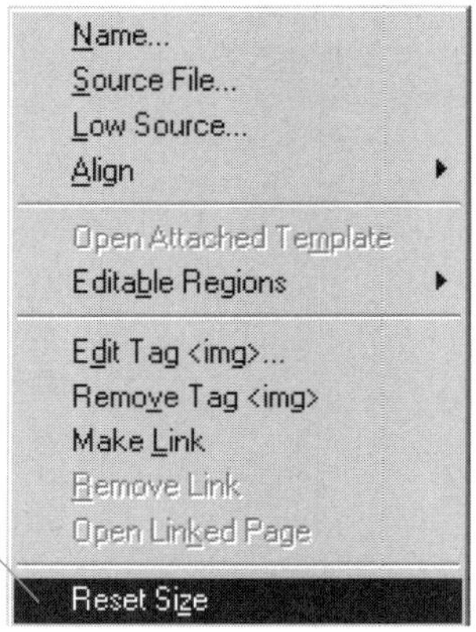

The Reset Size function can also be applied by selecting an image and clicking on the Reset button on the Properties Inspector.

Do not change the size of an image too many times. If this is done then the quality of the image will deteriorate noticeably.

6 The image size that was specified in Fireworks is now applied to the image in Dreamweaver

Fireworks HTML

Fireworks can create certain elements that are a combination of both HTML and images. These include slices, hotspots, pop-up menus and rollover images. This can create a number of different documents in Fireworks which can then be imported into Dreamweaver for use on Web pages. This is a powerful device as it can add considerable functionality to Web pages. The basics of creating HTML documents in Fireworks and then importing them into Dreamweaver are:

For more details about slices and hotspots, see Chapter Seven. For more information about pop-up menus and rollover images, see Chapter Nine. These include more information about exporting these elements once they have been created.

1 Create a slice, hotspot, pop-up menu or rollover image

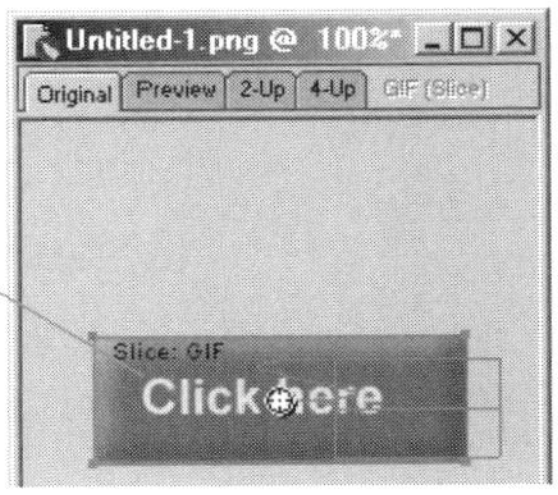

2 Select File>Export from the menu bar

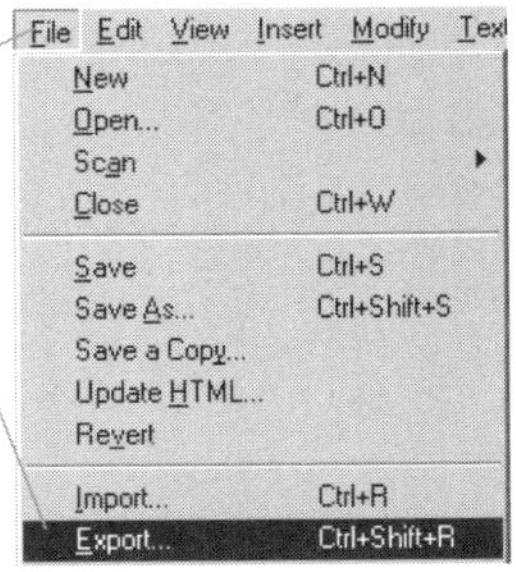

The export settings for each item are covered in greater detail in the relevant chapters.

3 In the Export dialog box, select the required settings

4 Select Save

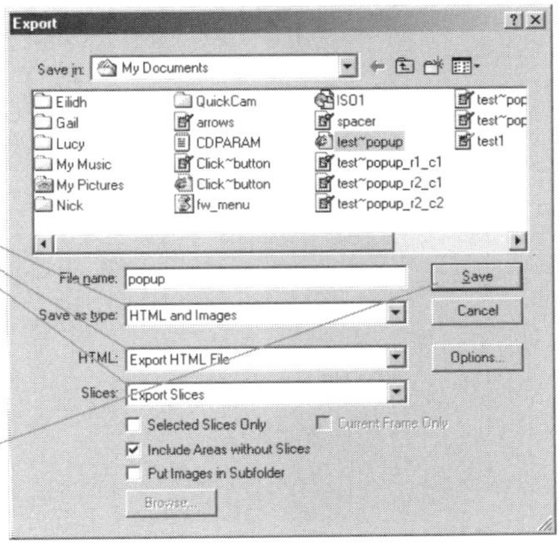

5 To import the effect into a Dreamweaver document, select Fireworks HTML from the Objects panel

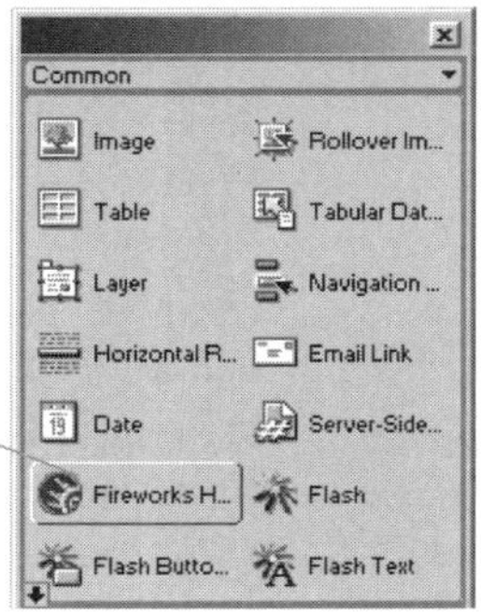

When Dreamweaver imports an HTML document created in Fireworks, it incorporates it into an existing HTML document, it does not open it as a separate one.

6 Select Browse to locate the required files

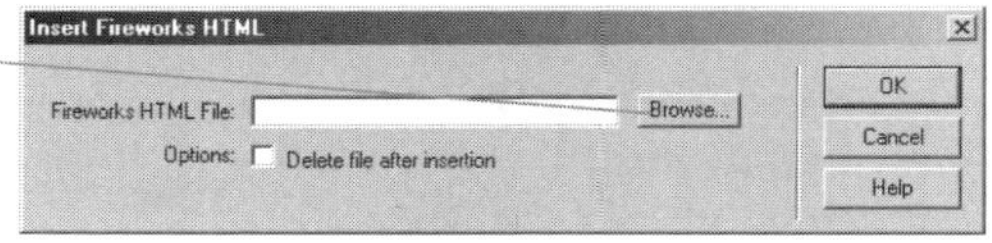

7 An HTML file and various image files will have been created. Select the HTML file and select Open

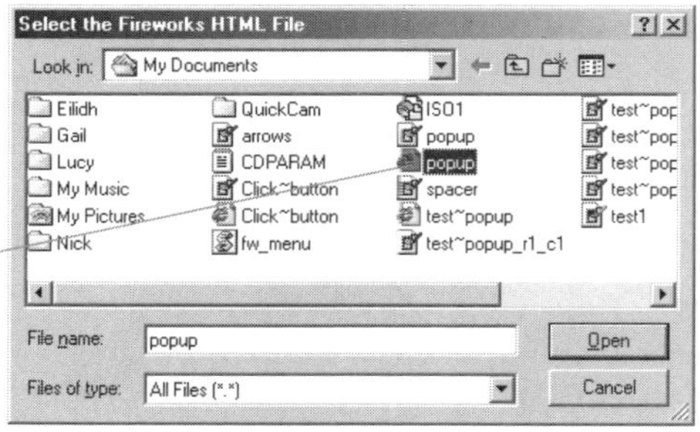

When Dreamweaver imports an HTML document it automatically includes any images in the correct places.

8 Select OK to insert the HTML document and any associated images into the Dreamweaver document. These will be active when previewed through a browser

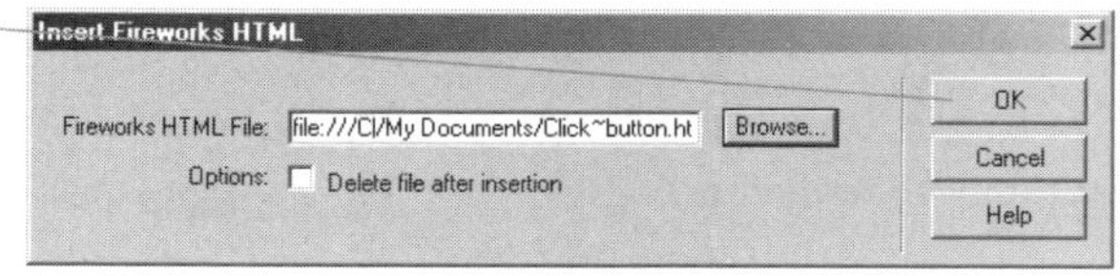

Updating HTML

HTML files that have been created in Fireworks can be updated as follows:

1. Make changes to an image that has been exported as HTML and select File>Update HTML from the menu bar

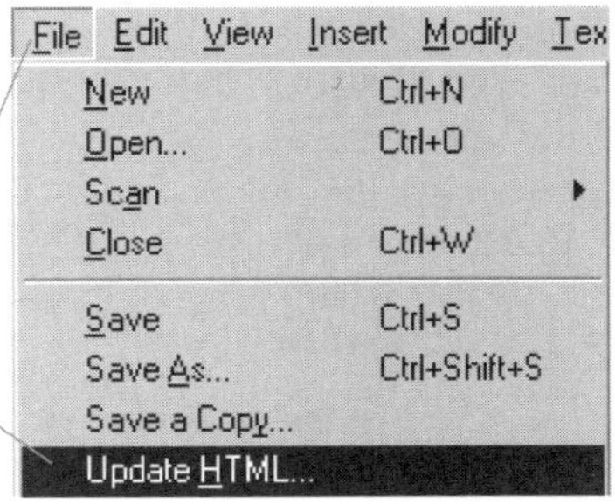

2. Select the file and select Open

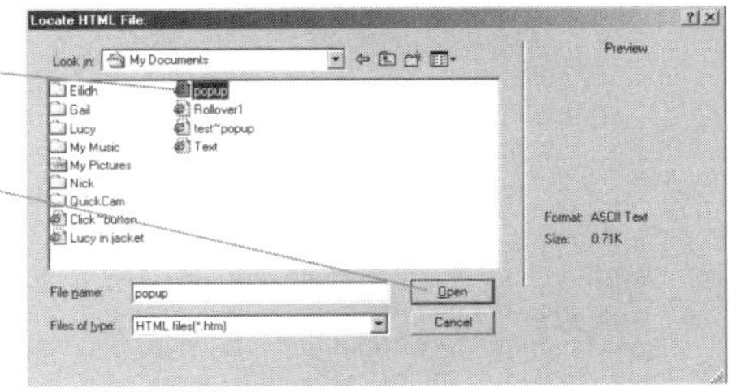

If you try and update a file that has no corresponding HTML file, Fireworks will insert a table so you can insert HTML at the end of the document.

3. Select the required updating options. Select OK

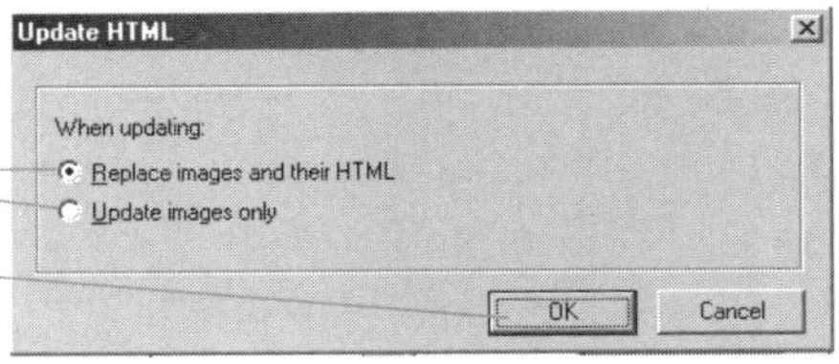

4. Select the folder where the images are contained and select Open. The required files will automatically be updated

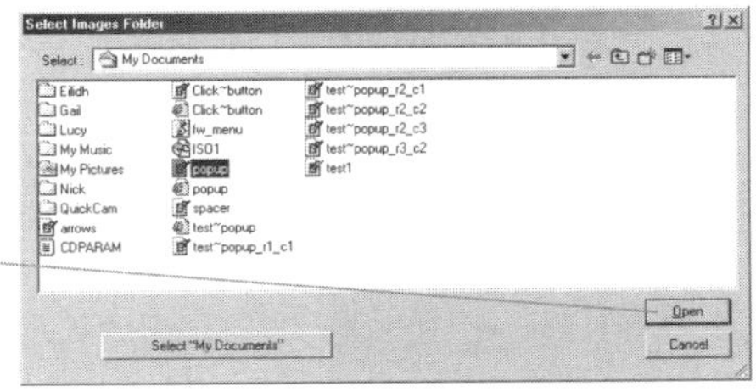

Using Photoshop files

Fireworks is becoming increasingly popular with users of Adobe Photoshop and this has been recognised in Fireworks 4, with increased flexibility for working with Photoshop files. When importing Photoshop files, various preferences can be set to determine how the files appear when they are imported:

Fireworks files i.e. PNG files, can also be exported into the required format for Photoshop files.

1 Select Edit> Preferences from the menu bar

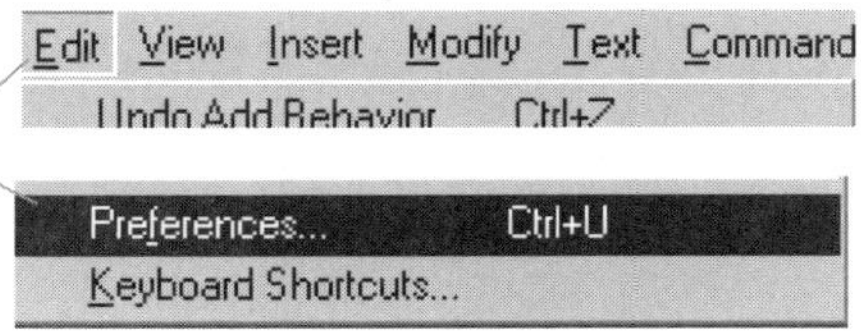

2 Select the Import tab

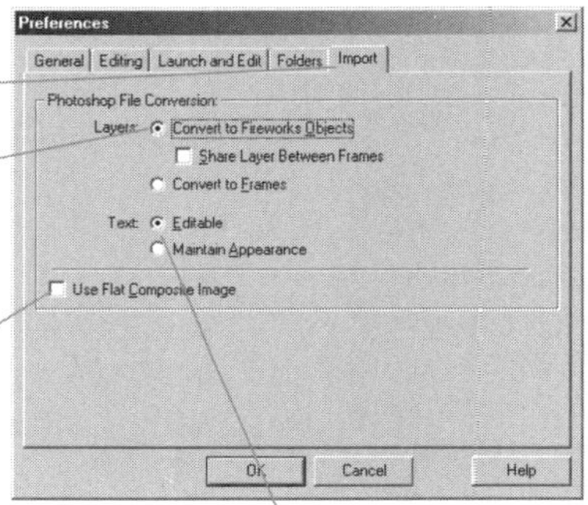

Click here to specify how layers are handled

Click here if you want the images to be imported without layers

Click here to specify how text is handled

Photoshop files have a PSD file extension. Other file formats that have been created in Photoshop, such as GIFs and JPEGs, can be opened and imported into Fireworks as normal.

Importing Photoshop files

To import files from Photoshop:

Select Edit>Open from the menu bar. Navigate to a Photoshop file and select Open

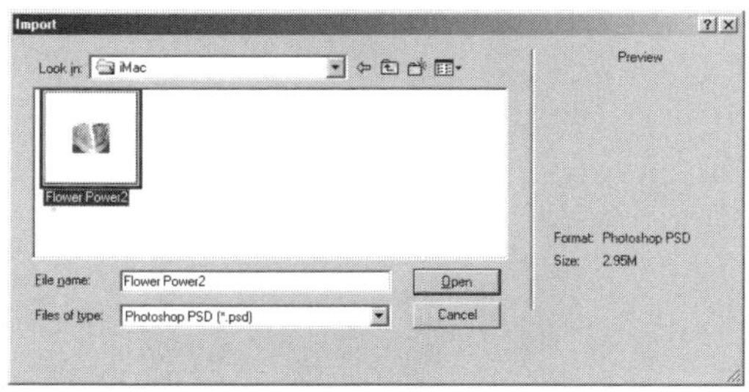

Photoshop files can be imported into an existing Fireworks document by selecting Edit> Import from the menu bar and navigating to the required file.

Slices, hotspots and layers

Chapter Seven

Slices and hotspots can be used to create HTML code that can give images increased functionality. This chapter gives an overview of slices and hotspots and shows some of the uses to which they can be put. It also shows how layers and masks can be used to combine graphics together into a single image.

Covers

About slices

Although slices take on a physical appearance within Fireworks, they are in fact HTML code that adds certain elements of functionality to images. Slices can be edited within a Fireworks document, and then the whole file can be exported for use within a Web page. Slices are used to cut up images into smaller parts and then various functions can be applied. The main uses for slices are:

Cutting up large images

When you see an image on a Web site that is being download a segment at a time, this is probably because it has been created using slicing.

Large images take longer to download on a Web page than a lot of small ones. With slices, it is possible to cut an image up into several smaller parts. Once it is exported and viewed as a Web page, the different parts are reassembled to display the entire image again. Since this uses a lot of smaller images, this results in faster downloading times. In addition, it is possible to optimise different parts of a sliced image. So if one area of the image does not have to be as prominent as another, this can be optimised to create a smaller file size.

Creating interactivity

For more information about creating rollover buttons, navigation bars and rollovers, see Chapter Nine.

Slices can be used to apply interactivity to certain areas of an image. For instance, a slice could be created for buttons, pop-up menus or rollover items. This is done by instructing the slice to display another item when the cursor is passed over it. In this way slices can be a very powerful tool for use on a Web page.

Swapping images

Sliced elements of an image are created as individual image files. These can then be edited independently of each other if required.

If there are a number of different elements within an image, slices can be used to update one image, without having to edit the whole thing. For instance, if there is an image that displays a weekly special offer on an e-commerce site, slicing could be used to update the special offer item without having to touch the rest of the image. In this respect a sliced image can be thought of as a jigsaw puzzle: it is cut up in Fireworks and then the pieces are put together within a browser. If you need to replace one piece, this can be done without disturbing anything else.

Creating slices

There are three ways to create slices in Fireworks:

Menu bar option

When a slice is created, Fireworks generates a table structure in which the slice resides. This is denoted by lines around the object that is being sliced.

Slices created in this way are always done so as rectangle. So if you insert a slice over an oval or a circle, it will cover a larger area than the object itself.

When a slice is created, the name of the file format of the image that is being sliced is displayed on top of the slice.

1 Select an object with the Pointer tool, or part of an object with the Marquee tool

2 Select Insert> Slice from the menu bar

3 The slice is inserted over the object and appears as a transparent green rectangle

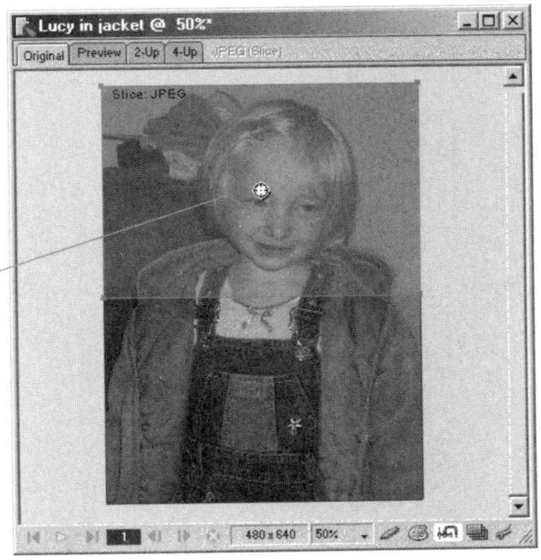

Slice tool option

1 Select the Slice tool from the Tools panel

2 Click and drag on an image to create a slice

When creating multiple slices on an object, be careful not to overlap them. This could effect the way they are viewed in a browser or any interactivity that is applied to them.

Polygon Slice tool option

1 Select the Polygon Slice tool from the tools panel

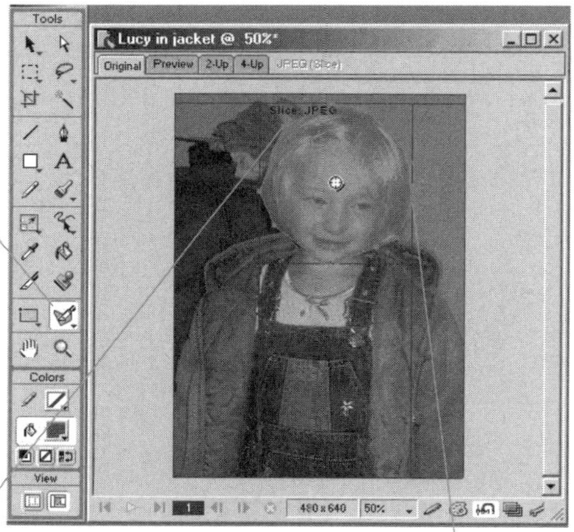

2 Click at the point where you want to begin the slice

3 Click at each point where you want to create a change of direction. Create an irregular slice object in this way

To access the Polygon Slice tool, click on the black triangle next to the Slice tool on the tools panel.

When using the Polygon Slice tool, click back at the starting point to finish creating the polygon shape.

Slice options

Once a slice has been created it can be edited and manipulated with the Object panel and the Layers panel:

Hyperlinks are used on slices to create the interactivity needed for buttons and navigation bars.

Object panel

The object panel can be used to add a URL (hyperlink) to a slice and specify its name and colour:

1 Select or create a slice and select Window>Object from the menu bar

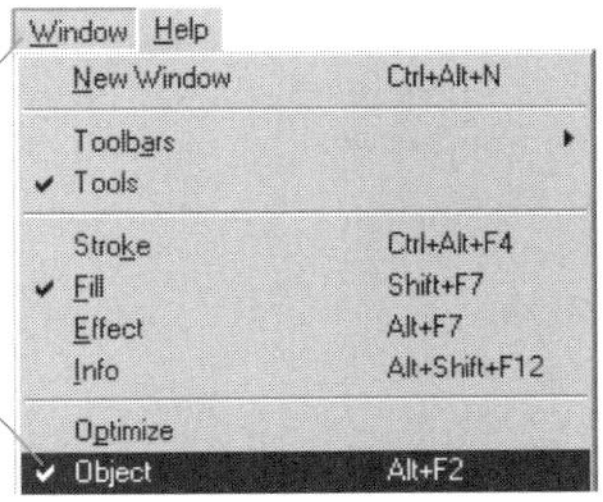

Alternative (or Alt) text is the text that appears when the cursor is moved over an image in a browser. It also appears if a browser is set to not display images. The target location is a function that is used to specify where a page opens when it is part of a frames structure in a Web page.

2 Enter a URL, alternative text and a target location (if required)

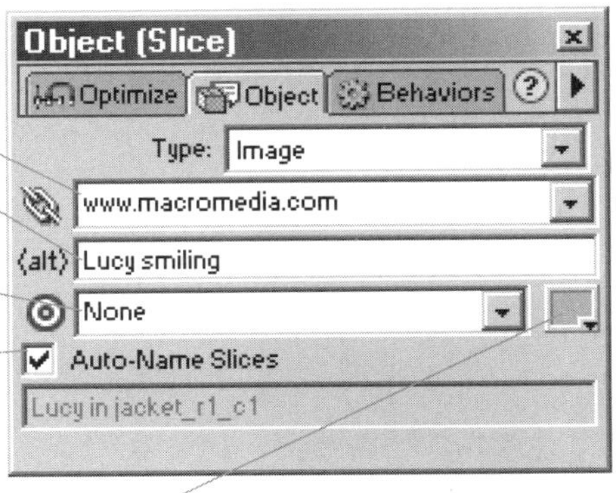

4 Check this if you want slices to be given names automatically

3 Click here to select a colour for displaying slices

If the Auto-Name Slices box is checked in the Object panel then each slice will be given a name that is derived from the base image. For instance, if the image on which the slice resides is named Home the slice will be named Home_r1_c2.

Tools panel

The Tools panel can be used to hide slices so that the images underneath them can be edited. To do this:

The Show/Hide buttons can also be used to show and hide any hotspots within an image.

Click here on the Tools panel to hide all slices

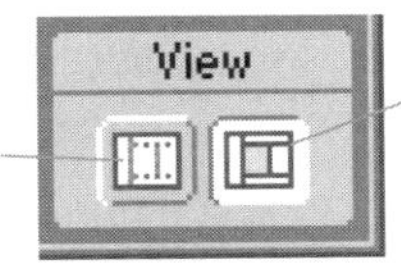

Click here on the Tools panel to show all slices

Optimising slices

Slices can be optimised in the same way as optimising whole images. However, it is possible to apply different levels of optimisation to different slices:

When slices are exported the sliced area becomes an image in its own right, with code inserted into an HTML document that instructs a browser how to reconstruct the whole sliced image.

1. Select an image that contains two or more slices. Select one of the slices by clicking on it once with the Pointer tool

2. Apply optimisation attributes in the Optimize panel

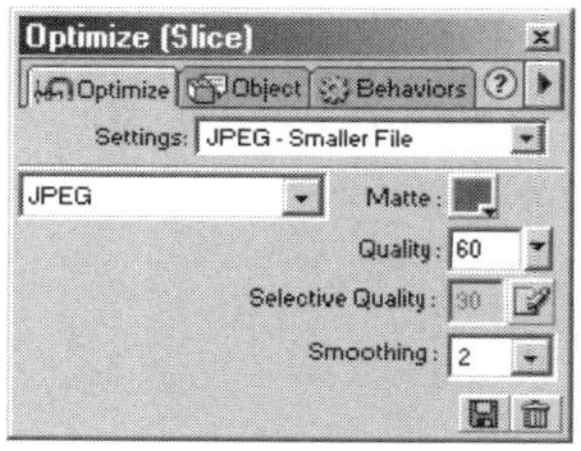

Slices on a single image can be optimised in different file formats i.e. you can mix GIFs and JPEGs. When the image is reassembled in a browser, the different file formats will appear together.

3. Select another slice

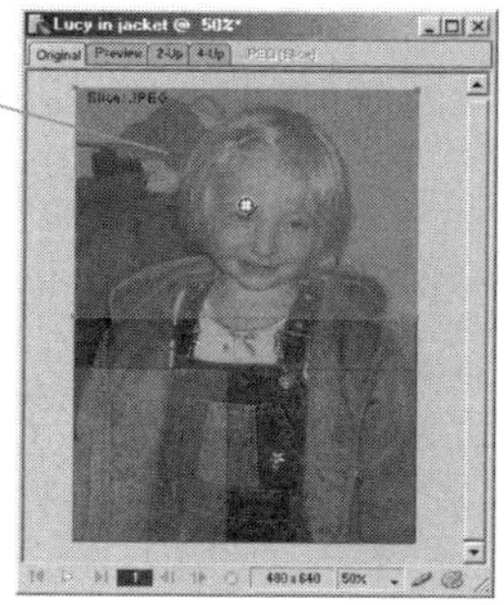

4. Apply different optimisation settings to this slice

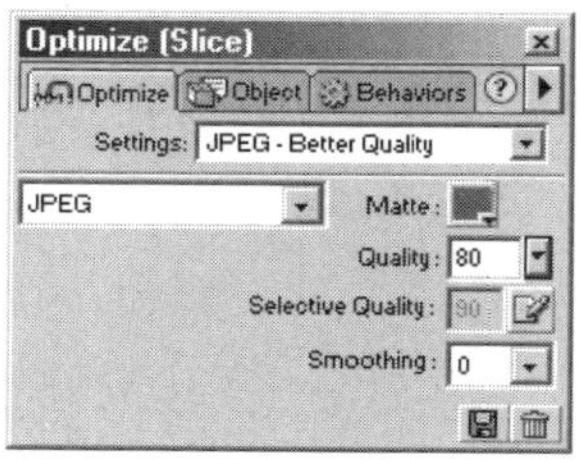

Exporting slices

Slices have to be exported for all of the sliced images and HTML code to be saved in a format that can then reconstruct the image in a browser. To export slices:

1 Create an image with all of the relevant slices inserted. Select File>Export from the menu bar

The Export process is the same for an image that has been sliced into smaller parts or an item such as a pop-up menu or a rollover image.

2 Select HTML and Images option

3 Select Export HTML file

4 Select Export Slices

5 Select Save

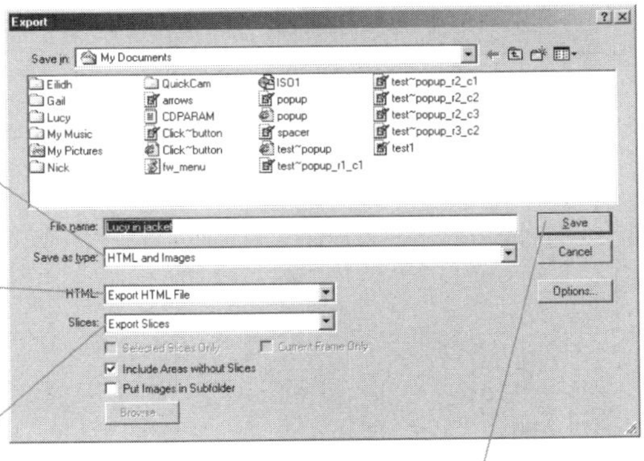

When a sliced object is exported the HTML file that is created contains the code for reassembling the image and also any interactivity that has been applied to the slices.

6 An HTML file is created and each slice is created as a separate image file

Text slices

Slices can also be used to create text on images. This is done by converting text into an image file. It is then possible to update the text without affecting the rest of the image. To create a text slice:

1 Insert a slice on an image

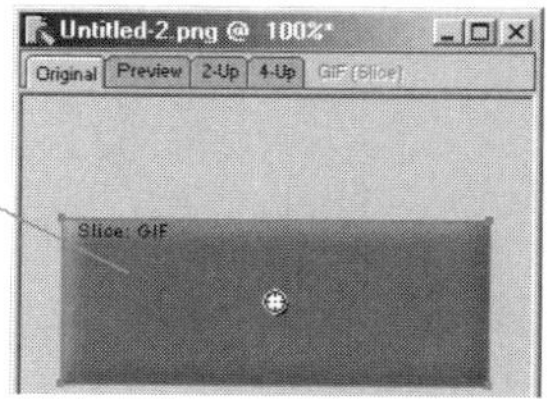

Text on a slice can be formatted by inserting HTML tags around it in the Object panel.

2 In the Object panel, click here and select Text

3 Enter the text you want to appear on the image

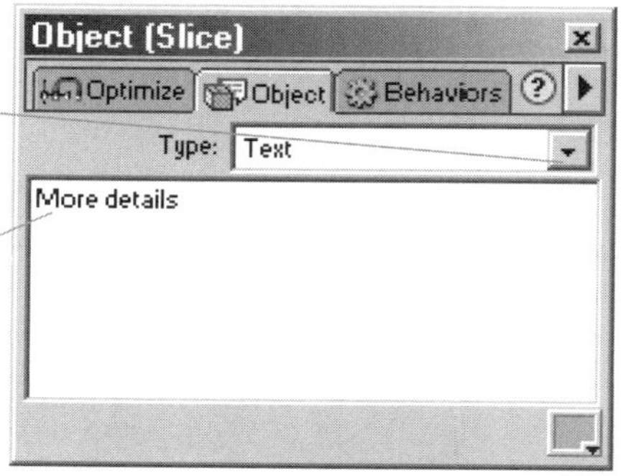

Text slices can be used for items that need to be updated regularly, such as the date or a latest news function.

4 Select File> Export from the menu bar and select Save in the Export dialog box

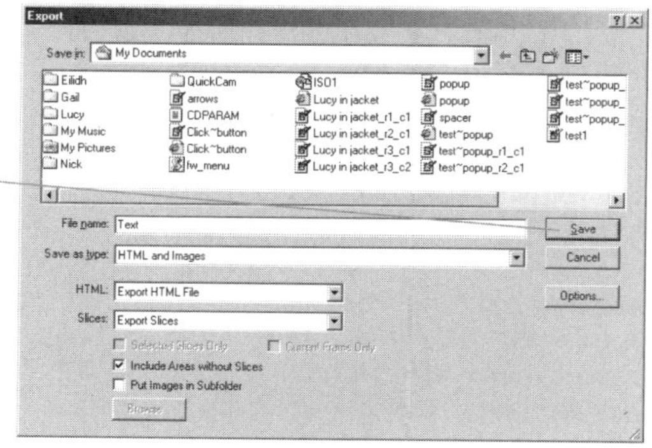

5 When the image is viewed through a browser, the text appears as a slice

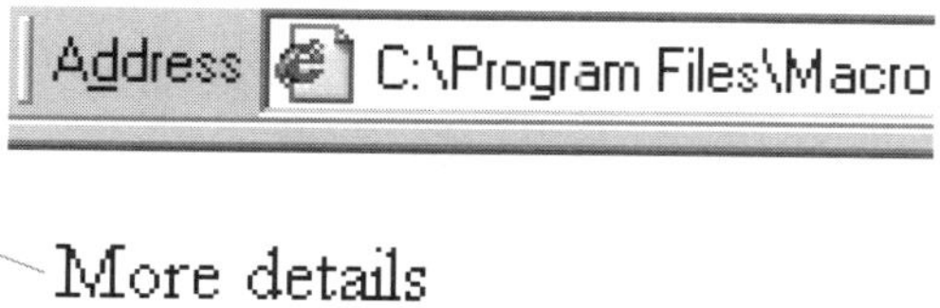

Creating hotspots

Hotspots can be used to create hyperlinks to different addresses, from within the same image. This end result is known as an image map and it can be used as a useful navigation device on a Web page. For instance, it could be used on a physical map to link to pages containing information about a particular country, or an e-commerce site could contain an image with hotspots over each product. When the user clicks on that product the hotspot takes them to details about that item. To create hotspots:

Hotspots and image maps are also an effective way to create navigation bars. To do this, create the design for the navigation bar and then create an image map by drawing hotspots over each area that will navigate to another part of the site.

1 Select the Rectangle or Circle Hotspot tool from the Tools panel

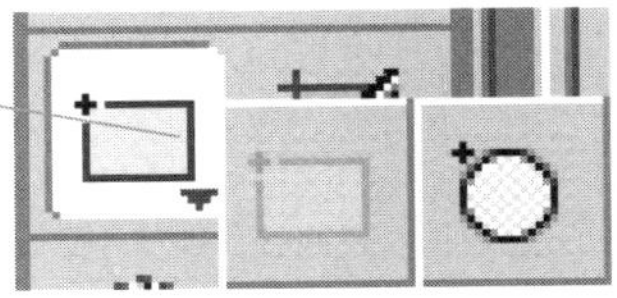

2 Draw hotspots on the image as required

The third hotspot option is the Polygon Hotspot tool. This is used to create irregular hotspots as opposed to symmetrical ones. These can be created in the same way as creating irregular slices (see page 98).

3 Select each hotspot and in the Object panel enter a URL, alternative text and a target location (if required)

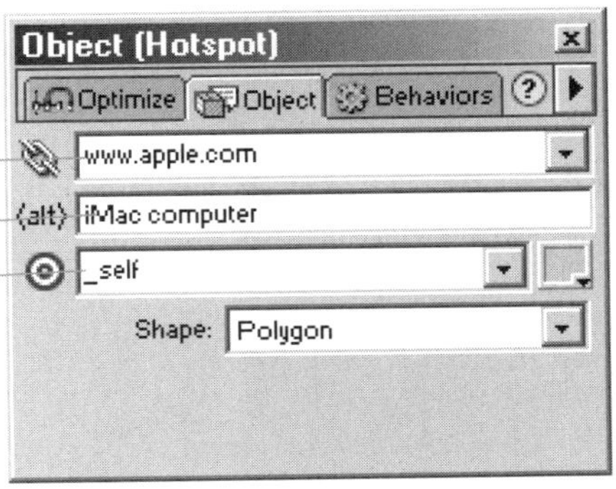

Exporting hotspots

Once an image map has been created it can be exported so that it can then be used on a Web page. To do this:

Fireworks creates client-side image maps, which means all of the relevant code is stored on the user's Web pages, rather than on the server that is hosting the pages.

1 Add hotspots to an image and select File>Export from the menu bar

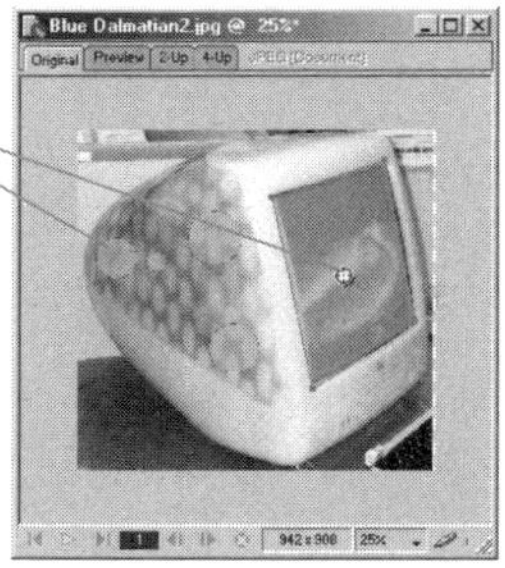

If you select Copy to Clipboard as the HTML option, the image map code can then be pasted into an HTML authoring program such as Dreamweaver. However, make sure this is done in Code view (or HTML view in some HTML editors) rather than Design view.

2 Select the location where you want the files to be saved. Select HTML and Images

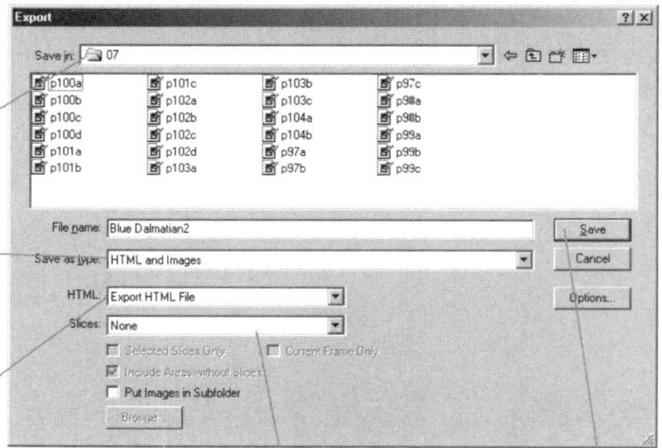

3 Select Export HTML File

4 Select None

5 Select Save

Make sure that hotspots do not overlap in an image map. This can result in the wrong page being accessed when a hotspot is clicked on.

6 When viewed in a browser each hotspot links to a different page

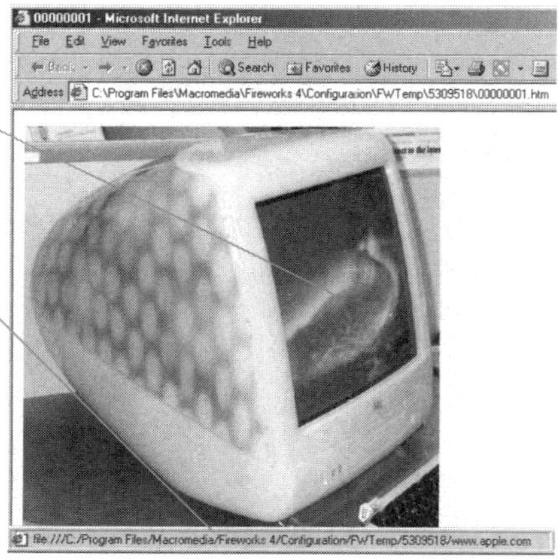

Creating layers

Layers are used in Fireworks to place items on different levels within the same image. It is similar to drawing objects on several pieces of transparent film and then combining them to create the overall image. By using layers, images can be edited independently of one another and they can greatly simplify things when working with complex images. In addition, blending and masking techniques can be used to merge images together. Working with layers is done with the Layers panel. To access the Layers panel and create layers:

The top layer in the Layers panel is always the Web layer. This contains Web objects such as hotspots and slices, and they always reside on this layer, regardless of how many Web objects there are. For more on this, see the next page.

1 Select Window> Layers from the menu bar

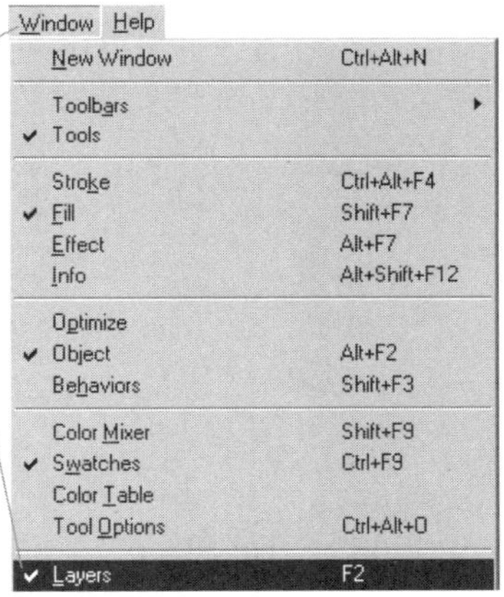

Numerous images can be added to a layer. However, if they do not need to interact with each other then it would be better to include them on separate layers.

2 The active layer is denoted by the pencil icon

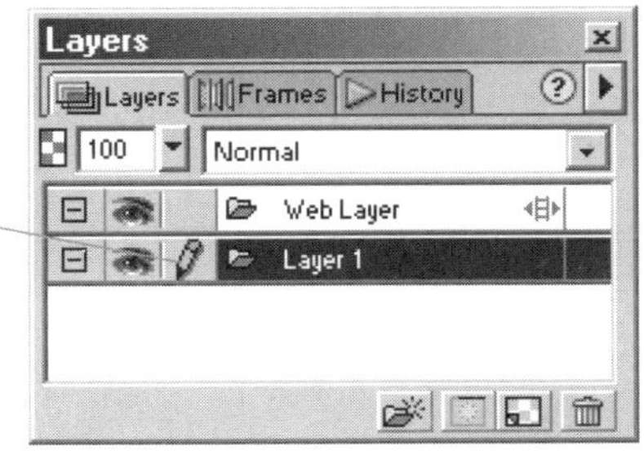

3 Add content to the work area. This is shown underneath the active layer

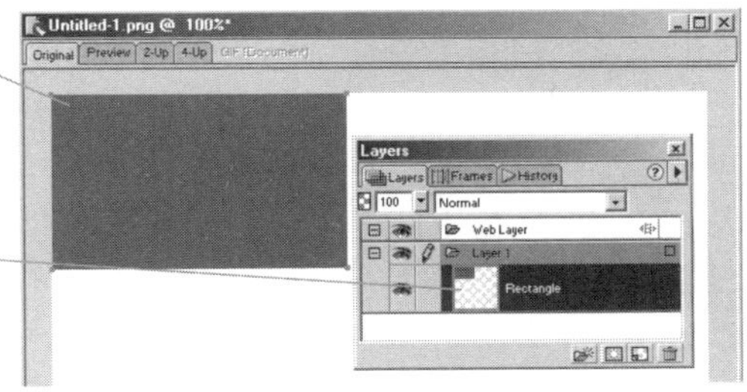

Web layer

The top layer in the Layers panel is always the Web layer, which contains Web objects such as hotspots, slices and rollovers. Even if these items are inserted when another layer is selected they will automatically be placed in the Web layer. To use the Web layer:

The Web layer cannot be deleted or renamed, although the items within it can be.

1. With the Layers panel showing, insert a hotspot or a slice on the work area

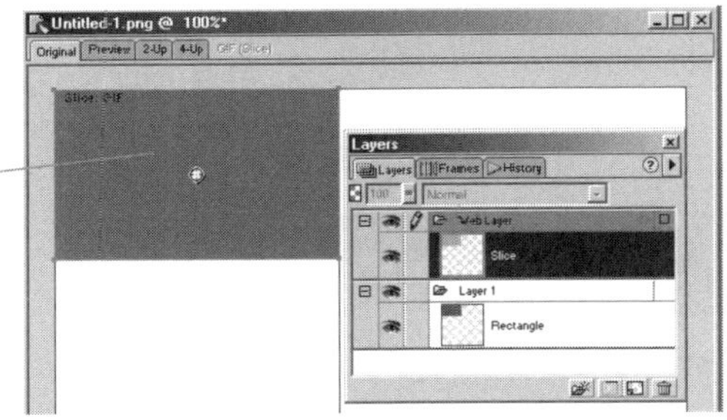

Objects in the Web layer are visible across all frames within an image.

2. The Web object appears under the Web layer

3. Double-click on the Web object and type a new name

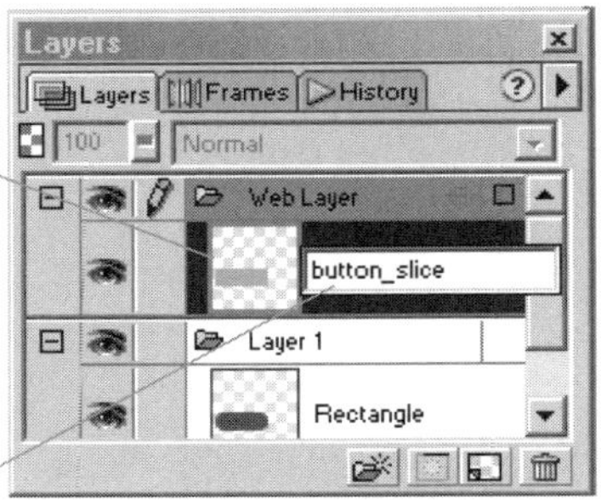

4. Select a Web object and click on the wastebasket to remove it from the Web layer and also the active document

Working with layers

Using the Layers panel, it is possible to edit and manipulate layers in a number of ways:

Adding layers

1 Click here to add a new layer

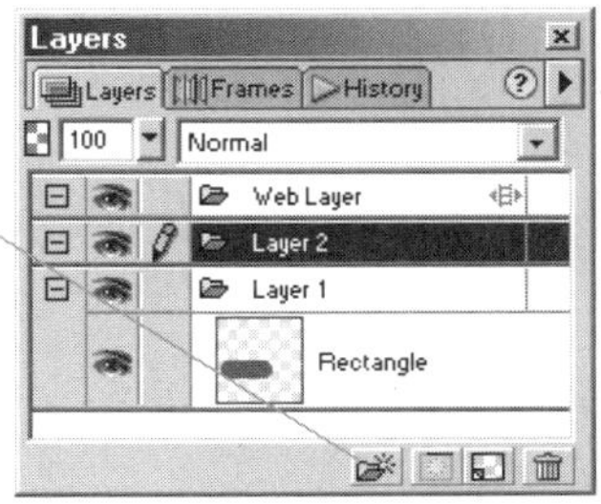

Items on layers at the top of the stacking order i.e. those nearest to the Web layer, will overlap the images on the layers below them.

2 Add content to the new layer. Although this can overlap items on other layers it does not interact with them

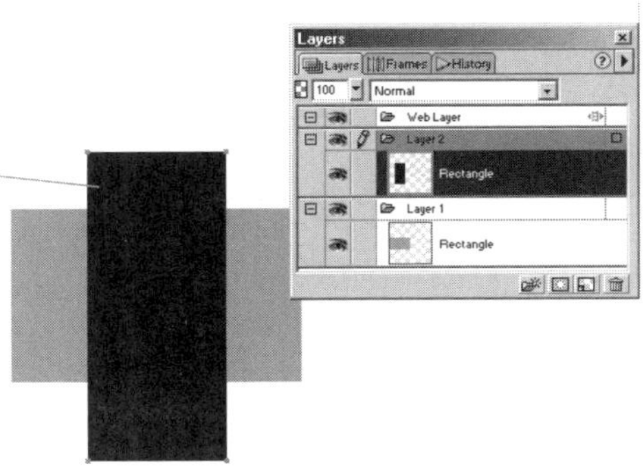

Naming layers

Items within individual layers can be renamed by double-clicking on them and typing over their existing name.

1 Double-click on the layer name

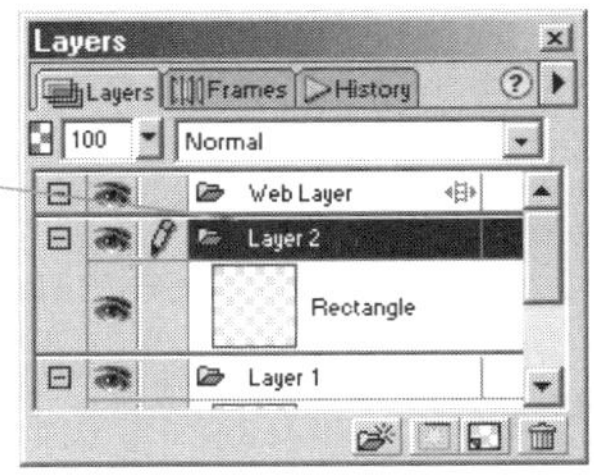

2 Enter a new name for the layer and press Enter or Return

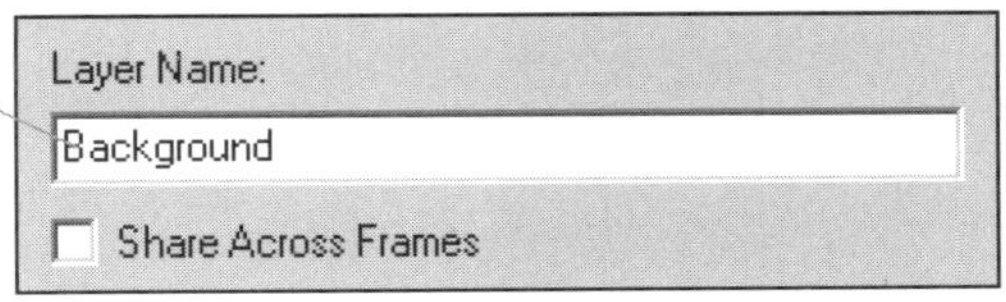

Selecting layers

If you are trying to edit a particular item and the changes are not taking effect, make sure that the correct layer is selected.

Click on the layer in the Layers panel

or

Click on an item in the work area

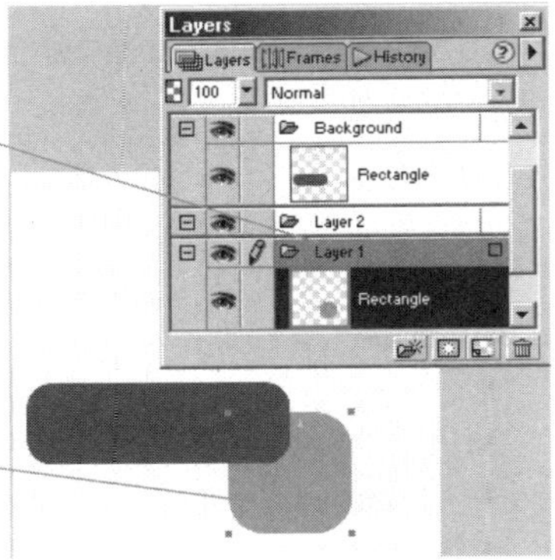

Individual items can be deleted from layers by selecting them rather than the entire layer.

Click here on the Layers panel to add a new bitmap object to a layer.

Deleting layers

Select a layer and click here

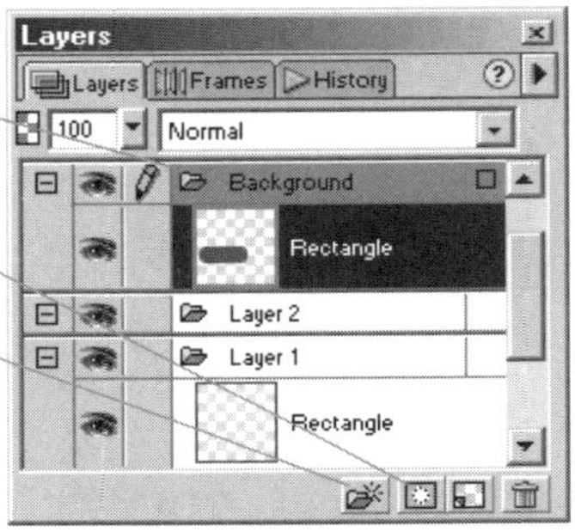

Hiding layers

When a layer is made invisible, the items on it are still in place, they are just hidden from view.

1. Click here so that the eye icon disappears

2. The items on the selected layer are no longer visible

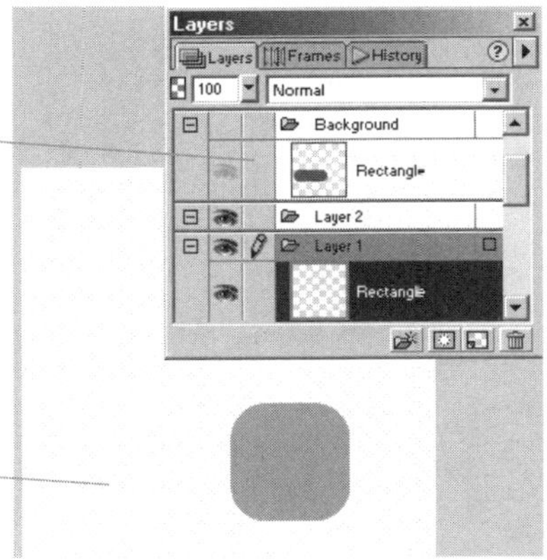

Locking layers

When a layer has been locked, it cannot be selected and the items on it cannot be edited. This is a useful option if you want to ensure you do not change any items on a layer by mistake. To unlock a layer, click the padlock icon.

Click here to display a padlock icon

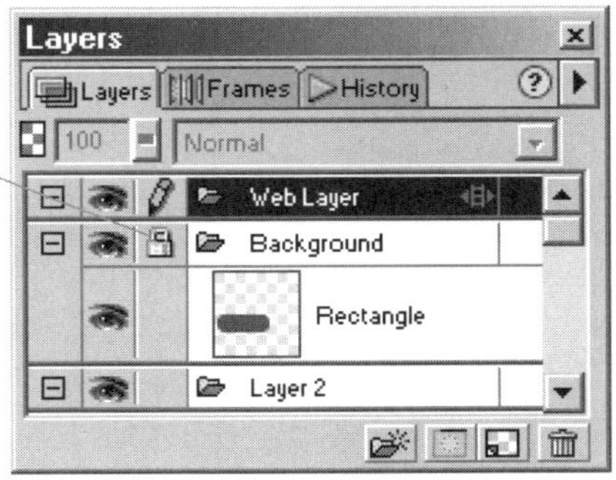

Setting transparency

1. Select an item in the work area

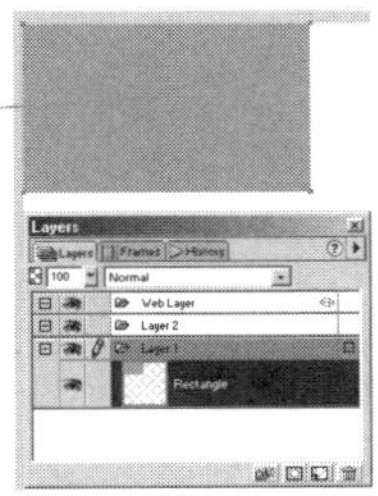

Different items within a single layer can have separate opacity settings applied to them.

2. Click here and drag the slider to set the level of opacity

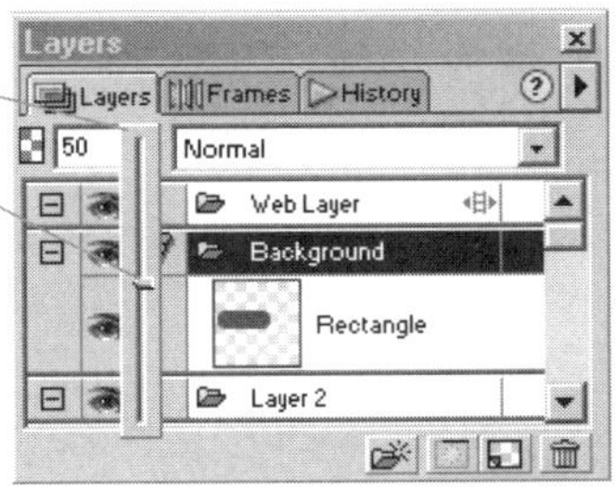

Select Modify>Flatten Layers to merge all of the layers in an image into a single layer.

3. The item on the layer will display the new opacity setting

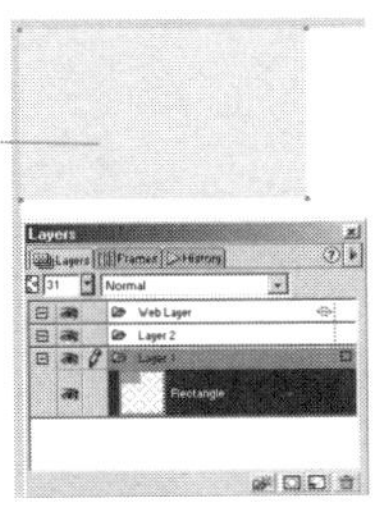

Blending

When two objects of different colours are blended, the one on the bottom is known as the base colour, the one on the top is known as the blend colour and the combination of the two is known as the result colour.

The available blend options in the Layers panel are as follows:

- *Normal, which applies no blending;*
- *Multiply, which results in a darker colour;*
- *Screen, which results in a bleached effect;*
- *Darken, Lighten and Difference, which use the darker or lighter colours of the blend and the base colours, or the difference between them, to create the result colour;*
- *Hue, Saturation, Color and Luminosity, which create the result colour using various combinations of these;*
- *Invert, which inverts the base colour;*
- *Tint, which adds grey to the base colour;*
- *Erase, which removes all of the base colour*

Blending can be used to create artistic effects by combining the colours of different objects. Blending can be used between objects on the same layer or different layers. To use blending:

1. Select an object that overlaps another one

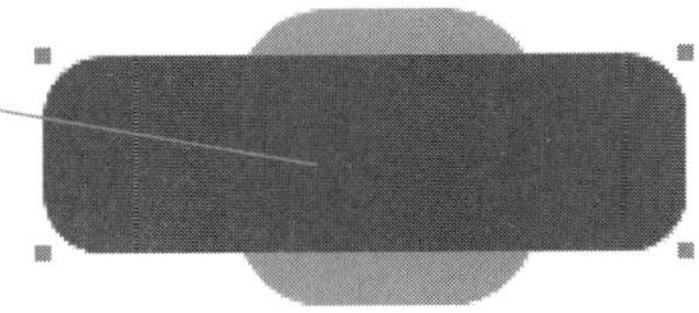

2. Click here to select a blend effect

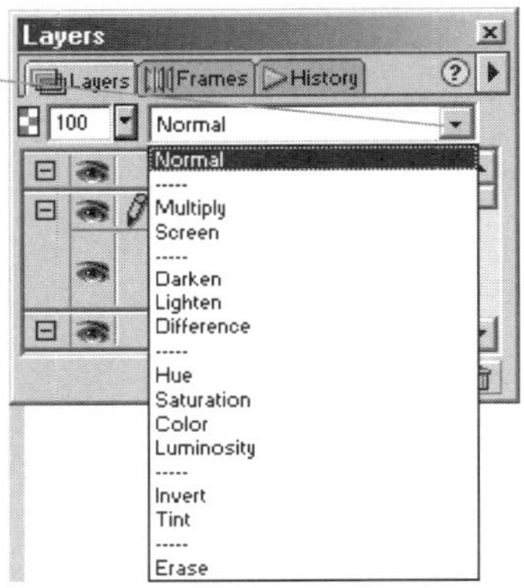

3. The effect is applied to the selected item in the work area. In this case the effect is Darken

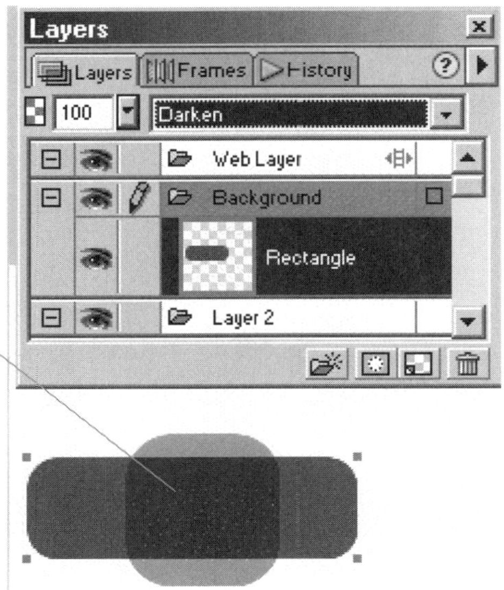

Creating masks

Masks can be created to cover existing objects and determine the area that is visible. When a mask is placed over an object, only the area covered by the mask is visible. To create a mask:

Existing objects can also be converted into masks. To do this, select the object and select Edit>Cut from the menu bar. Then select the object to be masked and select Edit>Paste as Mask from the menu bar.

1 Create an object which is going to be masked, or import a bitmap image

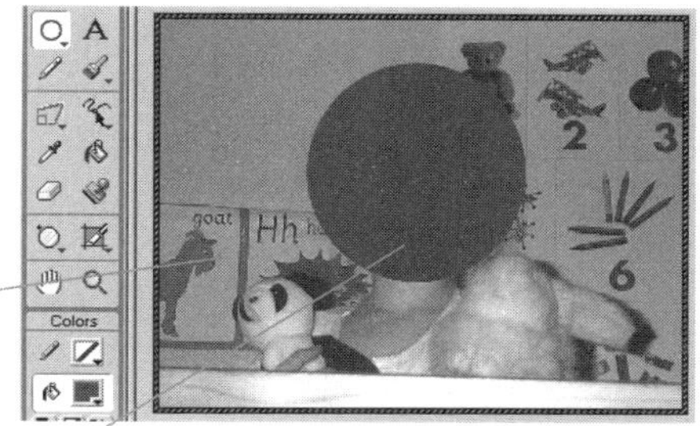

2 Create the mask object, in vector mode, with the drawing tools

Text can also be used as a mask. To do this, create the text using the Text tool and then cut it and paste it as a mask, as in the tip above.

3 Select the mask object and select Edit>Cut from the menu bar

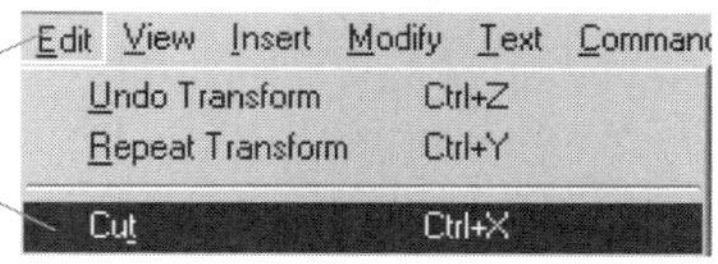

4 Select the original object and select Edit>Paste as Mask from the menu bar

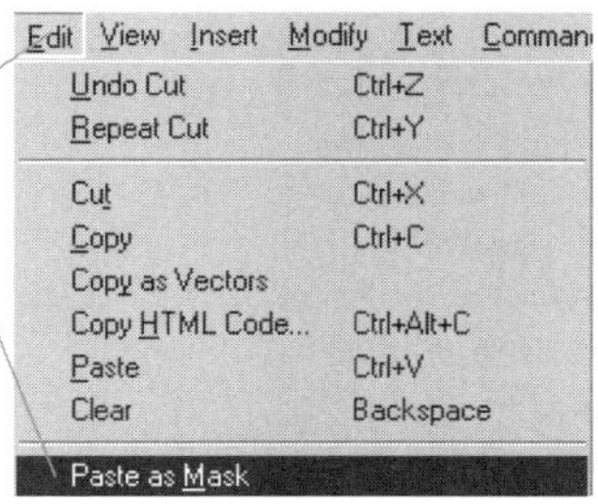

The Marquee tools can also be used to create masks. To do this, make a selection with a Marquee tool, then select Modify>Mask>Reveal Selection from the menu bar.

5 The original object is now only visible through the mask

Editing masks

When masks are applied to an image or graphic, the two objects become linked. However, it is still possible to edit them separately:

When the mask is selected, this is denoted in the Layers panel by a circle within a rectangle icon. When the graphic is selected, this is denoted by a pencil icon.

1 Click here to remove the link between the mask and the graphic

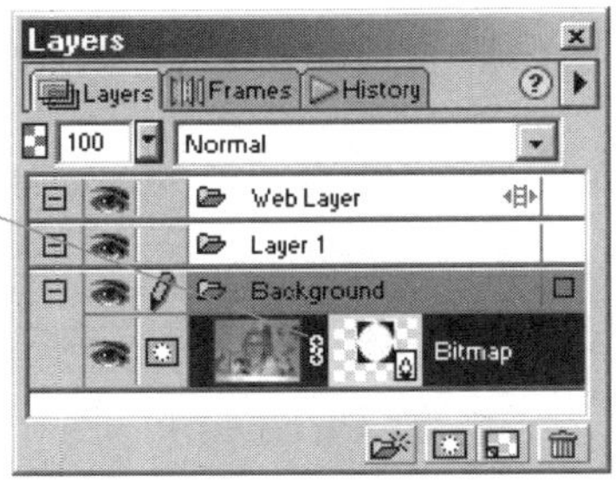

If the mask and the graphic are linked, they can be moved as one item. This is shown by them both moving in the thumbnails in the Layers panel.

2 Click here to select the mask

or

Click here to select the graphic

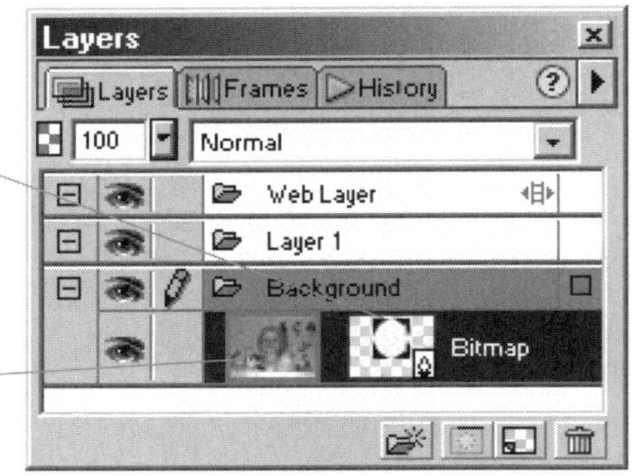

To remove a mask, select it in the Layers panel and select Modify>Mask>Delete Mask from the menu bar. Then select Discard in the dialog box that appears.

3 Click and drag to move the location of the mask or the graphic

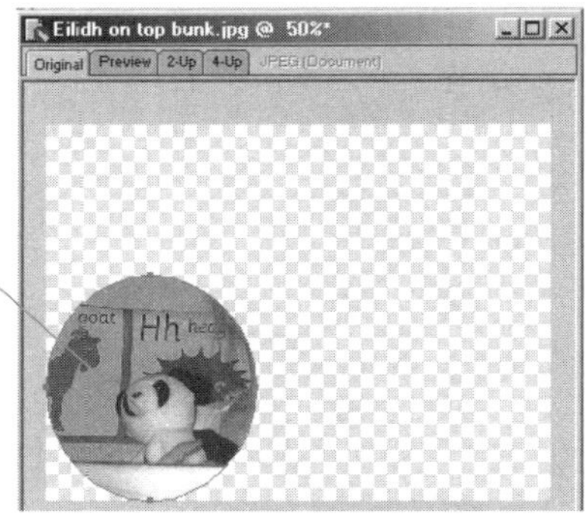

Masks can be scaled, rotated, skewed or distorted in the same way as any other object.

Navigation devices

Buttons and navigation bars are two of the most popular devices for providing navigation around Web sites. These are images that have interactivity added to them so that they can change appearance and also take the user to other Web pages. This chapter shows the processes for creating buttons and navigation bars.

Covers

Chapter Eight

About buttons

Buttons can be used as the basis for creating navigation bars. For more information on this, see pages 122–124.

Buttons are a common device used on Web pages to give them a more pleasing design aspect. They are created using Javascript code and they change appearance according to whether they are untouched, the cursor is moved over them or they are in the process of being pressed. Most commonly, buttons have two states: a static one (Up) and one when the cursor moves over them (Over). In Fireworks it is possible to create designs for the way buttons will look and then all of the complicated Javascript code is inserted automatically.

Up state of a button

Over state of a button

Symbols

For more information on symbols and instances see Chapter Ten.

Buttons that are created in Fireworks are a type of symbol, which means they can be stored in the Library and instances can be inserted into documents. An instance is a reference back to a symbol and, as such, it does not occupy a physical presence itself. If the original symbol is altered, then all instances that are based on it are changed too.

Symbols and instances help to keep the sizes of files and images as small as possible, which decreases downloading time when viewed on the Web.

Buttons in Fireworks are a very flexible device, which can be quickly edited using the Button Editor. They can also have text added to all elements of the button in one operation, there is no need to go into each state separately to update it.

If you want to give your Web pages an added touch of class then creating buttons in Fireworks is an excellent way to start.

Creating buttons

Buttons are created in the Button Editor, which is similar to the normal Fireworks work area, except that it contains panels for creating the different states of a button. The content for the button can be added in the same way as when creating objects in the normal work area. The Button Editor can only be accessed when a document has already been opened. When the button has been created it will appear within the original document. To create a button:

The Button Editor is a device that is contained within the currently active document. It cannot be opened if there is no document opened.

1. Open a new document and select Insert>New Button from the menu bar

The Button Editor can be used to insert buttons into images that already contain content. This is generally done if you are creating more complex elements for Web pages, rather than just straightforward buttons.

2. The Button Editor opens in the Up state panel

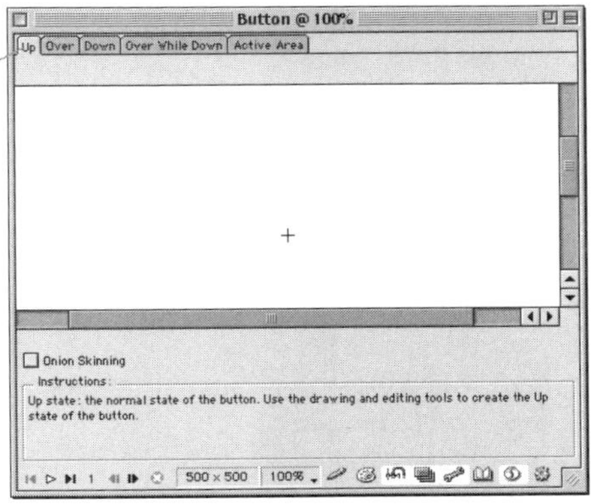

If the Onion Skinning box is clicked on, this will show an outline of the buttons in the other states. This can be used if you want to line up the different states in a particular way. If the buttons are in the same position in each state, then Onion Skinning will have no effect.

3. Enter content for the Up state of the button. This can be an object with a fill, style and stroke

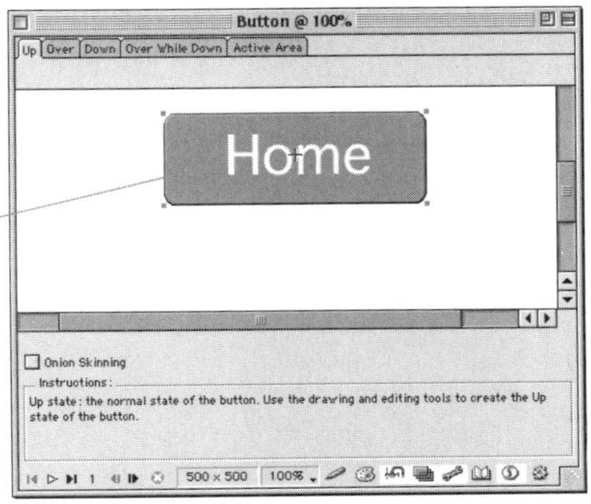

The most common technique when designing the Up and Over states of a button is to keep the text the same and just change the fill colour of the button. This achieves an effective transition from one state of the button to another.

4 Click on the Over tab. Click on the Copy Up Graphic button if you want this state of the button to be similar to the Up state

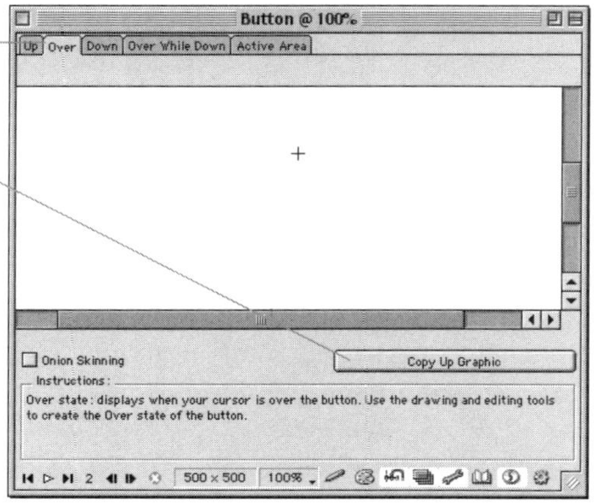

5 Edit the button for the Over state

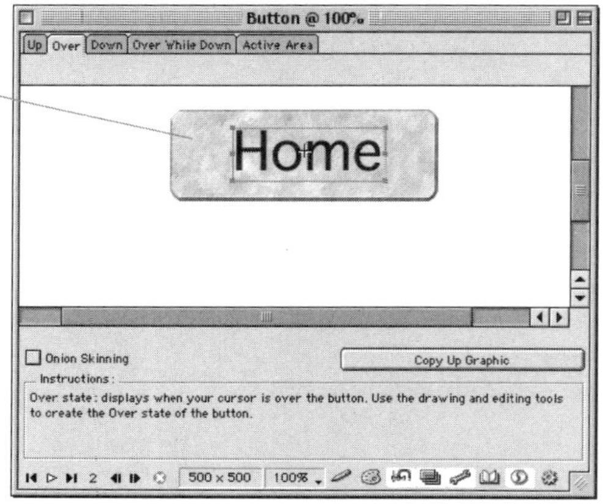

The content for the Down and Over While Down states can be copied from the previous states in the same way as the Over state is copied from the Up state.

6 If required, add content for the Down and Over While Down States

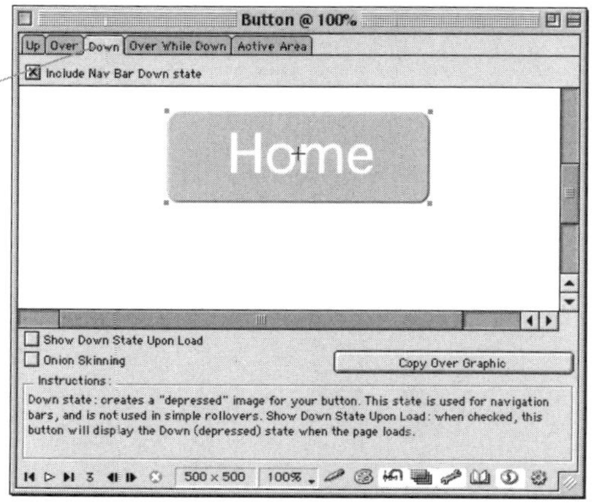

7 Click on the Active Area tab. This is the area that the user will click on to activate the button. Click here to set the Active Area automatically

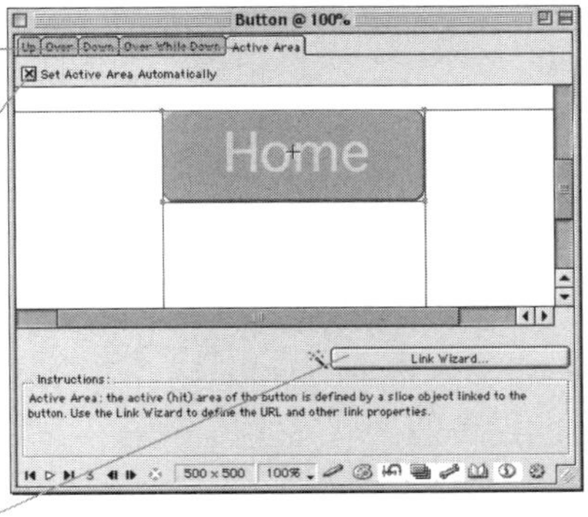

When a button is exported and viewed on a browser, the cursor will turn into a pointing hand when it moves over the active area of a button.

8 Click here to add a hyperlink and other attributes to the button

Although the Active Area will appear to contain content, this is just to show the area that it covers. The fill and stroke can be anything, as it does not appear in the finished button.

9 Click the Export Settings tab and click here to select attributes for when the button is exported

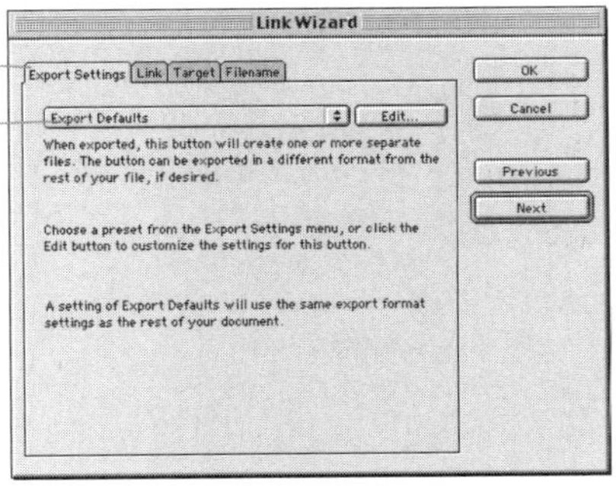

The active area of a button should generally be the same size as the button itself. If not, it could cause confusion when the button is viewed on a browser.

10 Click the Link tab and enter a URL (Web address) to which the button will take the user when it is clicked on a Web page

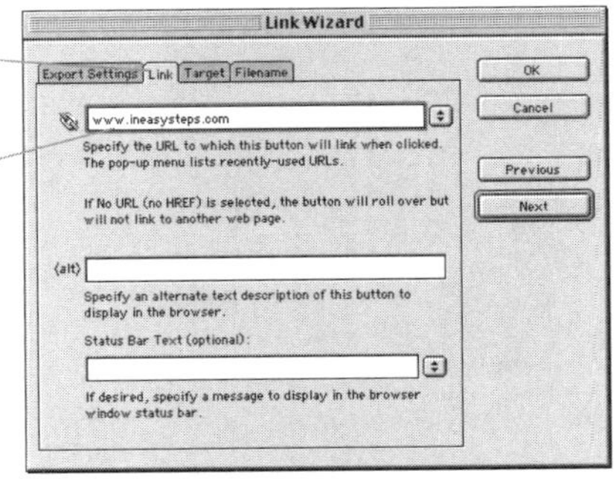

When adding a link, add Alt text too. This is the text that will appear when the cursor is moved over the button or if a browser has been set to not display images.

The Link Wizard can also be used to target links i.e. specify which frame they are opened in if a Web site is designed using a frames structure.

11 Click OK to apply the settings made in the Link Wizard

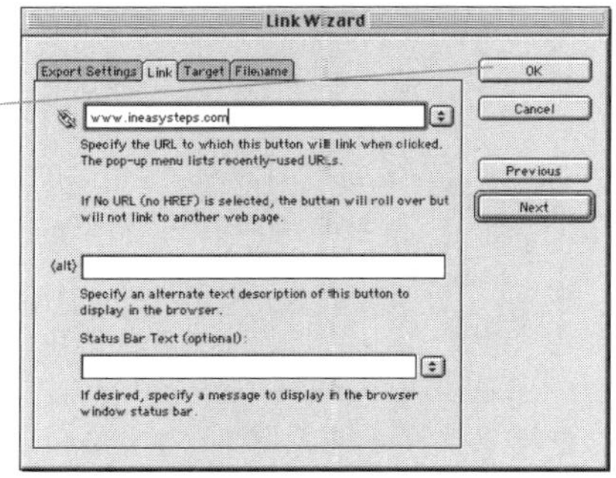

12 Close the Button Editor in the normal way for closing a window in Windows or on a Mac

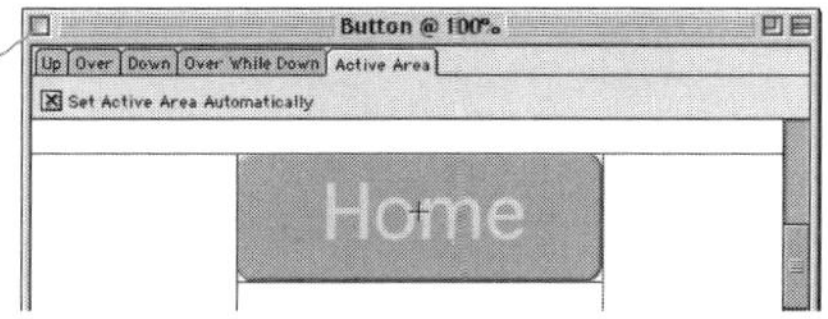

When a button is created, it is automatically placed in the Library as a symbol. This can then be placed into documents directly from the Library.

13 The button appears in the active document. The Active Area is shown by a slice over the button content

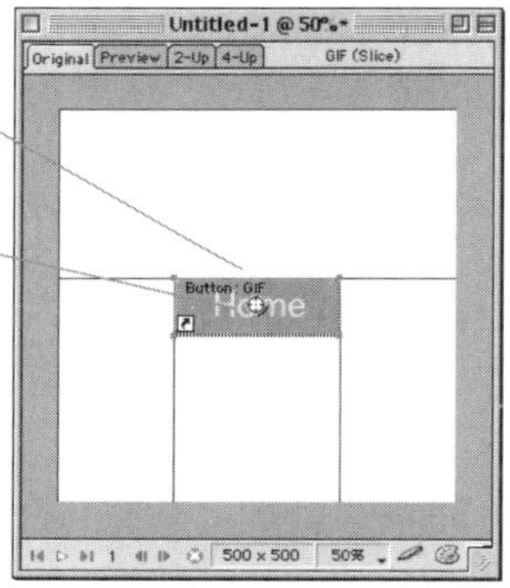

If the canvas is not trimmed to size, there may be unwanted space around the button when it is exported and then viewed on a browser. Make sure that only the button is visible.

14 Select Modify>Trim Canvas from the menu bar to make the canvas the same size as the button

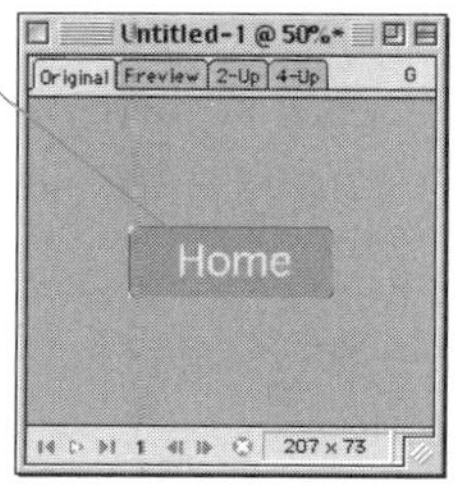

Editing buttons

All states of a button can be edited at any point before the button is exported. Fill, stroke and text can all be edited in the Button Editor. Text can also be edited on its own, using the Object panel.

Button Editor

To view the Library, select Window> Library from the menu bar.

1 Double-click the button in the work area or in the top panel of the Library

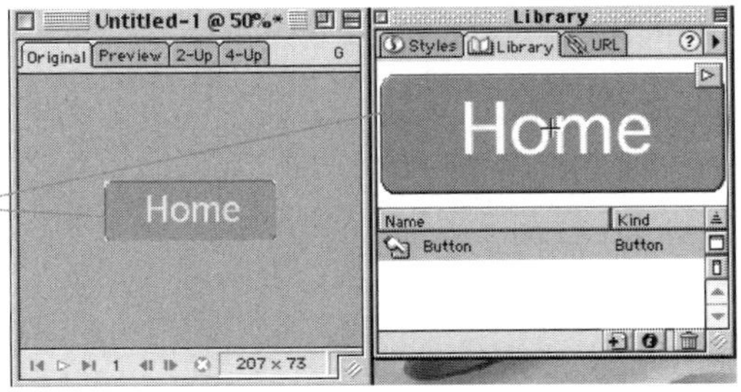

2 Edit the fill and stroke of one or all of the states of the button

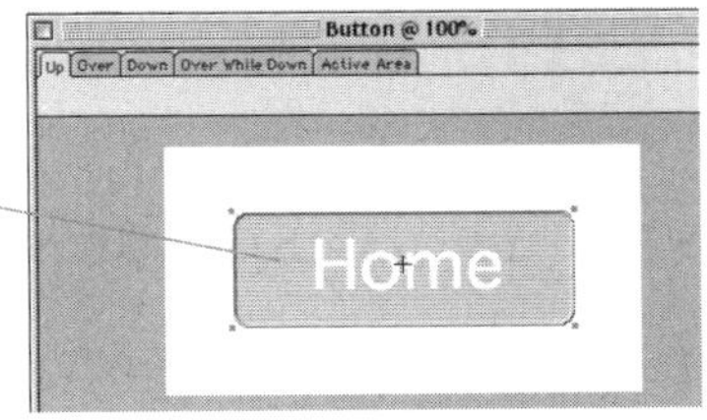

3 Double-click on the text in the Up state and edit it in the text editor. Select OK

4 Select Yes to update the text in the other button states

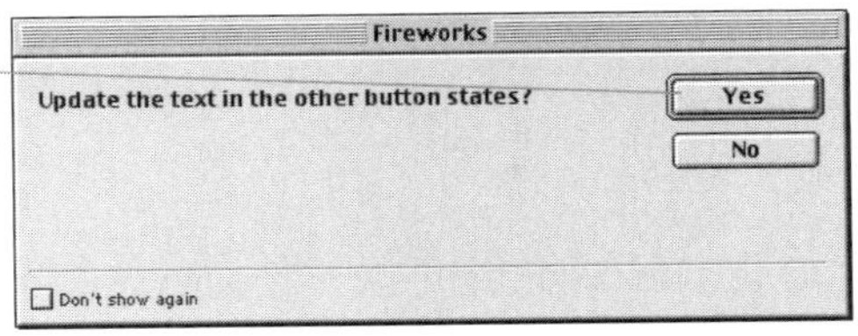

Unless you have a good reason not to, keep the text the same for all states of the button. There may be occasions when you will want to change it for different states but, in general, consistency is better.

5 Close the Button Editor to apply the changes and return to the work area

Object panel

1 Select a button in the work area and select Window> Object from the menu bar

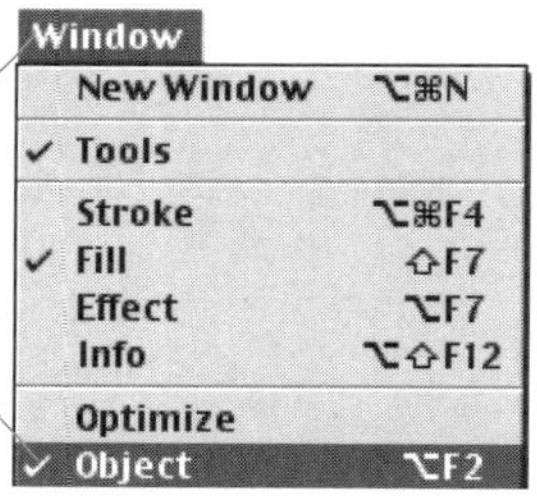

When a button is selected in the work area, the Object panel can also be used to edit the link attributes of the button. To do this, click on the Link Wizard and change the attributes as required.

2 Double-click here and over-write the text. This will apply to all states of the button. Click anywhere outside the Object panel to apply the changes

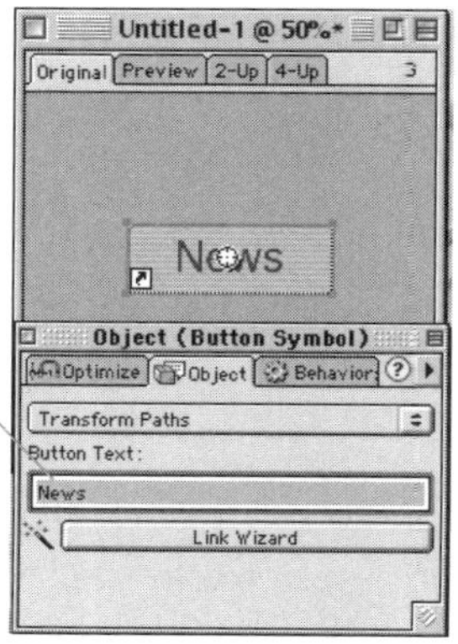

Exporting buttons

Once buttons have been created, they then have to be exported so that the necessary code can be created for them to be able to function on a Web page. When a button is exported, image files are created for the different states and an HTML file is created for the code. To export a button:

Before a button is exported, select the Preview, 2-Up or 4-Up panels, to see how the button will function when it is active i.e. viewed on a browser. Rollover the button and click it to preview its different states.

1 Select File>Export from the menu bar

When a button is exported, more image files are created than there are button states. This is a device in Fireworks that ensures that the button can be reassembled and displayed correctly on a browser.

2 Enter a name for the button; Select HTML and Images; Select Export HTML file; Select Export Slices

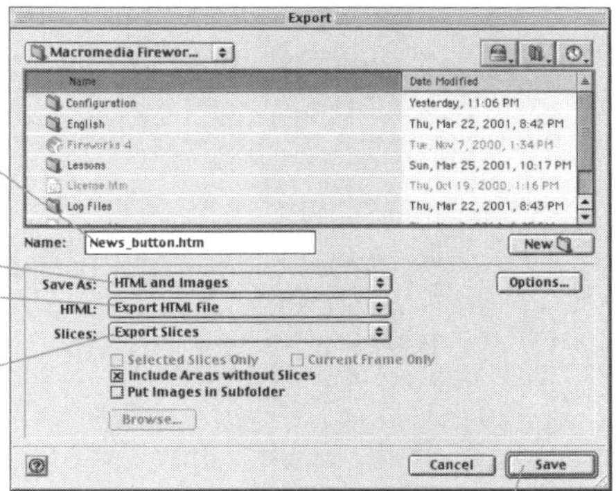

3 Select Save

Once a button has been exported it can be inserted into a Dreamweaver document by using the Insert Fireworks HTML command on the Object panel and then selecting the HTML file that is created during the export process.

4 View your file structure to check that the HTML and image files have been created

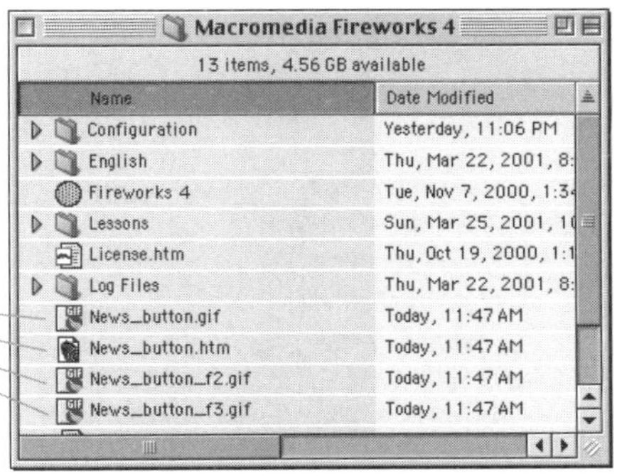

Creating a navigation bar

Plan the contents of a navigation bar carefully before you start creating it. This could save you from having to go back and redo it due to missing out one or more elements.

Always include a link back to a site's Home Page on a navigation bar. This way, users will have a quick way to get back to the point where they started and, if the navigation bar is on all the pages of the site, they will not feel as if they are lost within the site.

When duplicating buttons, it may be necessary to increase the canvas size by selecting Modify>Canvas size from the menu bar.

Navigation bars are usually positioned at the top or left-hand side of Web pages.

Buttons can also be inserted by selecting the original in the Library and then dragging it onto the work area.

A navigation bar is a collection of buttons that are displayed horizontally or vertically on a Web page. Ideally, it should also appear on all of the pages within a specific Web site. This means there is a consistency on all pages and users will feel comfortable when they are navigating around the site. To create a navigation bar:

1. Create a button as shown on the previous pages

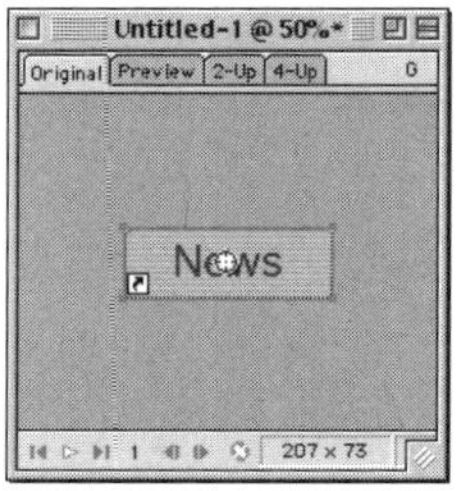

2. Select the button and select Edit> Duplicate and click and drag to position the new button

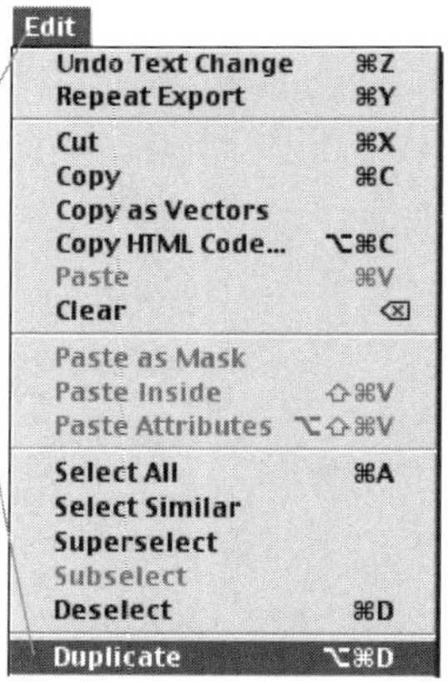

3. Select the duplicate button and enter new text in the Object panel. Click anywhere outside the Object panel

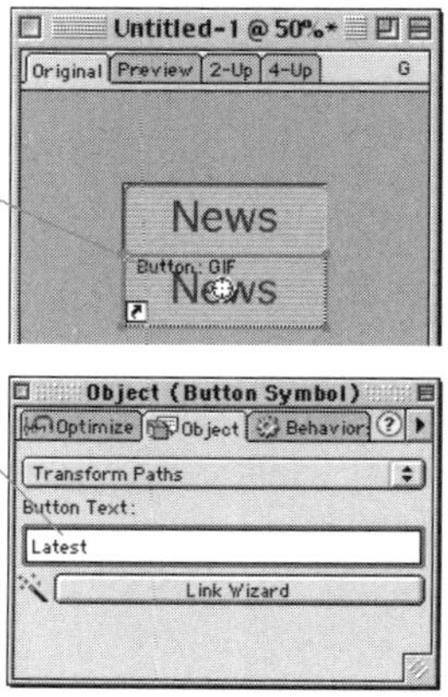

A button instance can be thought of as a copy of the original button that was created.

4 Select Current when prompted as to whether you want to update all instances of the button or just the current one

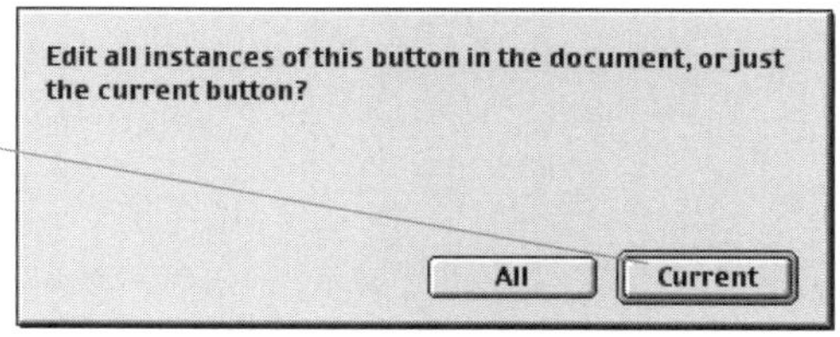

If you choose to update all instances of a button, then the new text will appear on all of the buttons that have been currently created.

5 Select the Link Wizard on the Object panel

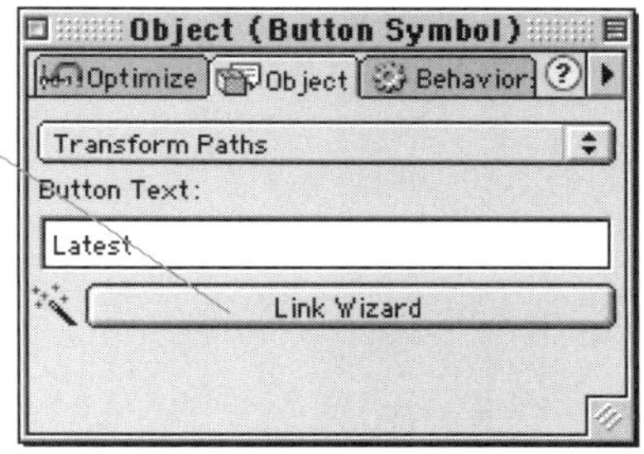

The design of buttons can be as simple or as complex as you like for use in navigation bars. However, make sure they all have the same appearance. The only items that should change from button to button are the button text and the link.

6 Enter a new link for the duplicate button. Select OK

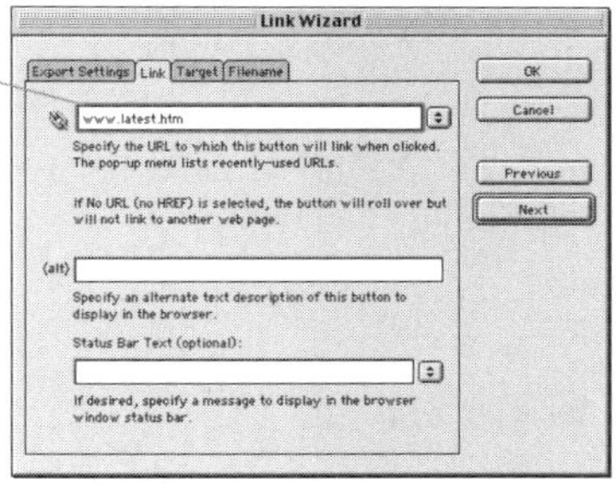

When all of the buttons have been created, align them as required by selecting Modify>Align from the menu bar.

7 Repeat Steps 2–6 for all of the buttons to be included in the navigation bar

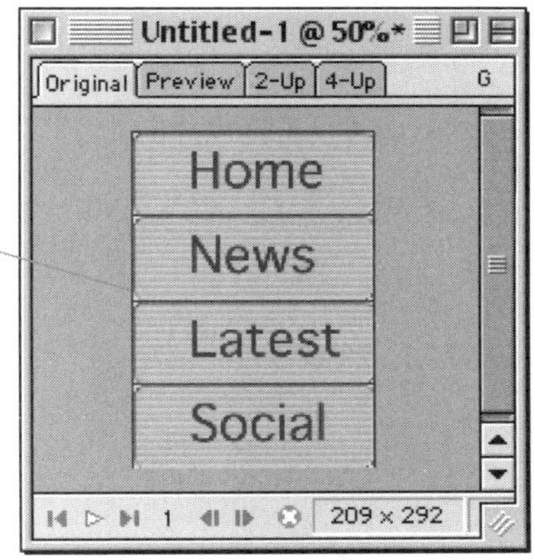

A navigation bar is a series of images, with interactivity added to them through the inclusion of Javascript coding.

8 Select File>Export from the menu bar and select the same options as for exporting a single button (see page 121)

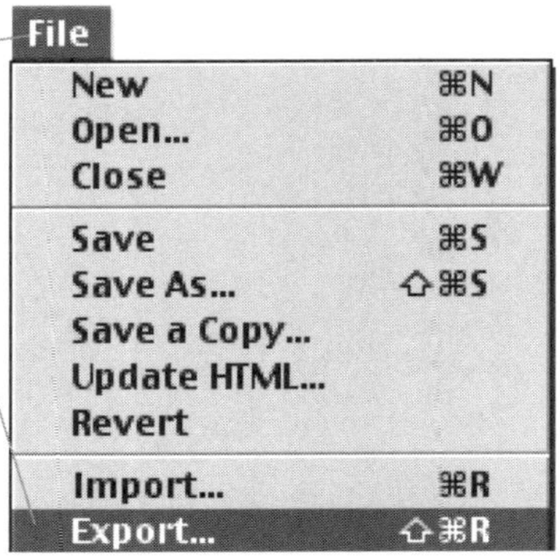

The links on the buttons of a navigation bar can be edited within the HTML code in a Web authoring program such as Dreamweaver.

9 When the navigation bar is imported into a Web authoring program such as Dreamweaver it appears as a single image. However, when it is previewed in a browser, each button on the navigation bar operates independently of the others

Navigation bars should be designed in the same style as the pages on which they are going to appear i.e. use the same colours, fonts etc.

Rollovers

Rollovers can be used to create some of the most eye-catching and effective elements on a Web page. This chapter shows how to create rollovers using different techniques. It also details how to create simple rollovers, disjoint rollovers and pop-up menus.

Covers

Chapter Nine

About rollovers

Rollovers are a frequently used device on Web pages. They are created with Javascript and can be used to created different types of effects when a cursor interacts with them on a Web page. A button, such as those shown in the previous chapter, is a simple example of a rollover: when the cursor rolls over the initial image, this is replaced with another one. However rollovers can be used to create complex and effective design features:

Rollovers are created using slices and frames. Different images are accommodated in different frames and the slices are used to connect the two and apply the required effect.

Swap one image with another when the cursor rolls over the initial image

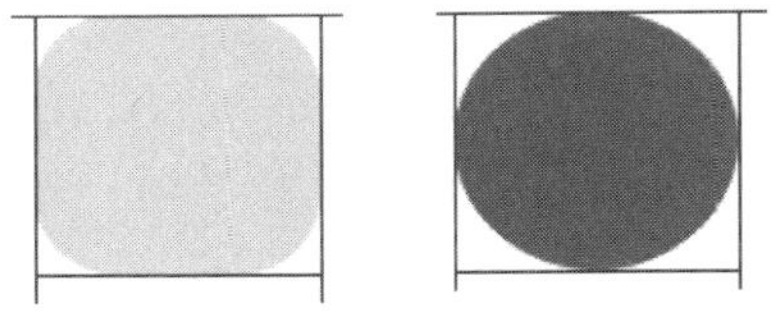

The two elements of a disjoint rollover should be kept within reasonable proximity of each other. Otherwise it may not be clear that they are connected.

Create a disjoint rollover, where an image or text appears at a different point from the initial image

Pop-up menus are very useful if you have a lot of sub-headings, or topics, that you want to link to one main heading or topic. The user can then navigate to the sub-heading without having to leave the main menu.

Create a pop-up menu for enhanced navigation

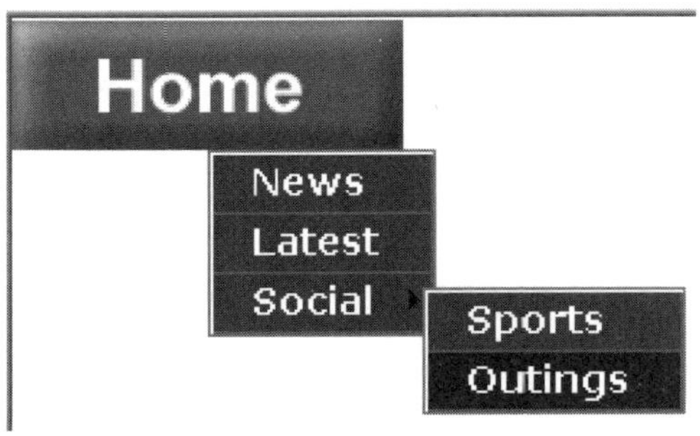

Creating rollovers with behaviors

Rollovers can be created by using the following elements:

- A trigger Web object. This is either a slice or a hotspot that has one or more behaviours attached to it
- Images. These are the images that are displayed in the rollover. In a simple rollover, the first image resides below the trigger object and the second image resides in the target area
- Frames. Images in a rollover are placed on separate frames within the document

In a simple rollover, an image from frame 1 is replaced by one from frame 2. However, for more complex rollovers, the replacement image can be taken from any other frame.

Rollovers can be created using either the Behaviors panel or drag-and-drop techniques. The most basic rollover is known as a simple rollover. This is when an image is replaced by one directly below it when the cursor moves over it. However, it is also possible to create more complex rollovers using the same techniques.

Creating simple rollovers with Behaviors

Slices can be inserted over an image by using the Slice tool on the Tools panel and clicking and dragging over the image. Alternatively, select the image and select Insert> Slice from the menu bar.

1 Select an image and insert a slice over it. The slice is the trigger object

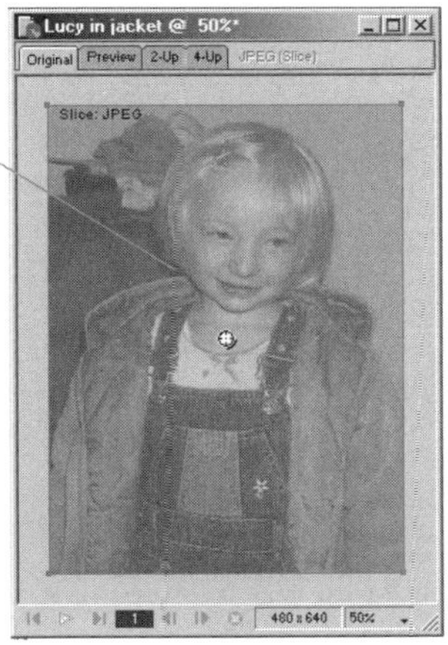

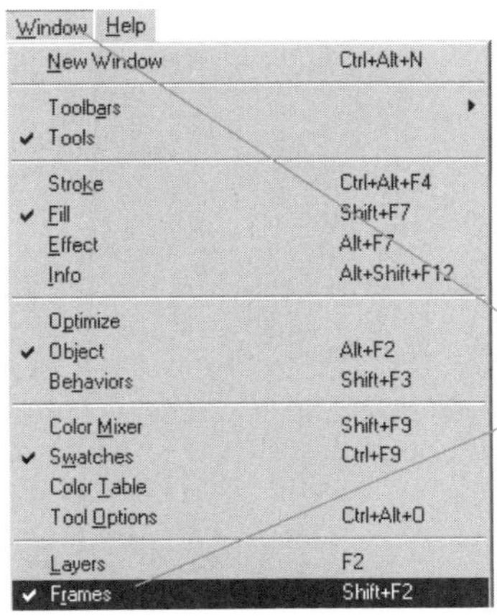

2 Select Window> Frames to display the Frames panel

The menu for the Frames panel can be accessed by clicking the black triangle at the top right of the panel. This provides options for adding frames, duplicating frames and deleting frames.

3 In the Frames panel, click here to add a new or duplicate frame

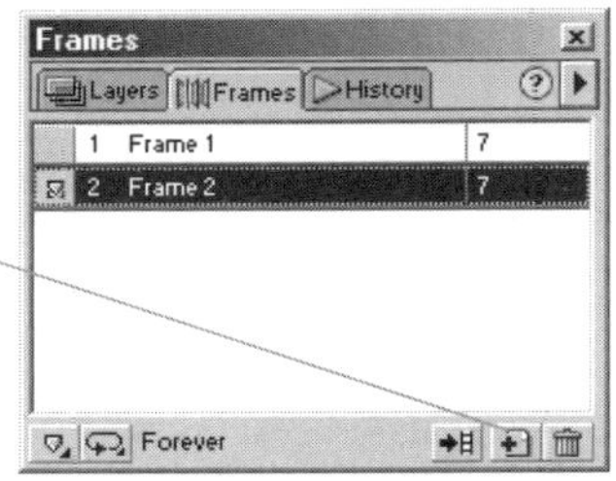

4 Draw a new graphic in the work area or import an image

As long as the view button on the Tools panel is selected to show slices/ hotspots, then you can select the slice or hotspot in any frame of the rollover.

5 Select either frame in the Frames panel and select the slice or hotspot

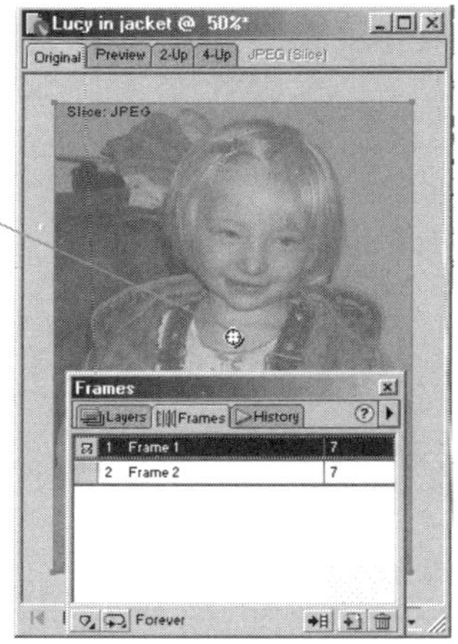

6 Select Window> Behaviors from the menu bar

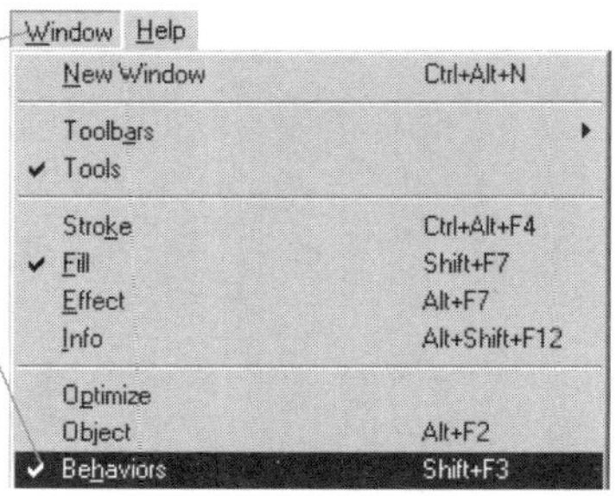

Behaviors are Javascript commands that add the interactive element to items such as rollovers.

7 Click here to access the available behaviors

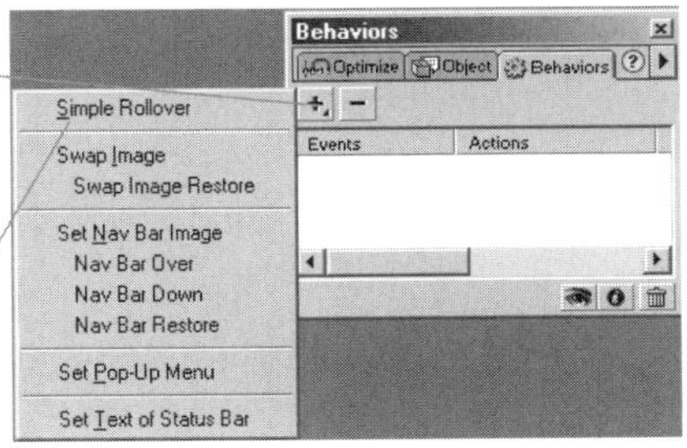

When a behavior is selected, the default event is also selected. An event is an action that triggers the behavior and is usually connected to the actions of the mouse i.e. onClick or onRelease. For a simple rollover the default event is onMouseOver, which means the rollover is activated when the mouse rolls over the image.

8 Select Simple Rollover as the behavior

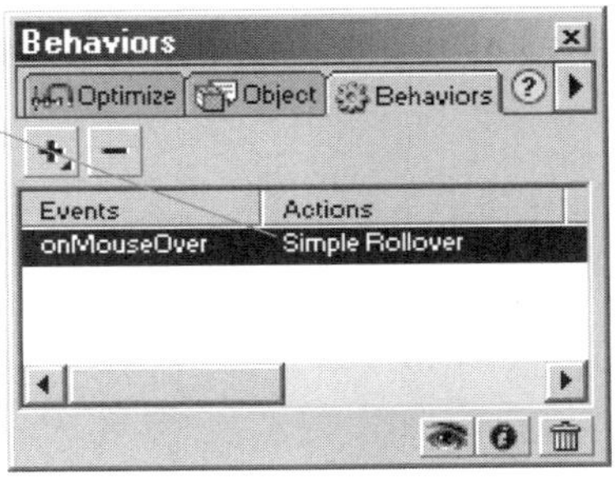

The preview of a rollover should be the same as how it will appear when viewed on a browser.

9 Select the Preview tab and roll over the image with the cursor to see the rollover take effect

Before the cursor rolls over

After the cursor rolls over

Creating rollovers with drag-and-drop

Creating rollovers with drag-and-drop techniques achieves the same results as using the Behaviors panel, but it can provide more flexibility, particularly when working with more complex rollovers. To use drag-and-drop to create a simple rollover:

1 Select an image and insert a slice over it

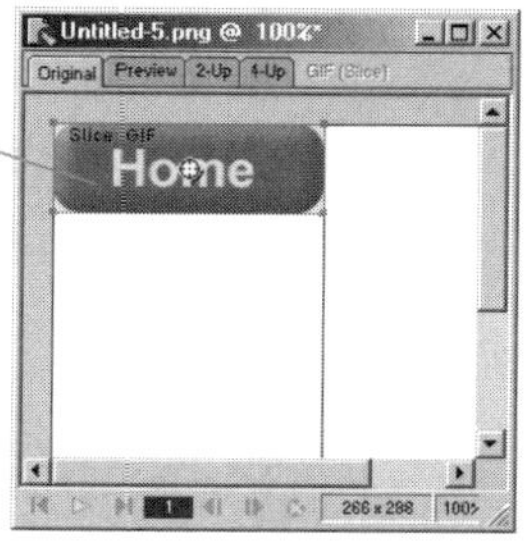

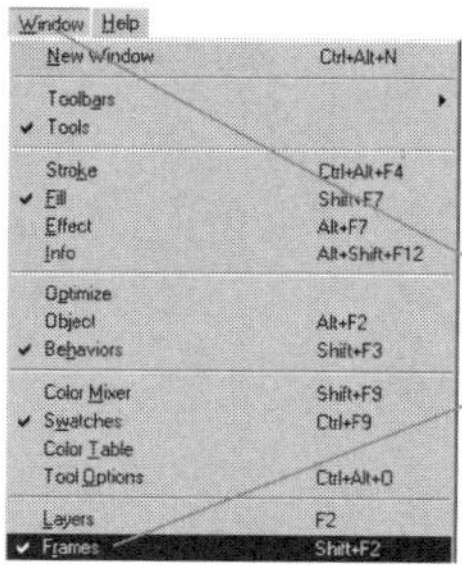

2 Select Window>Frames to display the Frames panel

3 In the Frames panel, click here to add a new or duplicate frame

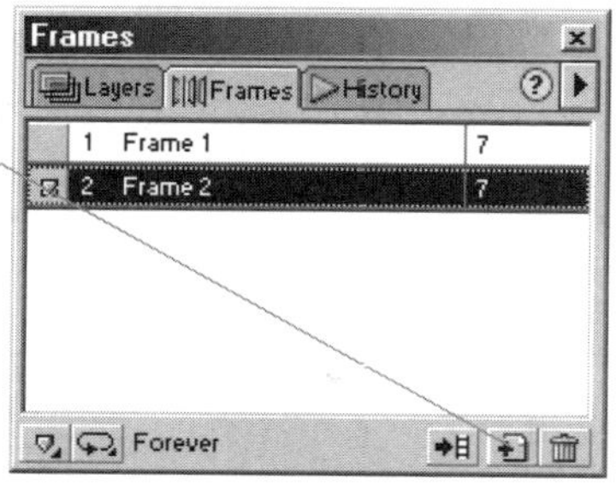

The two images or graphics used for a simple rollover do not have to be the same size or shape.

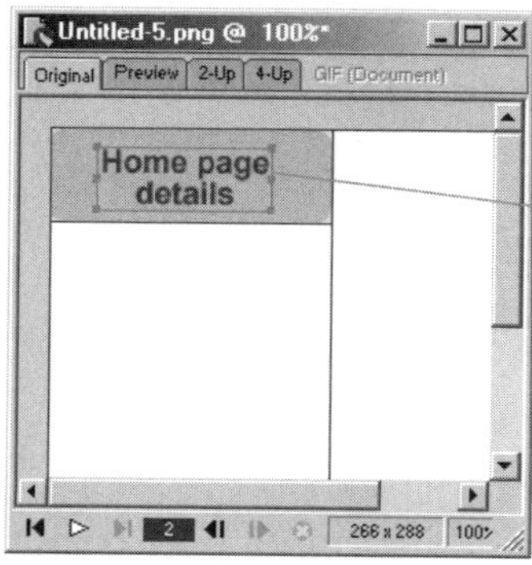

4 Draw a new graphic in the work area or import an image

The slice resides above the images in both frames and so can be selected from either one.

5 Select either frame in the Frames panel and select the slice or hotspot

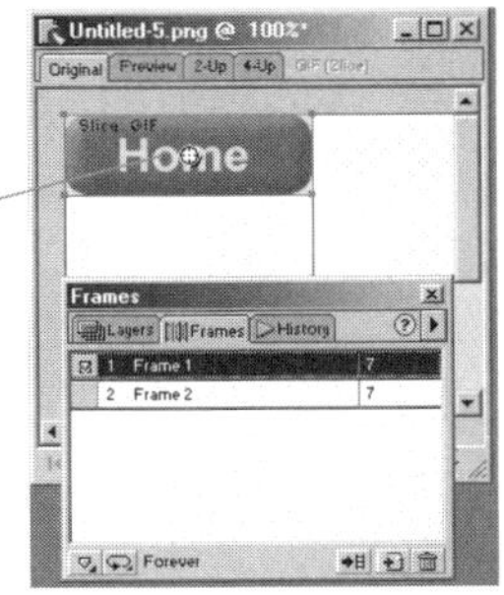

6 Click here and drag to the top left-hand corner. A blue line loops between the two points

The Swap Image dialog box has a More Options button that can be used to preview the image that will serve as the swap image and also to specify an image from another frame or select an image from a separate file instead.

7 Access the Swap Image dialog by selecting the '+' button under the Behaviors tab of the Behaviors panel. Select Frame 2 as the location for the second image. Select OK

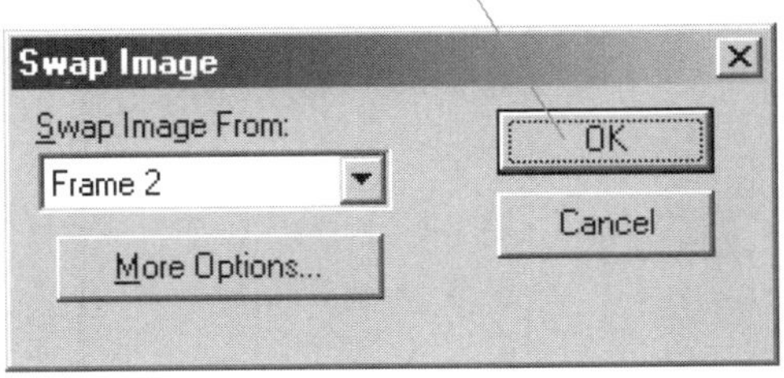

Rollovers can also be previewed in a browser by pressing the F12 key.

8 Select the Preview tab to see the rollover effect

Creating disjoint rollovers

Disjoint rollovers are ones where the rollover effect i.e. the second image, appears in a different location to the initial image. This is created by placing the disjoint image under a different slice, unlike a simple rollover, where both images are under the same, single slice. Disjoint rollovers can give a very sophisticated appearance to a Web page and they are particularly effective for displaying text in a different location to a trigger object. To create a disjoint rollover:

A disjoint rollover can consist of any combination of images and text, it does not have to be one or the other.

1 Select an image and insert a slice over it. The slice is the trigger object

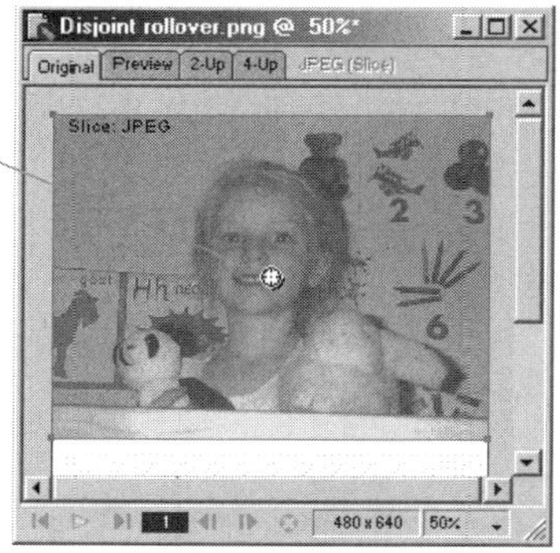

When creating a disjoint rollover, do not make the distance between the two elements too large. If it is, this could create too much unused space when the rollover is displayed on a Web page.

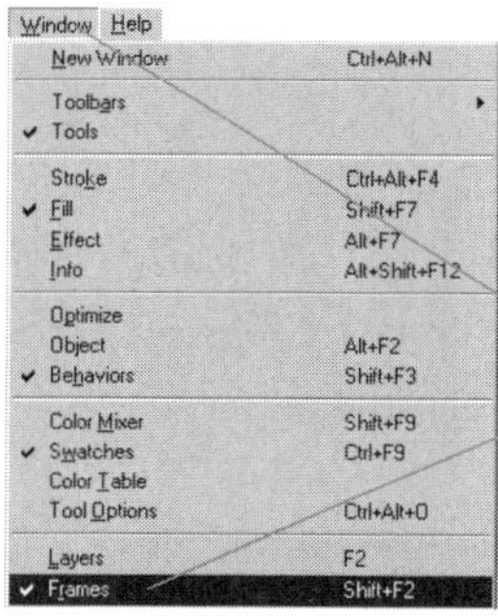

2 Select Window> Frames to display the Frames panel

With a disjoint rollover, the image that is initially displayed remains in place when the cursor is rolled over the trigger object. This displays the second image and so the two images are visible together.

3 In the Frames panel, click here to add a new or duplicate frame

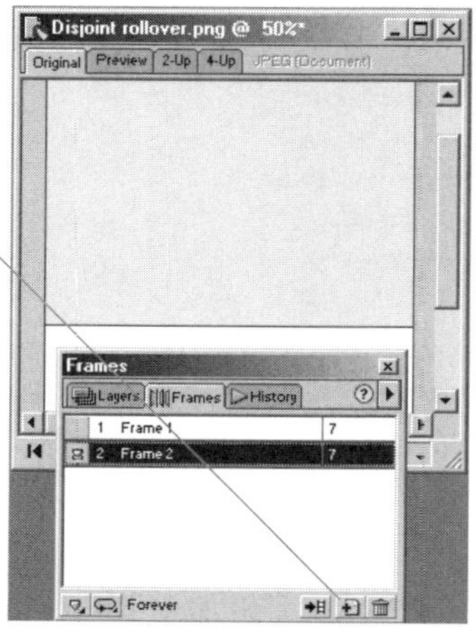

4 Draw a new graphic, import an image, or add text to the work area. Insert it at a different point to the image in frame 1

If the slice or hotspot is smaller than the item in the frame then not all of that item will appear when the rollover is previewed. Only the area under the slice will be visible.

5 Insert a slice or hotspot over the item in frame 2

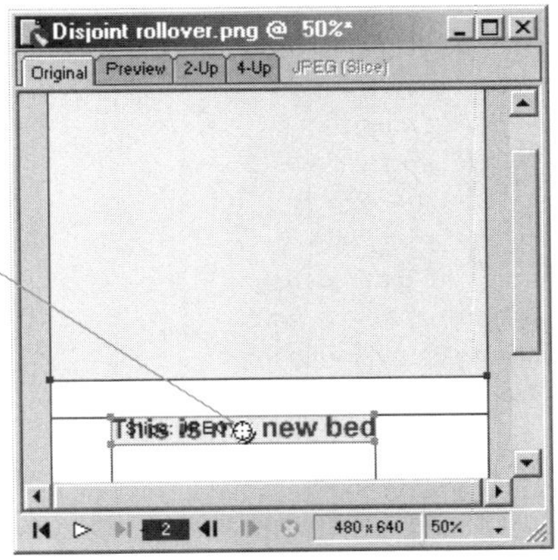

The trigger object for a disjoint rollover can only be linked with one other slice, even though it is possible to put numerous slices on a single frame.

6 Select any frame and click and hold here

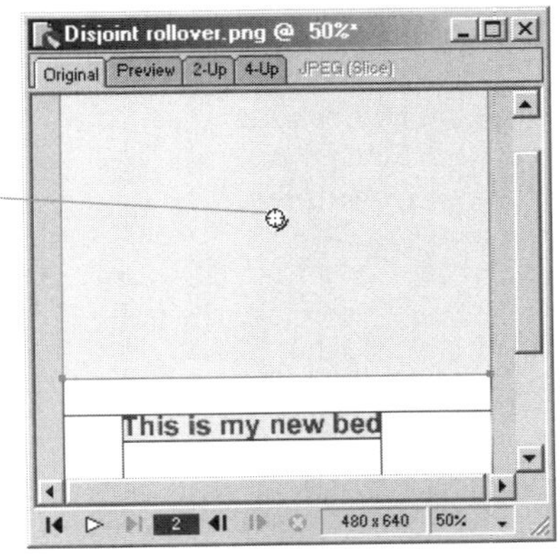

7 A pointing hand should appear. Drag it down to the item in frame 2. This should create a curved blue line between the two items

The disjoint rollover effect can also be achieved by selecting the slice in frame 1 and selecting Swap Image in the Behaviors panel. Then select the image to be displayed as the disjoint rollover.

8 Access the Swap Image dialog by selecting the '+' button under the Behaviors tab of the Behaviors panel. Select Frame 2 for the item that will appear as the disjoint image. Select OK

Links can be added to a rollover by using the Object panel. For a disjoint rollover, add the link to the trigger object in frame 1.

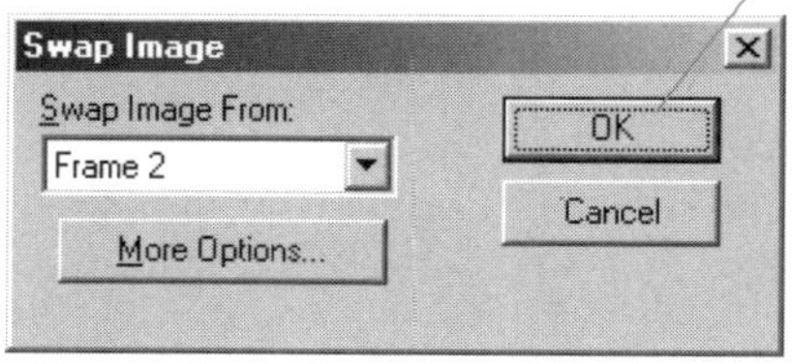

When the disjoint rollover has been completed, select Modify> Trim Canvas to. This ensures that the elements that are exported are no bigger than the largest area of the rollover.

9 Select the Preview tab or F12 to preview the rollover

Roll over here and the disjoint effect appears here

Creating pop-up menus

Pop-up menus are created with complex Javascript code and they were once only the domain of programming professionals. However, Fireworks 4 has changed all that and it is now possible for anyone to create pop-up menus, regardless of whether they know the first thing about Javascript or not. This is done through the use of slices and rollovers. Pop-up menus are menus where the user rolls over a graphic and this displays one, or more, subsequent menus. To create a pop-up menu:

Pop-up menus are an excellent navigation device for condensing a lot of items into one area.

Pop-up menus can be set to appear either horizontally or vertically with respect to the buttons from which they are activated. However, each level of the menu is then displayed vertically. This type of menu is also sometimes referred to as a drop-down menu.

1. Create a graphic that will be displayed initially, as part of the pop-up menu

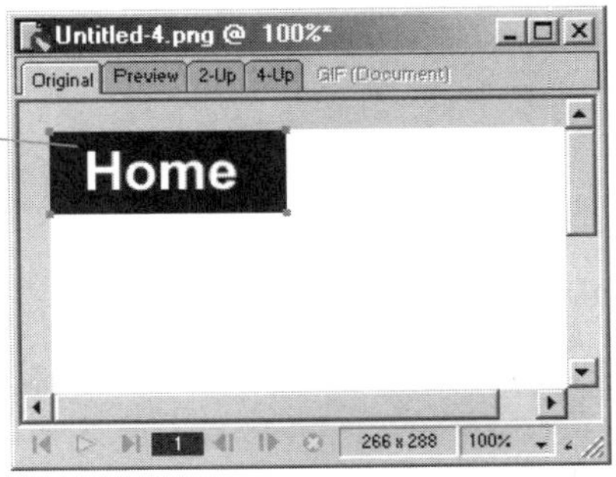

2. Insert a slice over the graphic, either through drawing one with the Slice tool or by selecting the graphic and selecting Insert>Slice from the menu bar

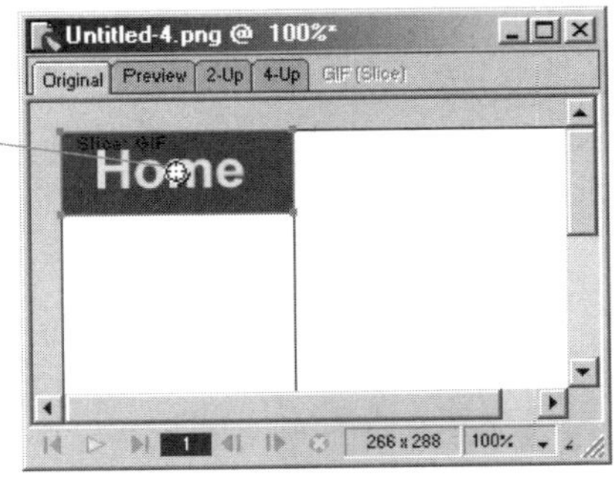

3. Select Insert> Pop-up Menu from the menu bar

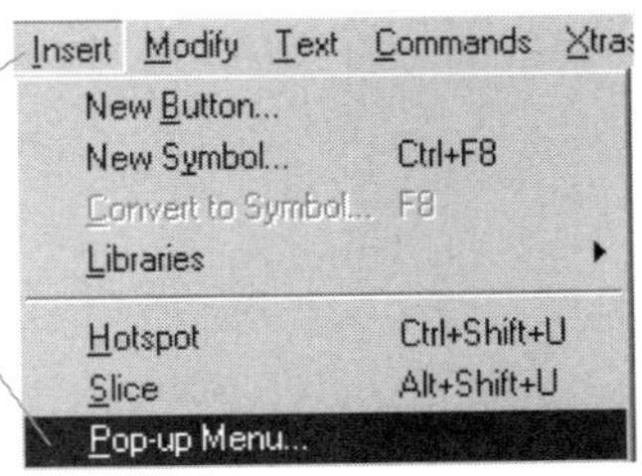

6 Click here to add the item to the pop-up menu

4 In the Set Pop-up Menu dialog box, enter a title for the first sub-menu here

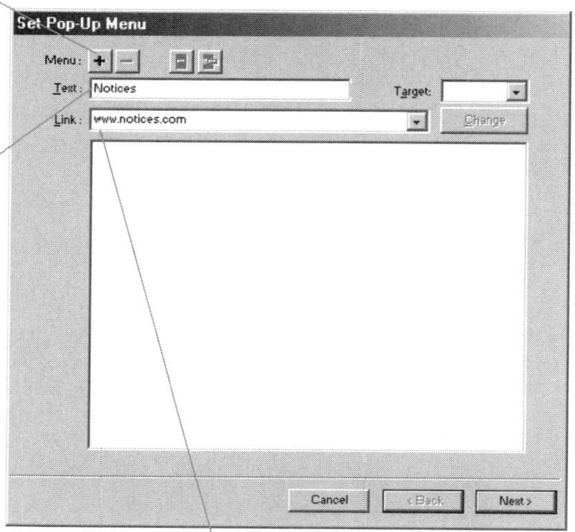

5 Enter a link here (if required)

If an item on a pop-up menu leads to another level of menus, there is probably no need to include a link with this item. The links should be inserted in the buttons for the final level of the pop-up menu as this is the point where the user will want to access another page.

7 Repeat Steps 4–6 for all of the items to be included in the first level of the pop-up menu

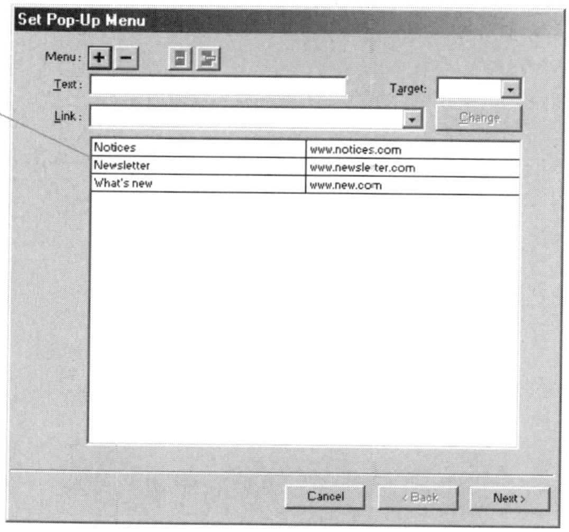

If pop-up menus have more than three levels it could become confusing for users, since there will be too many sub-menus to navigate through.

8 To create the next level for the pop-up menu, select an item and click here

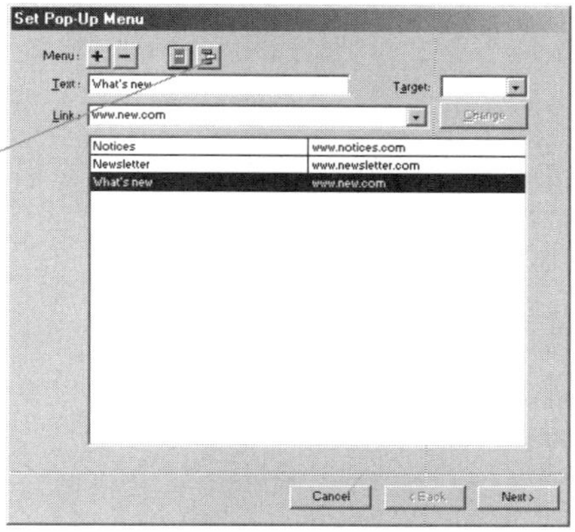

If you want to move an item in a pop-up menu back to its original level after it has been indented, click on the outdent button (to the left of the indent button).

9 Create the structure for the whole of the pop-up menu. Select Next

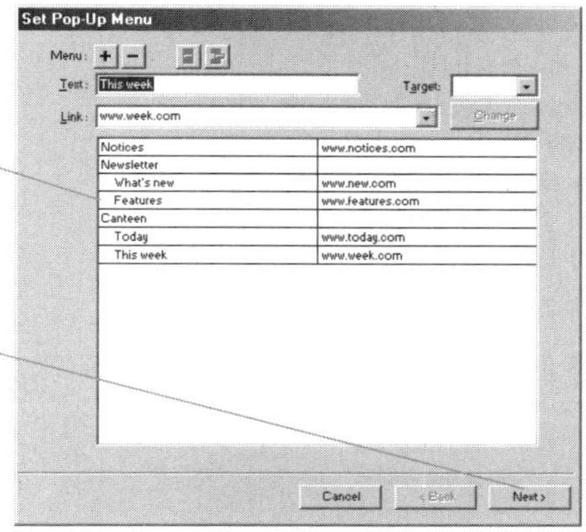

To edit a pop-up menu, double-click on it in the work area and then make any changes as required.

When formatting a pop-up menu, use a similar design to the graphic that was created at the beginning of the process (see Step 1).

10 Click here to format the font, size and formatting of the text used on the pop-up menu

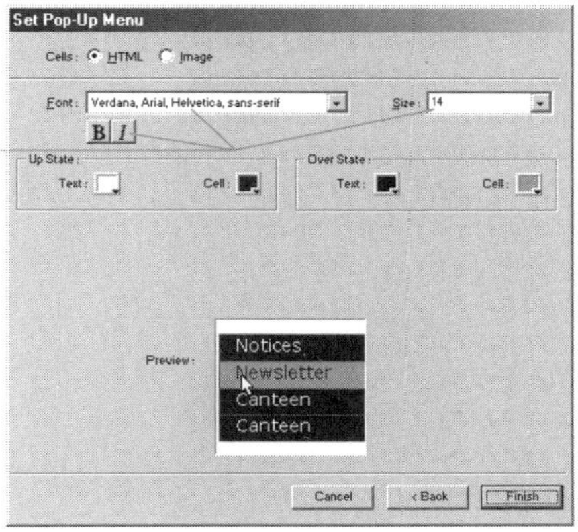

There can be some problems with the positioning of pop-up menus when they are exported to a Web authoring program such as Dreamweaver and then displayed on a browser. In some cases, the pop-up menu does not appear in the correct place in relation to the trigger object. There are three possible reasons for this:

- *The trigger object is positioned differently from when it was created in Fireworks;*
- *The default page margins have not been set to 0 in the Web authoring program;*
- *The trigger device has not been positioned absolutely.*

All of these problems can be resolved in a program such as Dreamweaver, although it can involve editing the HTML code.

For more information about ensuring pop-up menus are positioned correctly on a Web page see the Fireworks support page on the Web at www.macromedia.com/support/fireworks/ (no spaces).

11 Click here to format the style and colour for the buttons in the pop-up menu

12 Select Finish

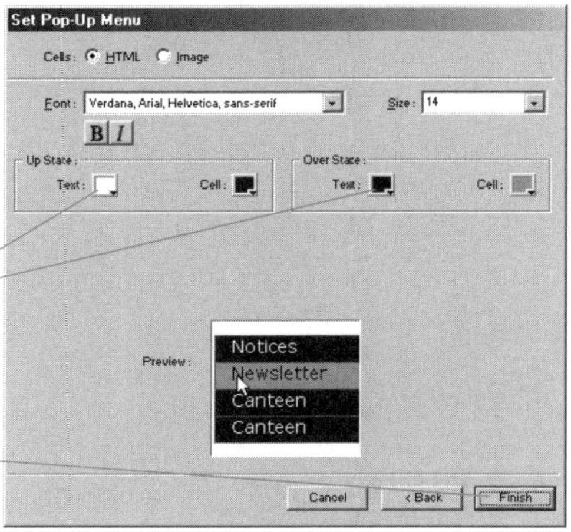

13 Select the Pointer tool and click and drag to position the pop-up menu

14 Preview the pop-up menu. Rolling over one button displays the available sub-menus

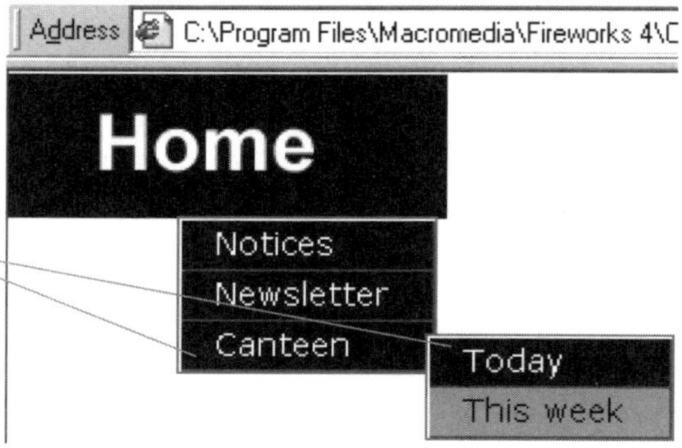

Combining slices and hotspots

Slices and hotspots can be combined to create another level of sophistication for rollovers. For instance, a slice can be inserted to swap an image or create a disjoint rollover and then a hotspot can be placed on top of it so that only that specific area triggers the rollover. To combine slices and rollovers (this is for a disjoint rollover, but the procedure is the same for a simple rollover too):

Creating a rollover with slices and hotspots gives a greater degree of precision for defining the area which will trigger a rollover. It means that you are not restricted to using complete images as the trigger area.

1. Create an object and add a slice to it

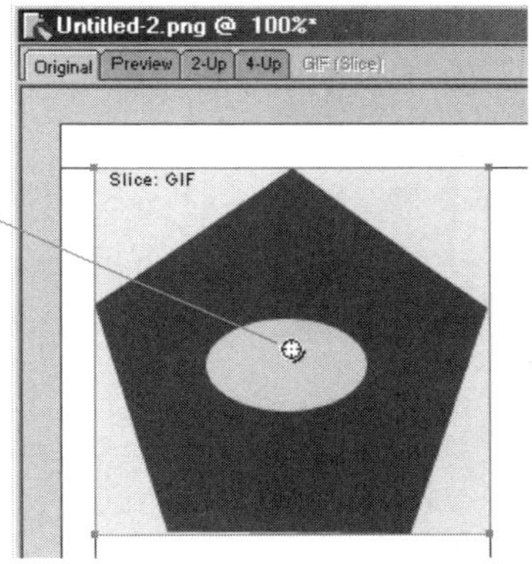

2. In the Frames panel, click here to add a new or duplicate frame

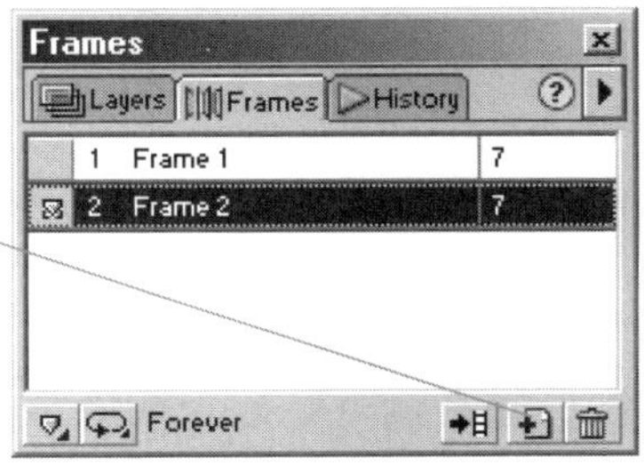

3. Draw a new graphic, import an image, or add text to the work area. Insert it at a different point to the image in frame 1

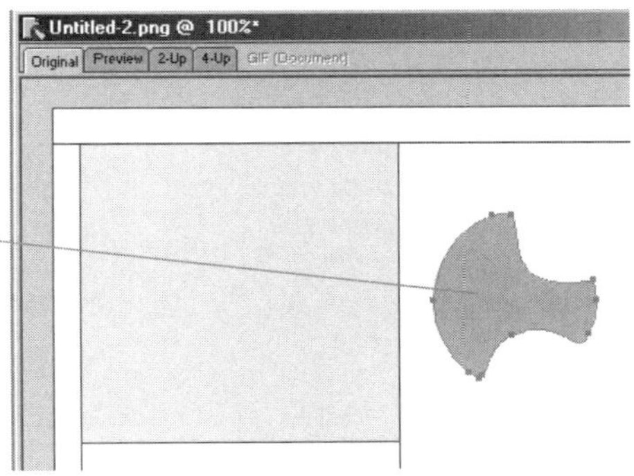

4 Insert a slice over the object in frame 2

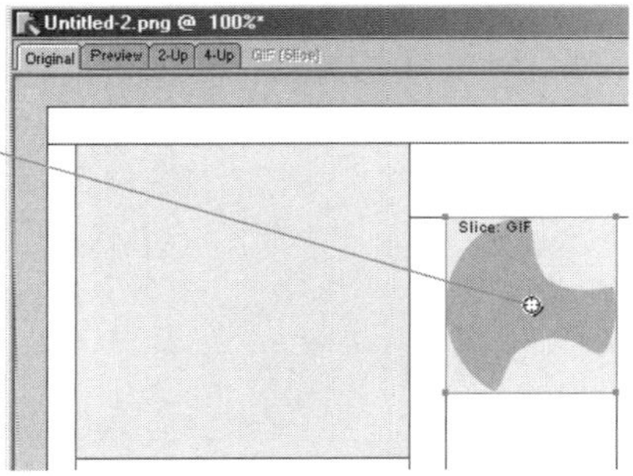

5 Select the slice over the object in frame 1 and select the Hotspot tool from the Tools panel

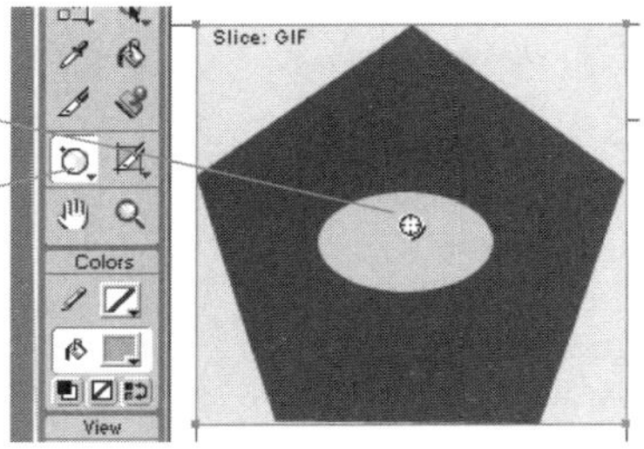

6 Draw a hotspot on top of the slice, covering the particular area that will be used for the trigger of the rollover

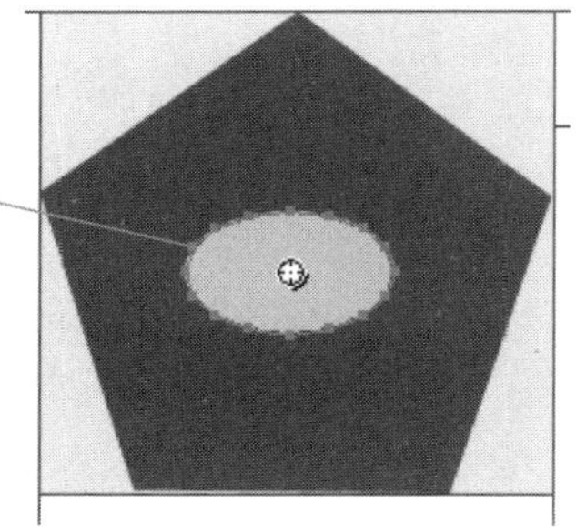

7 Select the Pointer tool and position it over the centre point of the hotspot until it turns into a pointing hand

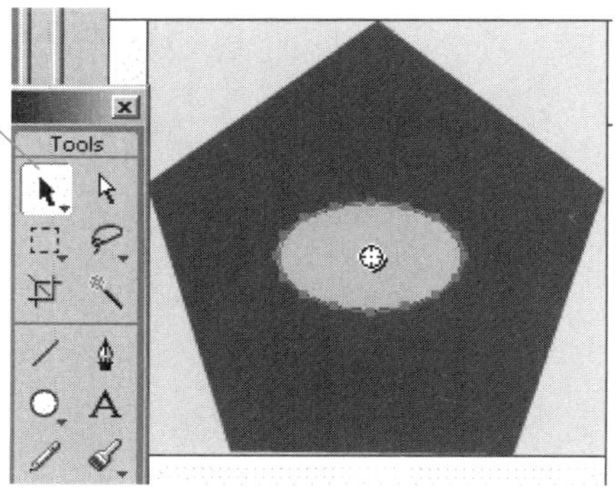

Slices can be inserted by selecting an image or graphic and selecting Insert>Slice from the menu bar. Alternatively, the Slice tool on the Tools panel can be used to draw a slice over the item.

When the hotspot is drawn over the slice, it becomes the trigger object, rather than the slice.

When adding a hotspot that is going to act as the trigger area make sure it is clear to the user that this is where they are meant to move the cursor. For instance, it could be over some explanatory text or a graphic such as an open door. If the user does not know how to activate the rollover, then its effectiveness could be lost.

8 Drag from the object in frame 1 to the object in frame 2. This is indicated by a curved blue line

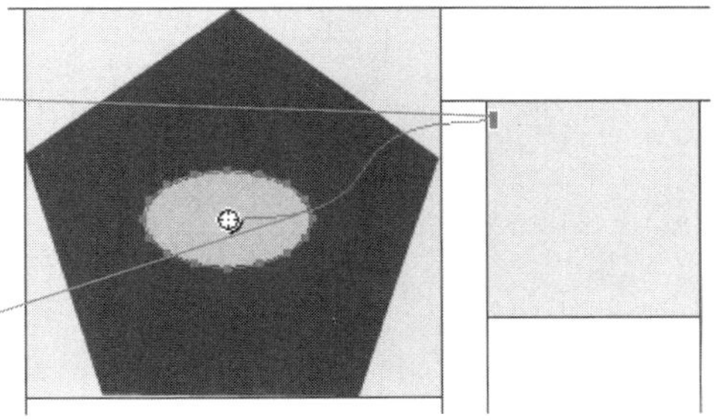

It is possible to add images in numerous different frames and then use these as the swap image, it does not have to be the one in frame 2. It is then possible to change the image if you want the rollover to include a different swap image. This could be useful if you had an e-commerce site displaying different special offers. Each week the rollover could be updated to show a different product by selecting a different frame for the swap image. It could also be used for a page such as employee of the month. The images of different employees could be inserted in different frames and then each month the site could be updated by selecting an image in a different frame.

9 Access the Swap Image dialog by selecting the '+' button under the Behaviors tab of the Behaviors panel. Select Frame 2. Select OK

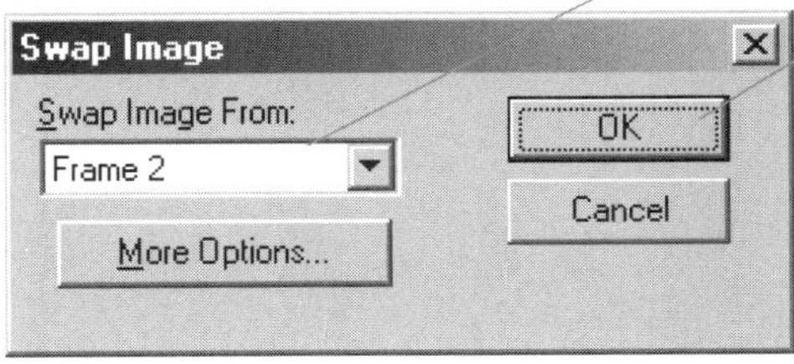

10 When the rollover is previewed or viewed on a browser the disjoint rollover will only be activated when the cursor rolls over the area covered by the hotspot

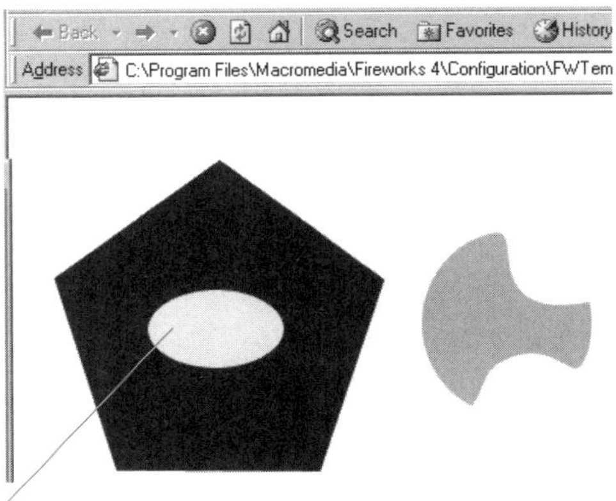

Editing behaviors

The Behaviors panel contains the details of how a rollover is triggered and what happens once this trigger has taken place. These are known as events and actions, respectively. It is possible to edit the events and actions for behaviors and also delete them.

Changing events

The default event for triggering a rollover is onMouseOver i.e. when the mouse rolls over the trigger object the rollover occurs. To change this:

Behaviors can only be added to slices or hotspots, rather than images or graphics created in Fireworks.

1 Click here on the Behaviors panel

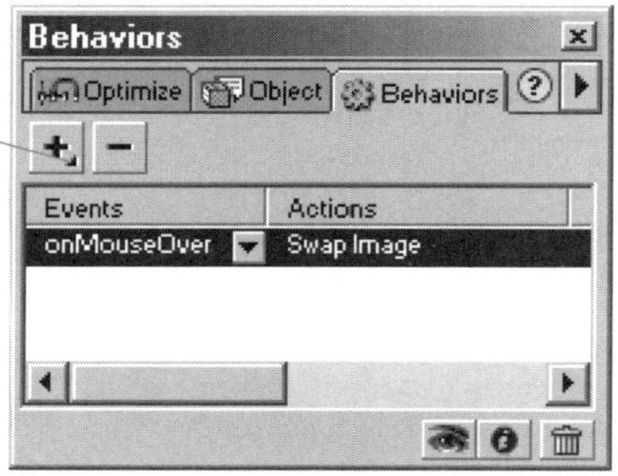

Several behaviors can be added to a single slice or hotspot. These are executed in the order in which they appear in the Behaviors panel.

2 Click here to select different events. These are:

- onMouseOut, which is triggered when the cursor is rolled over the trigger and then away from it;
- onClick, which is triggered by clicking on the trigger;
- onLoad, which is triggered as soon as the image is loaded into a browser

Adding actions

Actions can be added to a slice or a hotspot through either the Behaviors panel or by clicking on the drag-and-drop handle in the centre of one of these objects:

The Set Nav Bar Image actions can be used for specifying the Down and Over While Down states of buttons that are used in navigation bars.

1. Click here on the Behaviors panel

   or

   Click here on the handle on a slice or hotspot

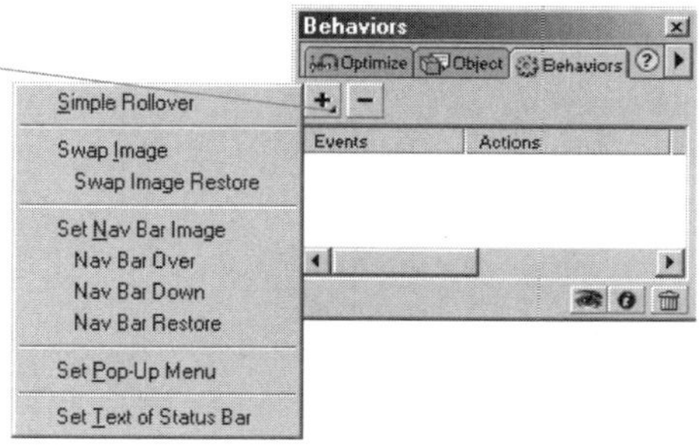

The Set Text of Status Bar action can be used to display text in the status bar at the bottom of a browser window. When this action is selected, text can be entered into a dialog box and this is what will appear in the status bar. This is a useful device for reinforcing a particular message, but it is best used sparingly on Web pages.

2. Select the required option from the menu

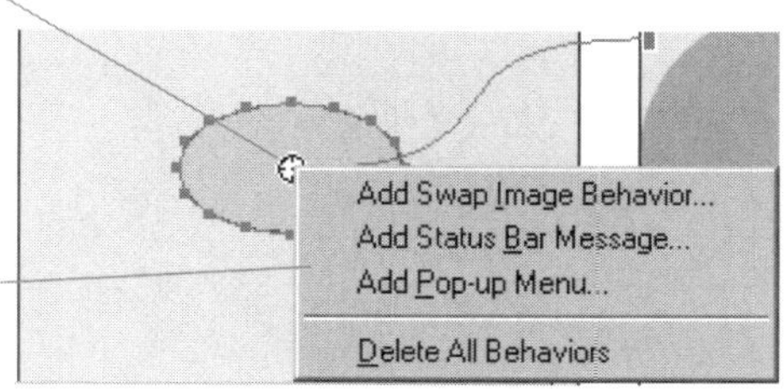

Deleting actions

1. Select the action in the Behaviors panel
2. Click here to remove the action

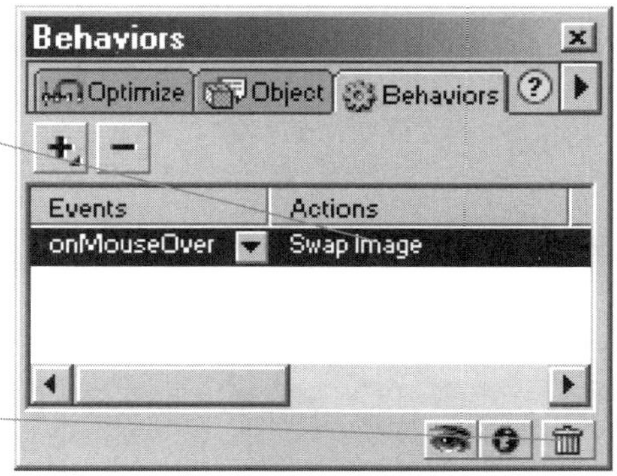

Exporting rollovers

When rollovers have been created they need to be exported so that they can then be included with an HTML Web page. The export process is the same for all types of rollovers and it involves exporting the images that have been created and also the HTML file that contains the necessary code. To export a rollover:

When a pop-up menu is exported, a Javascript file is also exported. The provides the functionality for the menu.

The name of the rollover is used as the root name for all of the images that are created for it.

Once a rollover has been exported it can be inserted into Dreamweaver using the Import Fireworks HTML button on the Objects panel. Select the HTML file and the image files will be included automatically.

When a rollover is exported, Fireworks creates a small image file called a spacer (spacer.gif). This is used to ensure that the elements of the rollover are correctly positioned within the HTML table that is created to accommodate them.

1 Select File>Export from the menu bar

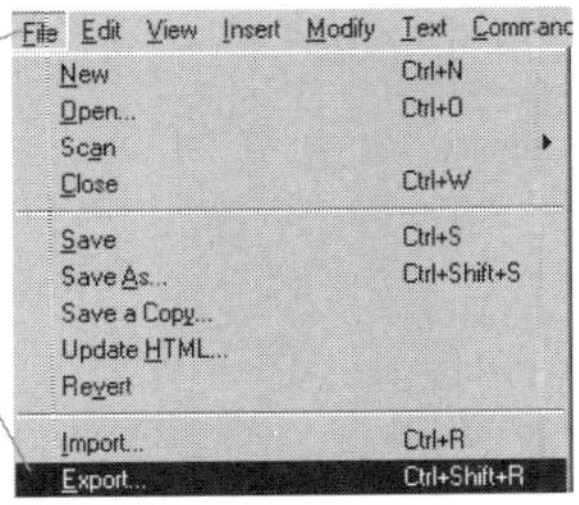

2 Select a location and enter a name for the rollover

3 Select HTML and Images

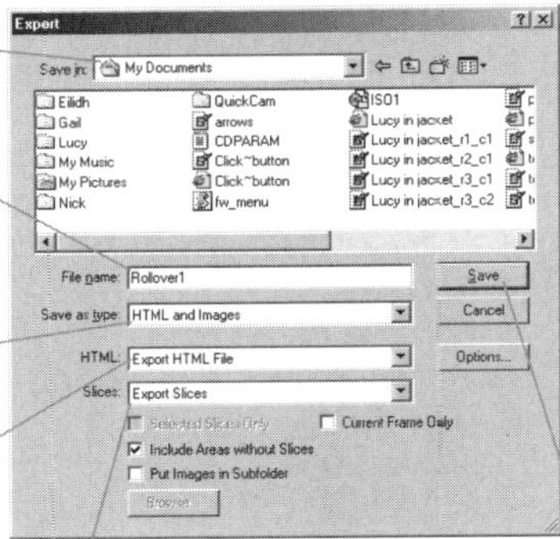

4 Select Export HTML file

5 Select Export Slices

6 Select Save

7 Check the rollover files are in your file structure

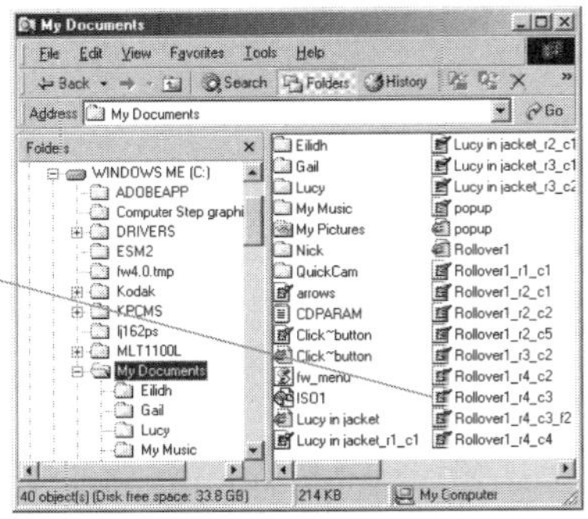

Animation

Animation can add a degree of real style and panache to a Web site. This chapter shows how to create simple animations in Fireworks and how to apply settings so that they can be exported into other programs.

Covers

Chapter Ten

Animation in Fireworks

Although Fireworks does not have the power to create the kind of sophisticated animations that can be produced in a program such as Flash, it can nevertheless be used to create some interesting animated effects. These include banner advertisements, animated logos or small cartoon animations:

For a detailed look at Flash, take a look at Flash 5 in easy steps.

Banner ads can be created to display different items

Banner ads were once all the rage on Web sites but their worth is being questioned more and more these days. However, there is still a place for well-designed and original banner ads.

Animated logos can be created for corporate or personal use

When creating animated logos, do not loop them continuously i.e. have them playing all of the time. One sequence is usually enough, particularly if people are going to be returning to the page a lot, in which case the animation will be activated again.

Budding cartoonists can give life to their drawings

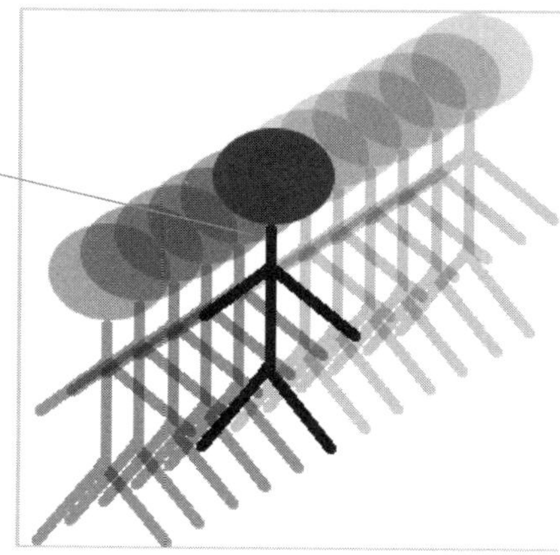

Animations in Fireworks are usually created as animated GIFs, which is a popular file format for this type of item. Fireworks can also export files into the Flash SWF format.

Animation basics

The theory of animation in Fireworks is the same as for creating an animated film: objects are created and then played in a sequence to create the animated effect. This requires working with different elements within Fireworks:

Symbols can be created as buttons, graphics or animations. All of these can then be used within a single Fireworks document.

- Symbols. The objects that are animated are known as symbols. These are normal graphics that are converted into a format that the program can then work with as animation. Symbols can be created from scratch or existing objects can be converted into symbols. When symbols are created they are placed in the Library. Copies of the symbol can then be used in the animation, while the original symbol remains in the Library:

Text blocks can be made into symbols. This is necessary if you want to create animated text.

Symbols are placed in the Library and then instances of them can be copied into the work area. Numerous instances can be created from one symbol

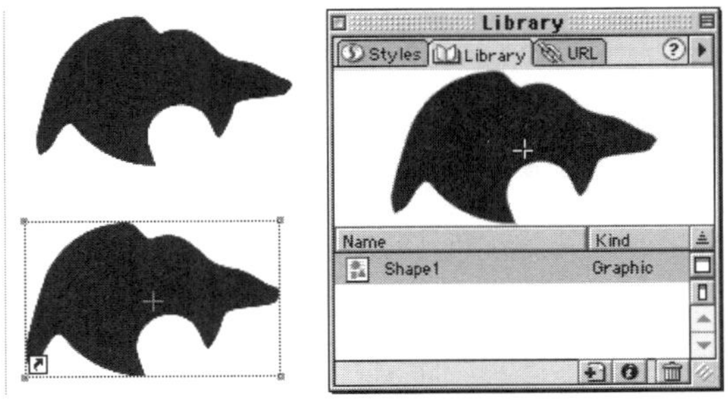

Tweening is an animation term that refers to the frames in between two points where an object changes position. Traditionally, in film animation, these are the frames that are created by the less experienced animators.

- Frames. In order for symbols to be animated they have to be placed on separate frames. When the animation is played, the frames are viewed in sequence and this creates the animated effect
- Tweening. This is the technique for creating the sense of motion between two points. In one frame the object is positioned at the start point; in another frame it is moved to a different location. Tweening can then be applied to animate it between the two points

Creating symbols

Symbols are the building blocks of an animation. Without them a lot of the functionality of an animation would be lost. Symbols can be created as graphics, buttons or animations. Single graphic symbols can be included in a document and then have animated effects applied to them, while animated symbols can be included as an animation within an animation. Symbols always reside in the Library and they can be created from scratch, or existing documents can be converted into symbols.

If you try and animate an object that is not a symbol, Fireworks will automatically convert it to an animation symbol.

Creating new symbols

1 Open a new document and select Insert>New Symbol from the menu bar

When graphic symbols are used to create an animation, the end product is created as a new, animated symbol.

2 In the Symbol Properties dialog box, give the symbol a name and select the type. Select OK

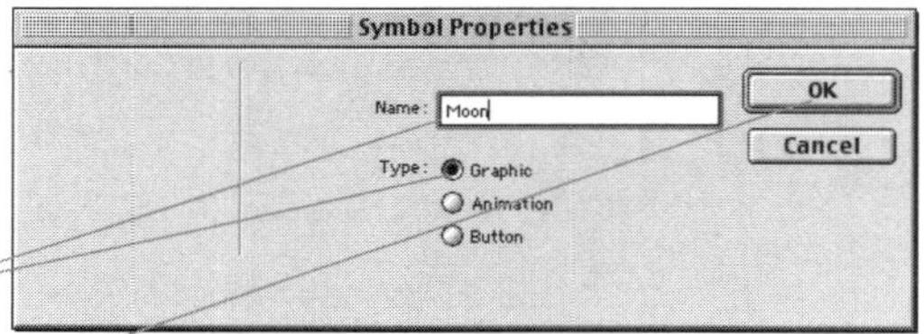

Graphic symbols are the ones most commonly used in animation. Animation symbols are like small animations that can be used independently or as part of a bigger animation.

3 The symbol window appears over the main document window. Think of this as residing inside the main window

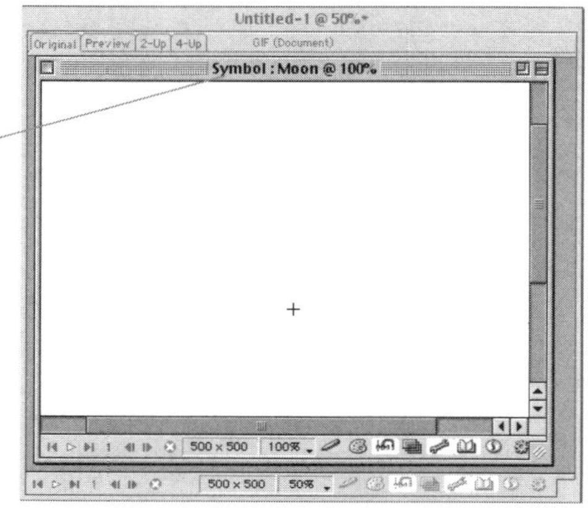

4 Enter the content for the symbol

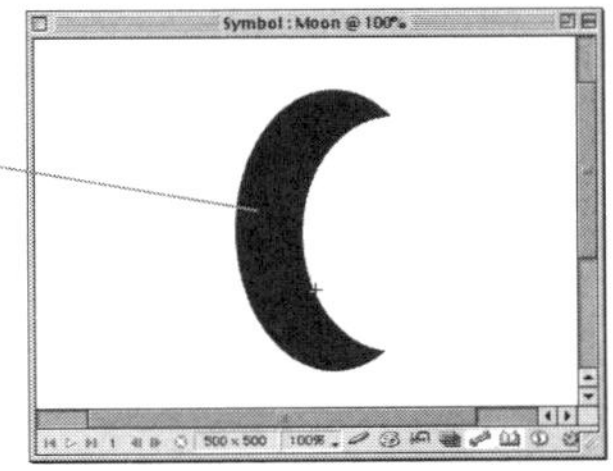

Select Window> Library from the menu bar to display the Library and its contents.

5 Close the symbol window. An instance of the symbol is placed within the work area and the symbol is placed in the Library

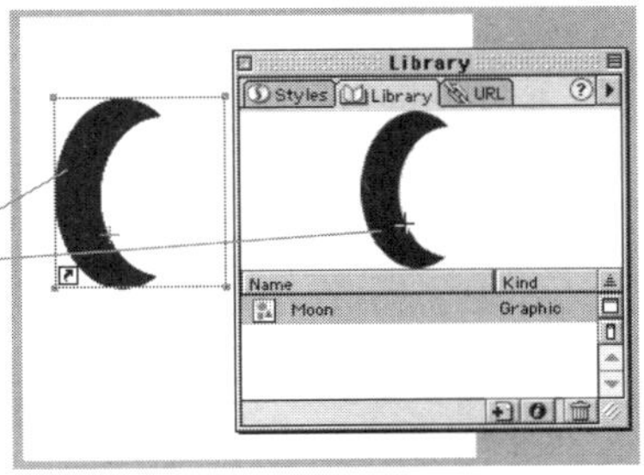

An instance of a symbol is a special type of copy that is referenced to the original symbol rather than just a straightforward copy of it. This means that it does not contain any content in its own right. This can be done because the symbol is created as a vector object rather than a bitmap one, so the instance is just another mathematical equation. This means that numerous instances can be used from the same symbol without increasing the file size of the document. This only changes if the original symbol is edited. When a change is made to a symbol, then this is also applied to all of the instances that have been created from it.

Converting objects into symbols

1 Create an object in the work area and select it

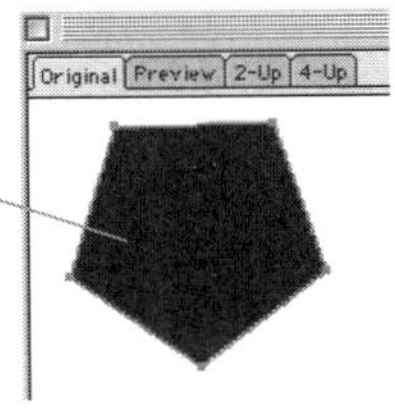

2 Select Insert> Convert to Symbol from the menu bar

3 In the Symbol Properties dialog box, give the symbol a name and select the type. Select OK

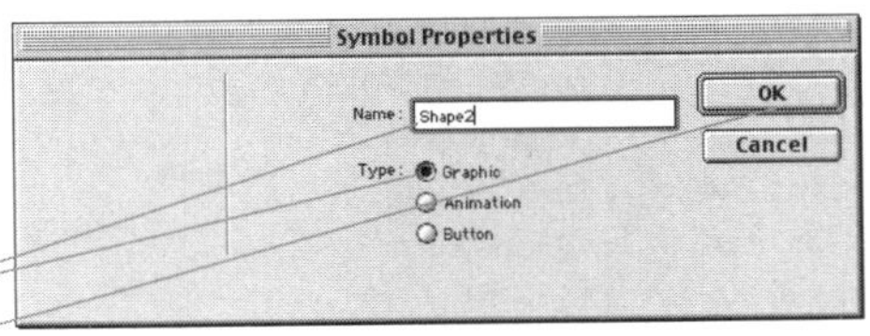

Working with the Library

Each symbol type is denoted by its own icon.

Creating instances

All symbols that are created are placed in the Library. They can then be placed within a document as an instance by inserting them into the work area:

1. Select a symbol from the list here

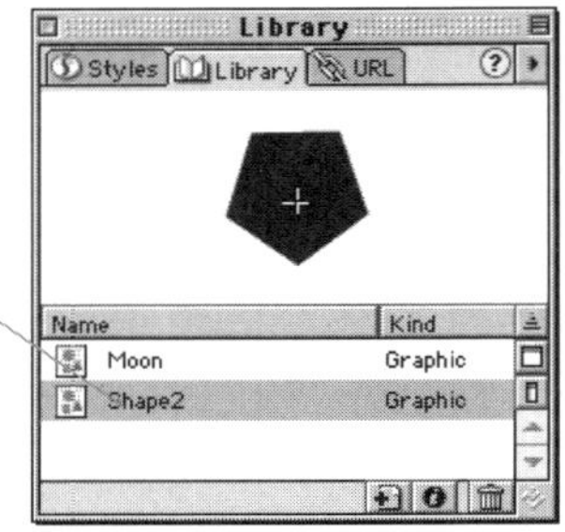

Symbols can be edited by double-clicking on them in the top panel of the Library. Any changes that are made will affect all instances of that symbol that have been added to a document.

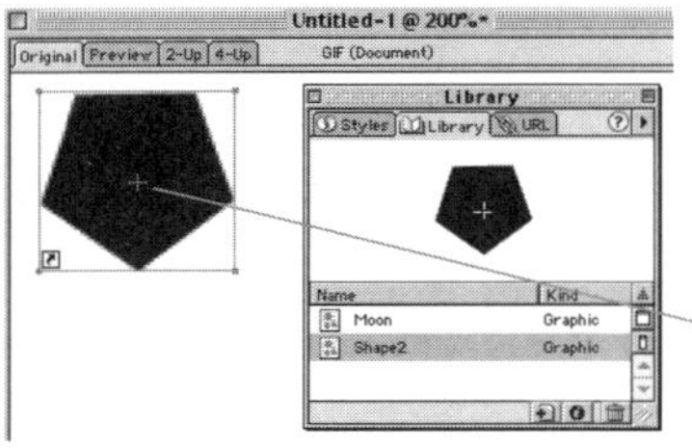

2. Click and drag the symbol onto the work area to create an instance

Creating symbols

The type of a symbol is also known as its behavior.

1. Click here to create a new symbol

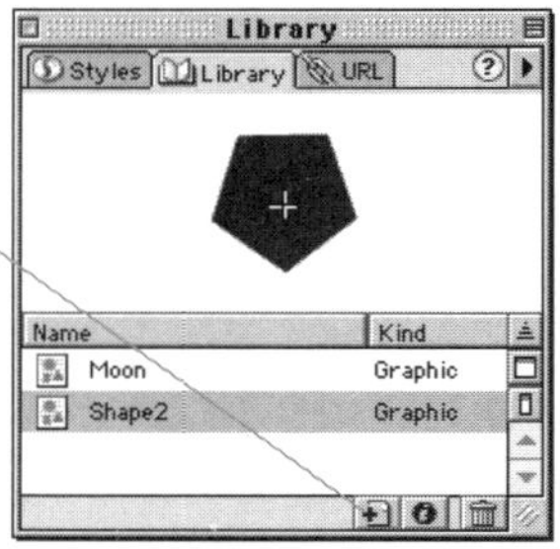

A symbol's properties can be edited by double-clicking on the symbol name in the lower panel of the Library. Double-click on the icon to edit the symbol itself rather than its properties.

2. Enter a name and type of symbol. Select OK and follow Steps 3–5 on pages 148–149

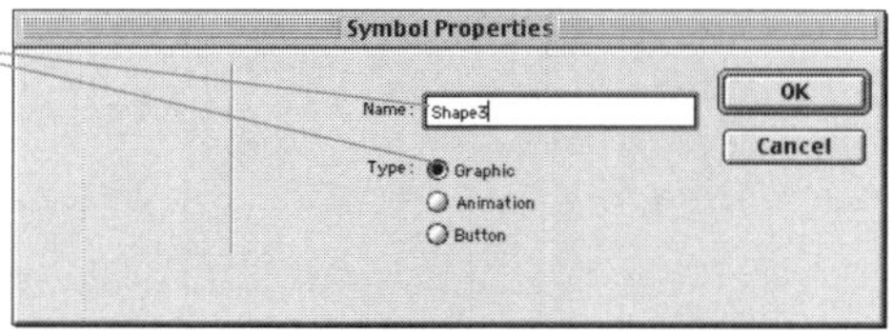

Deleting symbols

If a symbol is deleted from the Library, all instances of it that have been created will also be deleted.

Select a symbol in the lower panel of the Library and click here to delete it

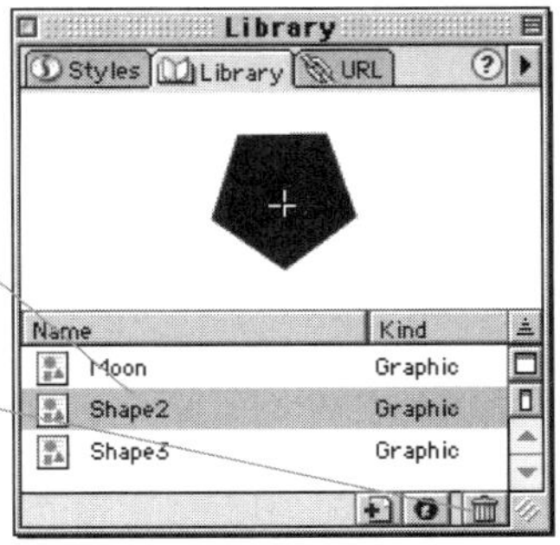

Editing the Library

If an instance of a symbol is deleted in the work area, this does not affect the original symbol.

1 Click here to access the Library menu

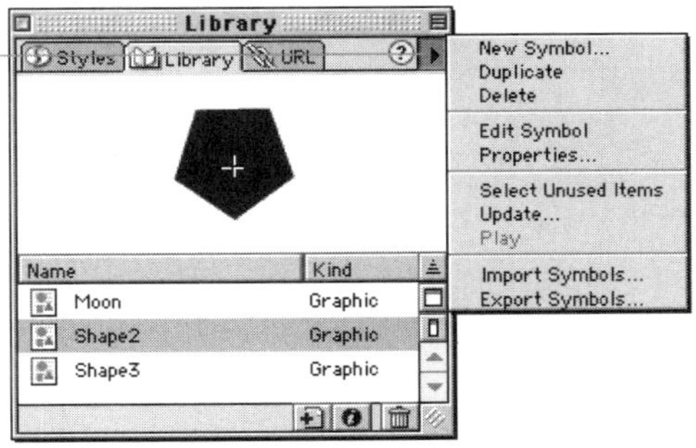

The options for displaying the items in the Library are (from top to bottom):

- *Show all columns, which displays the full details of each item;*
- *Minimize panel width, which shrinks the Library to its smallest width;*
- *Toggle sorting, which sorts the items in the Library in different orders.*

2 Select these buttons to determine the way the items in the Library are displayed

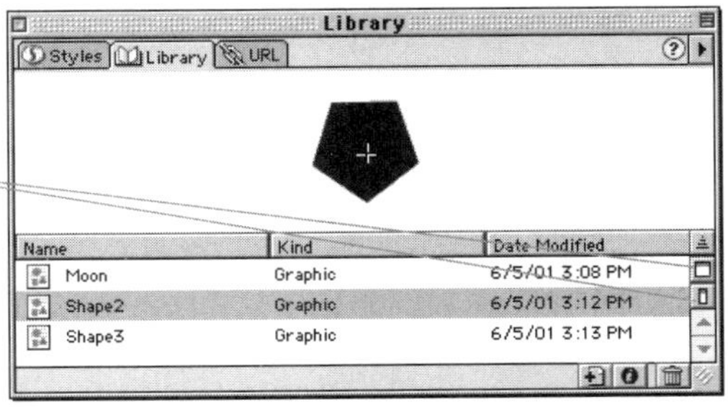

Creating a simple animation

Simple animations can be created by dragging a symbol from the Library and then animating it, or animating an object that has already been created, in which case it will automatically be converted into a symbol. To create a simple animation:

An instance in the work area is identified by a dotted line around it when it is selected.

1 Create an instance of a graphic symbol by dragging it onto the work area from the Library

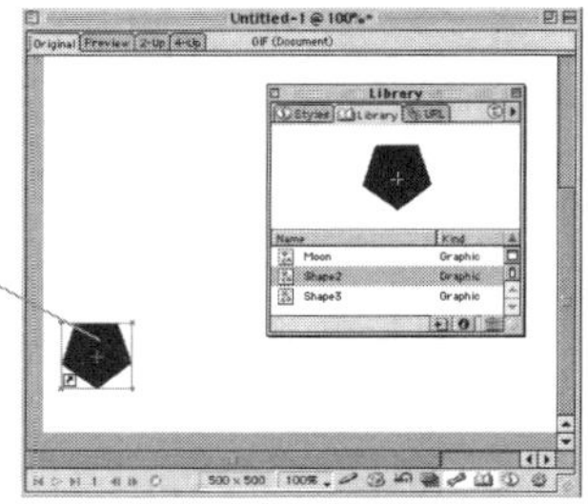

Make sure an item is selected before you try and animate it.

2 Select Modify> Animate>Animate Selection from the menu bar

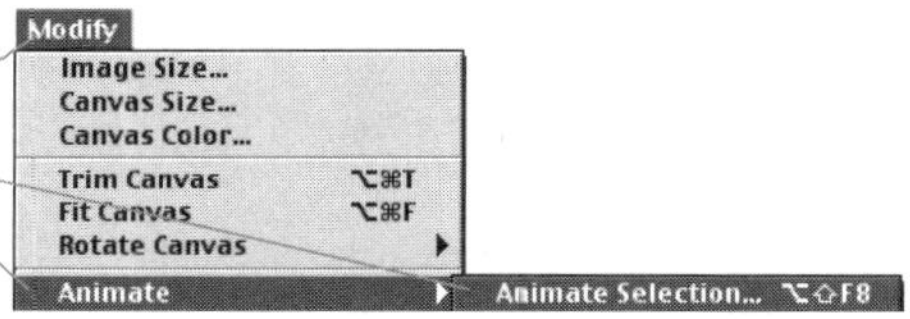

The Animate dialog box is looked at in more detail on pages 154–156.

3 In the Animate dialog box, leave the default settings as they are. Select OK

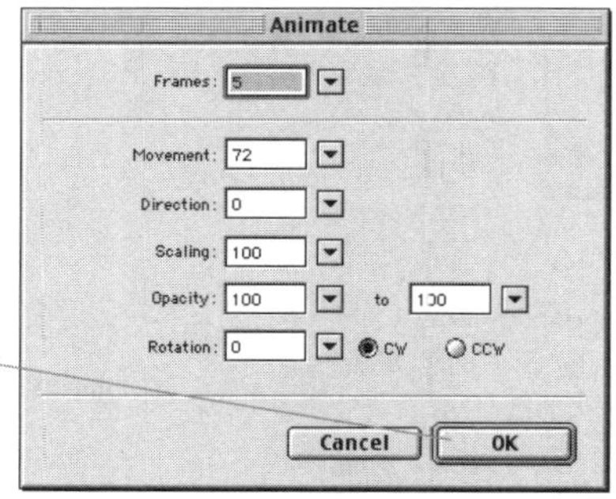

4 This dialog box may appear if the animation requires additional frames. Select OK

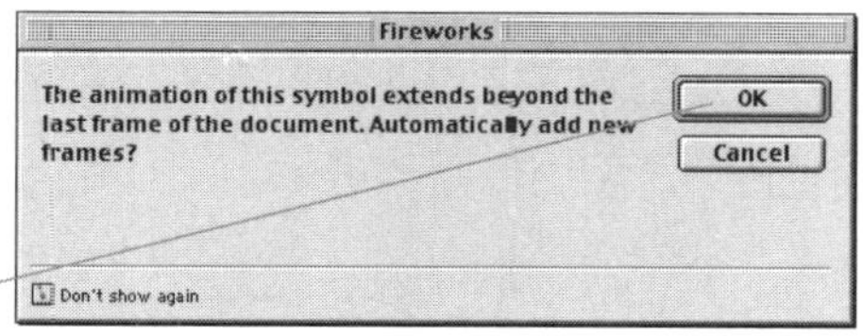

The centre-point of the object in the first frame is green and the one in the last frame is red. The centre-points of the in-between frames are blue. These colours remain the same regardless of the frame currently selected.

5 The centre-point of the instance in the different frames is shown here

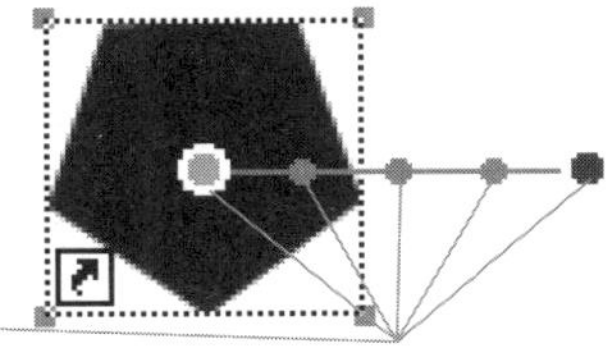

The animation control panel can also be used to move directly to the first or last frame in the animation.

6 In this animation the object will move from here to here

7 Click here to play and stop the animation

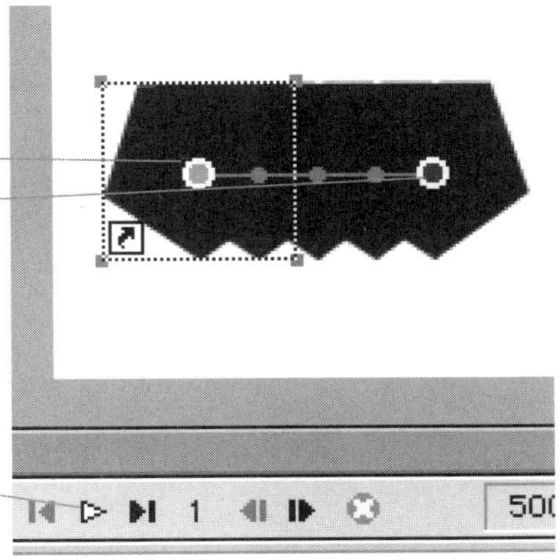

8 Select Window> Frames to view the Frames panel

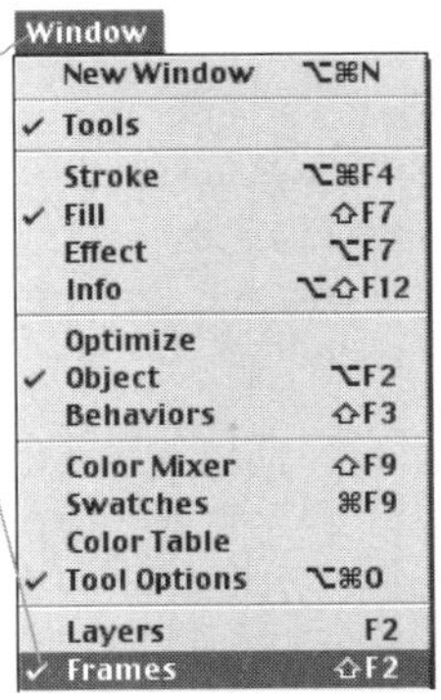

The number of times that an animation plays (or loops) can be specified by clicking here on the Frames panel and making a selection from the menu. This is only effective once the animation has been exported – when it is previewed in Fireworks, it will play continuously.

9 Click on a frame to see the position of the object at that point

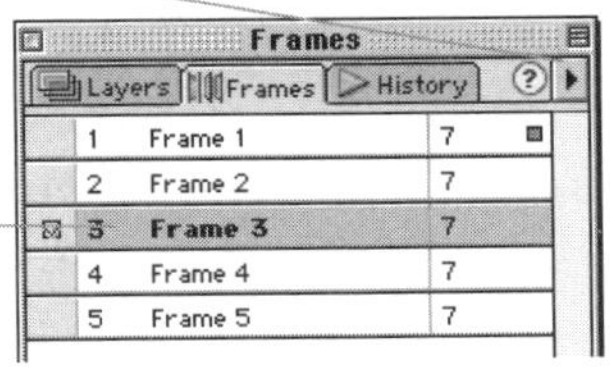

Animation settings

The way that an animation performs can be determined in the animation settings dialog box. This controls the distance an object moves when it is animated, the direction it moves in and its opacity. To determine animation settings:

The Animate settings dialog box can also be accessed by right-clicking (Windows) or Ctrl+clicking (Mac) and selecting Animate>Settings from the contextual menu.

1 Apply the settings in the Animate dialog box when an animation is first created. Or, select an animation and select Modify>Animate>Settings from the menu bar

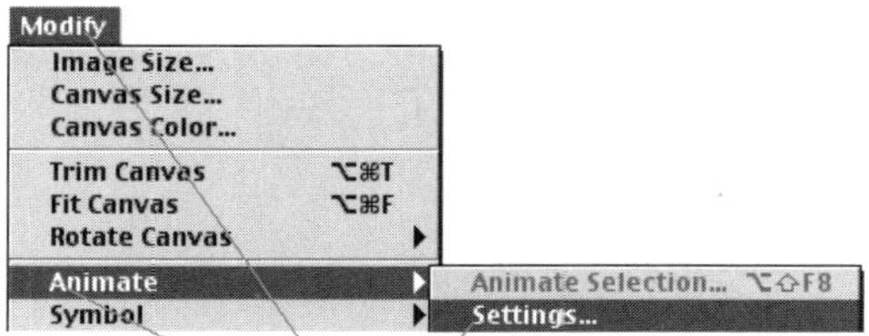

The maximum move value is 250 and the minimum is 0.

2 Enter a value here to specify how far (in pixels) the animated object moves in each frame

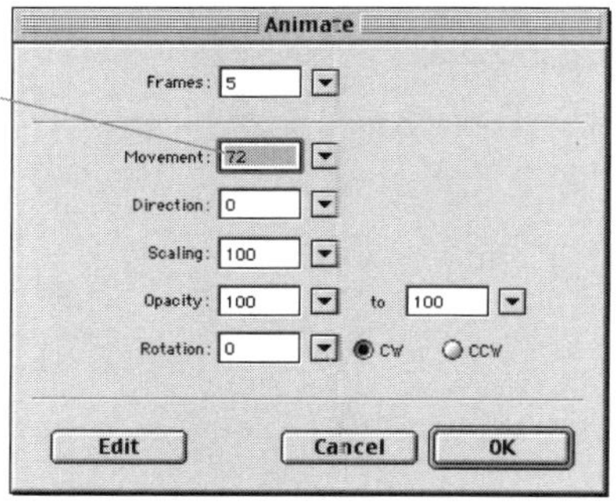

Select a move value of 0 if you want an object to animate at the same spot e.g. a spinning wheel.

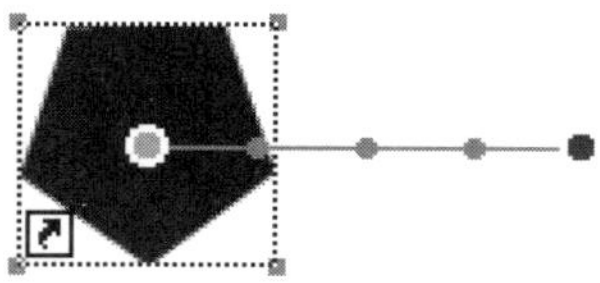

A move value of 100

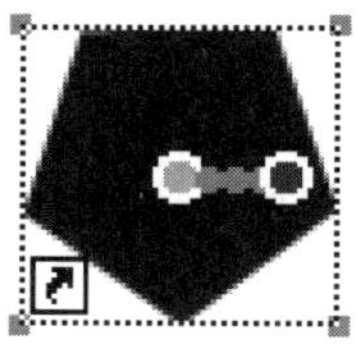

A move value of 20

3 Enter a value here to specify the direction (in degrees) in which the animated object moves

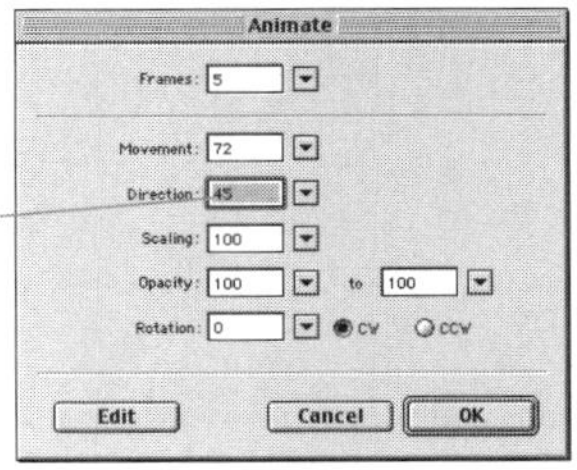

The direction setting can be changed by either adding a numerical value or by clicking on the down arrow next to the direction box and dragging the dial to the required direction.

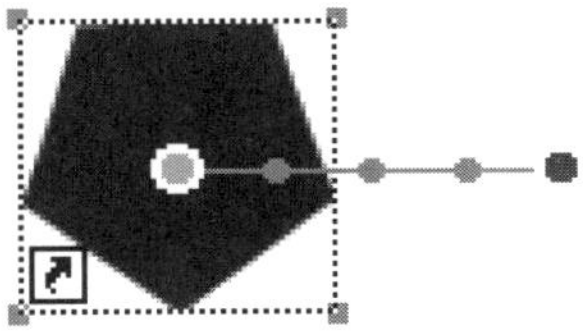

A direction value of 0

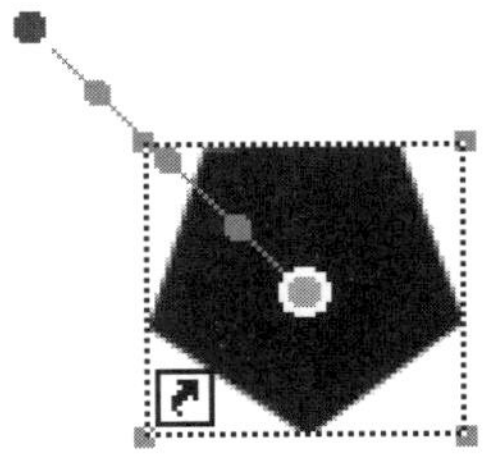

A direction value of 135

If the direction is set to 0, the object will move from left to right in a straight line.

4 Enter a value here to specify how the object is scaled i.e. how it changes size when it is animated

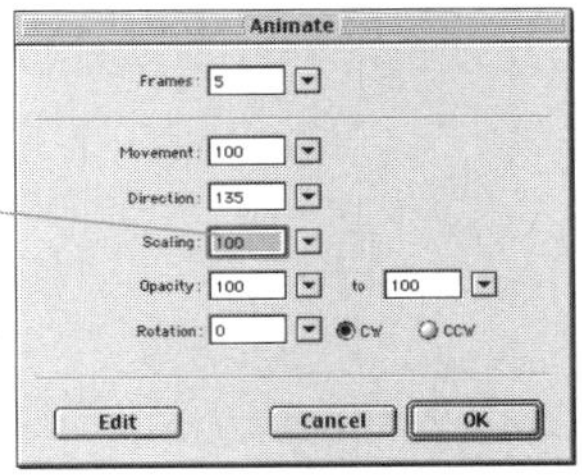

If the scale value is set at 0, this will make the object disappear at the end of the animation i.e. it will start at its normal size and then get progressively smaller until it disappears.

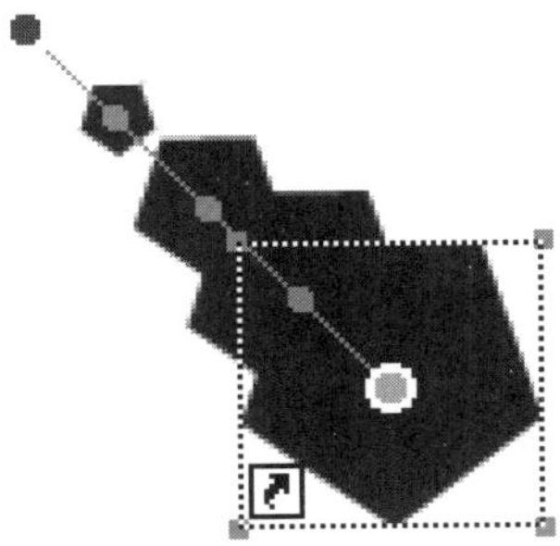

An object scaling to 0

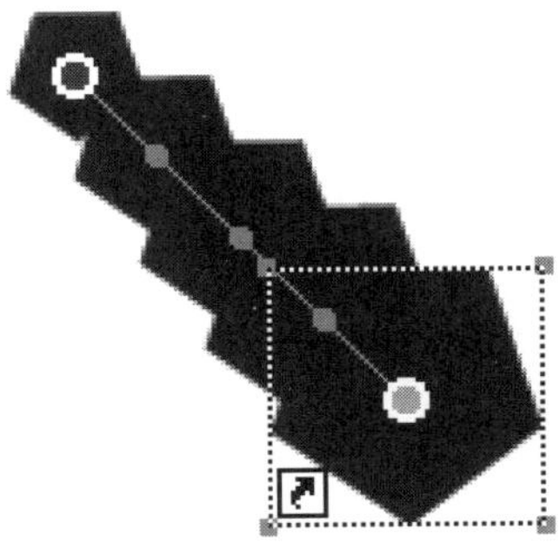

An object scaling to 50

5 Enter a value here to specify the opacity i.e. the level of transparency

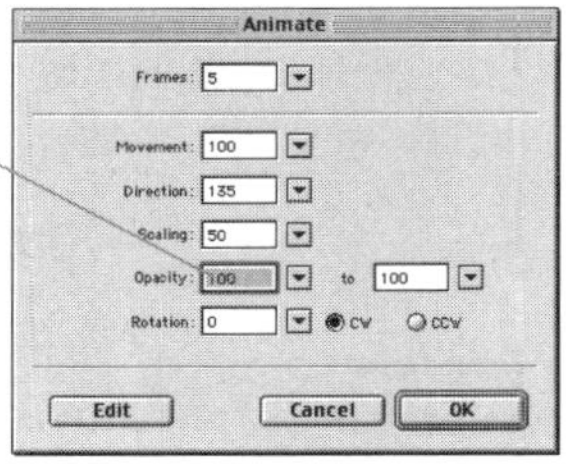

The opacity value in the first box is the one that is applied in frame 1. So if you want an object to begin completely transparent and then fade into view, enter a value of 0 in the first box.

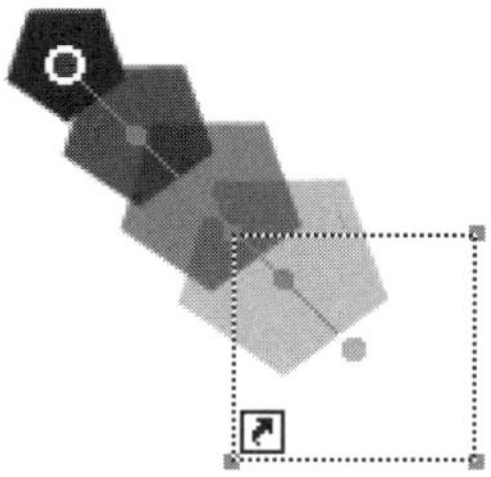

An opacity value of 0 to 100

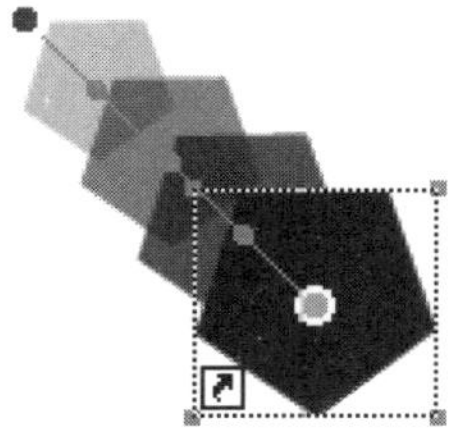

An opacity value of 100 to 0

6 Enter a value here to specify the amount (in degrees) that the object rotates during the animation

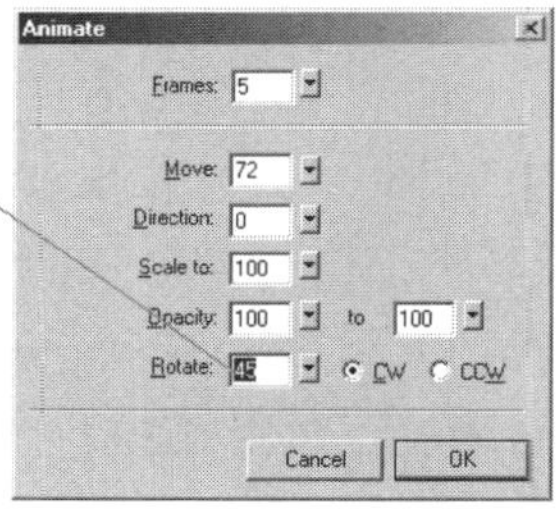

An object can be rotated in a clockwise or a counter-clockwise direction.

Once all of the animation settings have been applied, select OK.

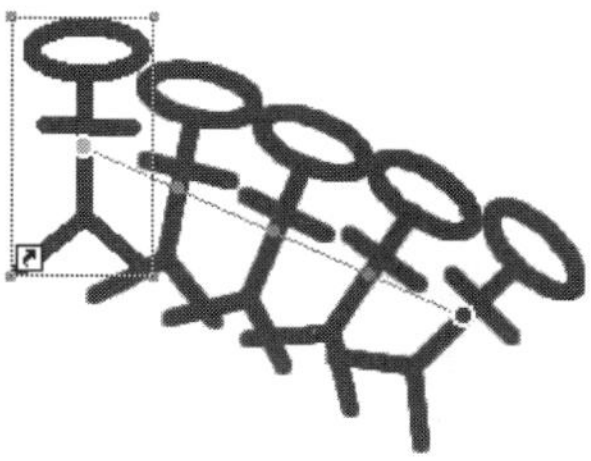

A rotation of 45

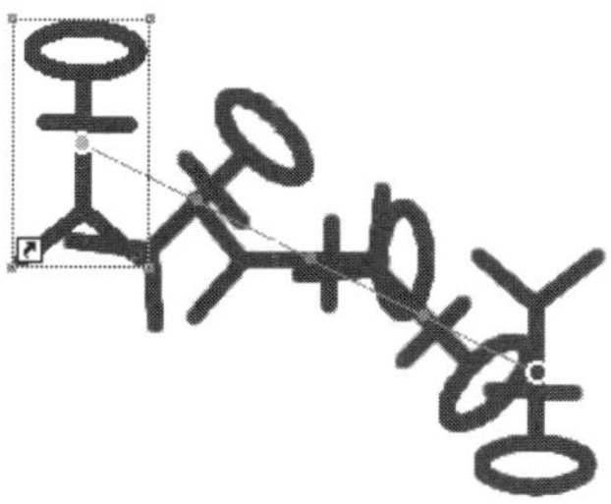

A rotation of 180

Optimising

When an animation has been completed, it has to be optimised and exported so that it is in a suitable format for displaying on the Web. To do this the image has to first be optimised as an animated GIF and then exported. To optimise an animation:

If an animation is optimised in a format other than an animated GIF, and then exported, the result will be a single frame, static image.

Animated GIFs are created as single files, even though they can contain numerous frames.

Animated GIFs are larger than comparable static images and so if a lot of them are being used,, downloading time could become an issue.

1 Create an animation and select Window> Optimize from the menu bar

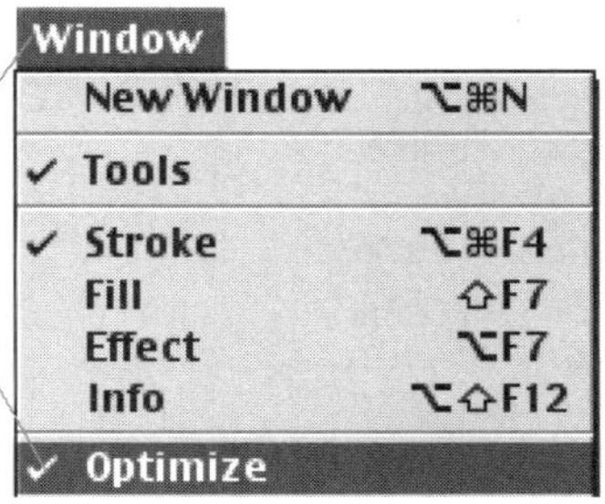

2 Click here to select the image format. Select Animated GIF. The settings for an animated GIF are the same as those for a non-animated one

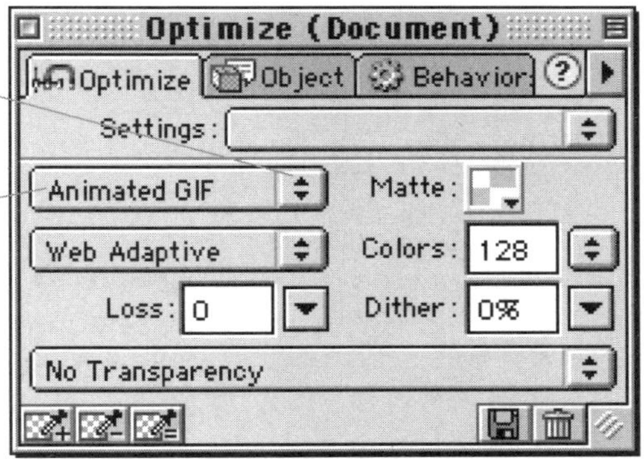

Exporting

Once animations have been optimised as animated GIFs they can then be exported into a variety of formats, including Flash SWF files.

Setting looping

Before an animation is exported its looping attributes can be set to determine how many times it plays after the initial sequence. To do this:

The looping number applies to the animation after it has played through one time. Therefore, if looping is set to No Looping, the animation will play one time and then stop.

1. Click here on the Frames panel

2. Select a looping option from the menu

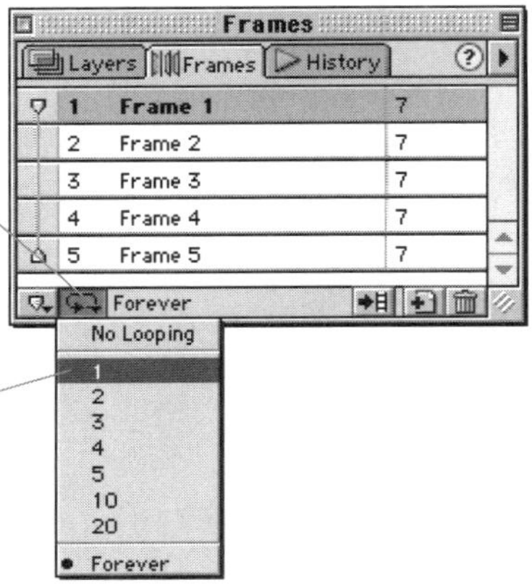

Animation that loops Forever, i.e. continuously, can get very annoying after a while and can actually detract from a Web site rather than add to it.

Exporting an animated GIF

One option for exporting animations is to do so in the same format in which they are optimised i.e. animated GIFs. To do this:

1. Select File>Export from the menu bar

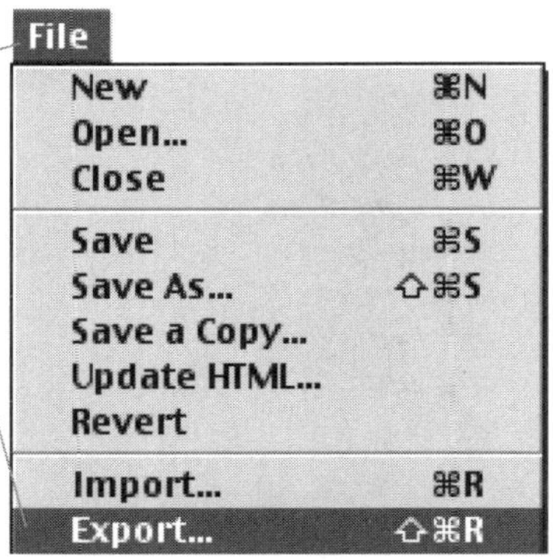

2 Give the animation a name and save it as Images Only. Select Save

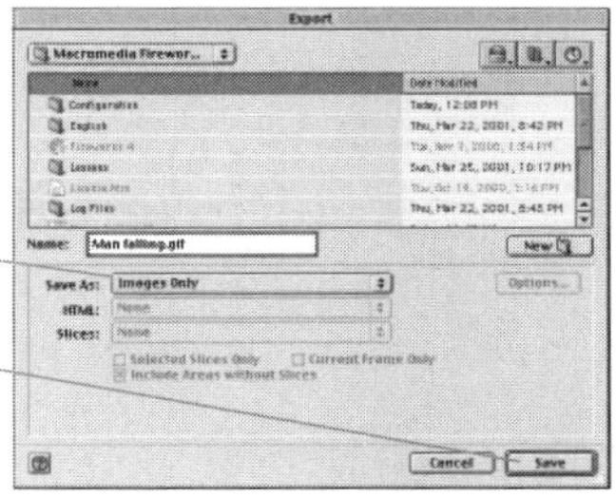

Exporting an SWF file

In addition to exporting animations as animated GIFs, they can also be exported as Flash files, which have the SWF file extension. These can then be edited within Flash or inserted directly into a Dreamweaver document. To do this:

Flash movies can be incorporated into HTML Web pages. When they are viewed on a browser, the Flash Player has to be installed. This is a plug-in program that enables the browser to play the Flash file. If the Flash Player is not already installed it can be downloaded from www.macromedia.com

1 Select File>Export from the menu bar

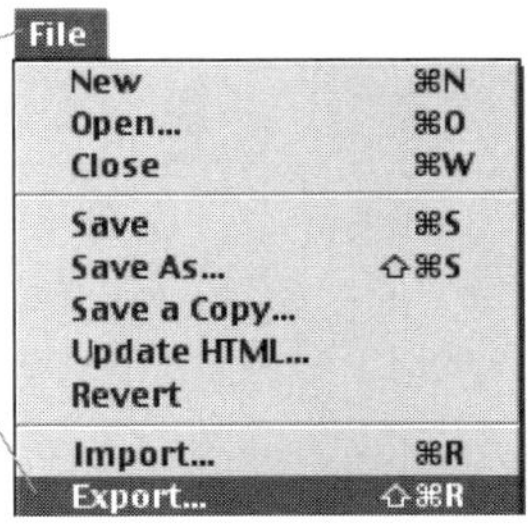

2 Give the animation a name and click here

3 Save as Macromedia Flash SWF. Select Save

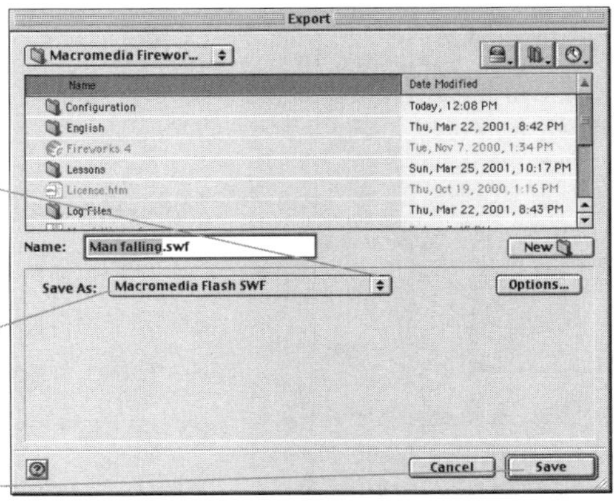

Using animation files

Using Dreamweaver, animated GIFs and SWF files can be incorporated in HTML Web pages.

Inserting animated GIFs

Animated GIFs can be inserted into a Dreamweaver page in the same way as a normal GIF image:

Animated GIFs appear the same as any other type of GIFs when they are viewed in the file structure. They do not have a different icon.

1. Insert the cursor where you want the image to appear and select the Image button on the Common panel

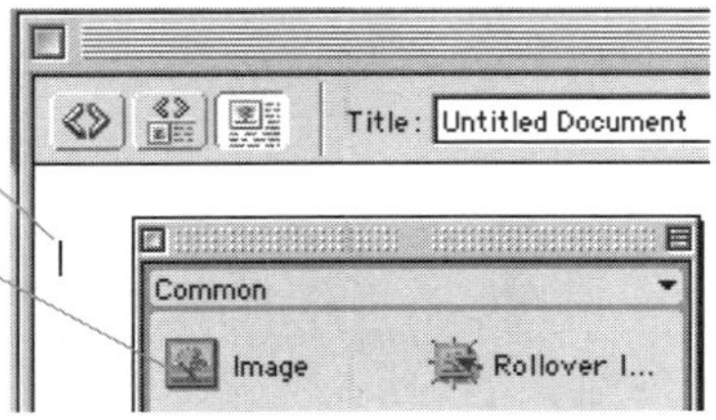

2. Select an animated image and click Select (Windows) or Open (Mac)

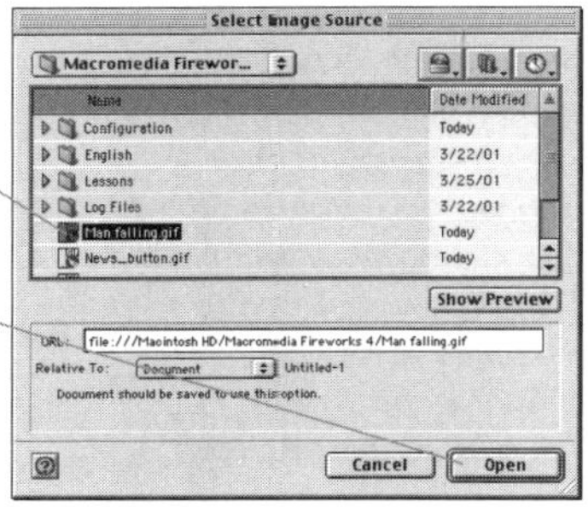

An animated GIF will only work when it is viewed on a browser. In Dreamweaver it will look like a single image.

3. The animation is inserted as a static image. Press F12 to preview the animation in a browser

Inserting a SWF file

When a Flash file is inserted into a Dreamweaver document, all of the code required for it to work with the Flash Player is inserted automatically.

Insert the cursor where you want the image to appear and select the Flash button on the Common panel. Select and preview the Flash image as in Steps 2 and 3 above

Further animation

Once the basics of animation in Fireworks have been mastered there is a range of techniques that can be looked at. This chapter shows how to edit animations, create tweened animations, work with animation symbols and create more complex animations such as a banner ad or similar.

Covers

Chapter Eleven

Editing animations

Modifying paths

When an animation has been created it is then possible to edit the path it takes. This can be done by dragging the animation's path to a new location and all of the frames are updated accordingly. To do this:

1 Create an animation and select it so that its entire path across all frames is showing

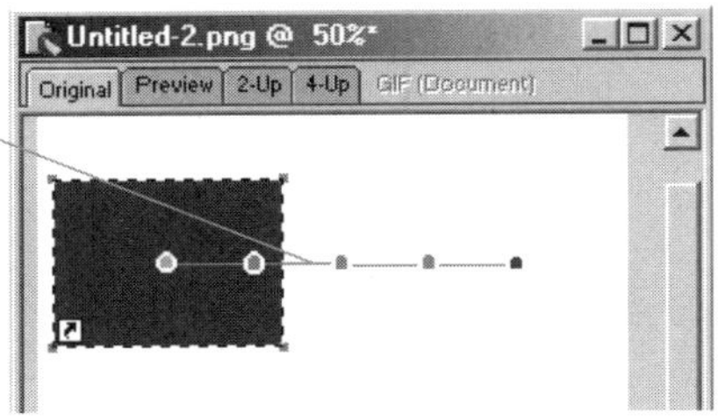

Click on one of the coloured dots on an animation's path to see the attributes of the object in that particular frame.

2 Click and drag here to move the start and end points of the animation. This can also be dragged to change the amount the animation moves between each frame

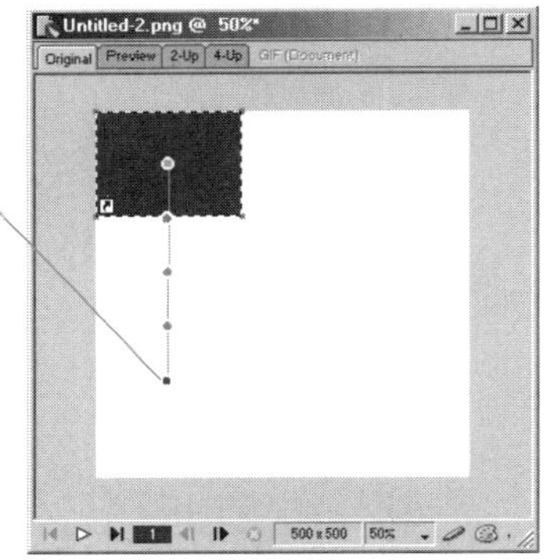

The direction in which an animation moves can also be edited by dragging the start and end points of its path.

3 Click and drag here to move the entire path without changing the amount the animation moves between frames

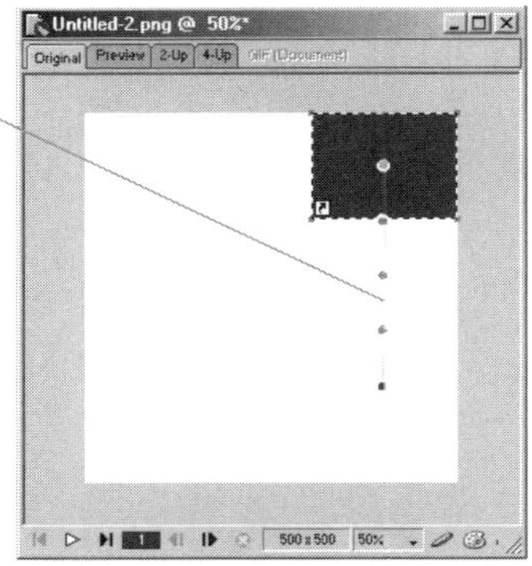

Onion skinning

When working with animations that cover several frames it is useful to be able to see how an object appears in different frames, while still being able to view and edit it in the current frame. This can be done with a technique called onion skinning. This enables you to see an outline of one, or more, other frames, to see the overall progression of the animation. To use onion skinning:

Onion skinning is an animation technique that refers to the practice of placing thin sheets of transparent paper on top of a drawing, to determine the location for the next frame of the animation.

If you have an animation covering a lot of frames, it can be confusing if you set onion skinning to Show All Frames. A better option may be to use Show Next Frame or Before and After. Alternatively, you could create your own settings in the Customize dialog box.

1 Select an animation

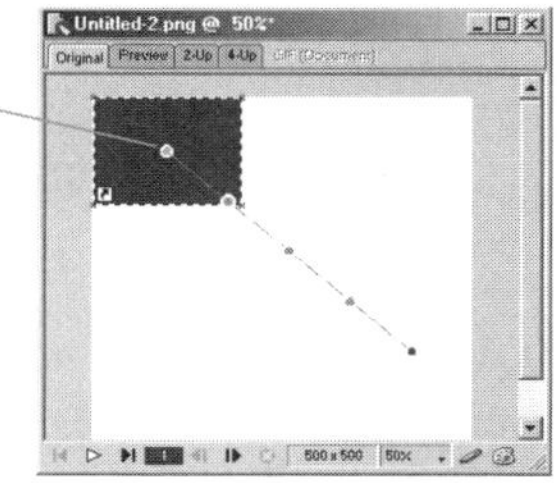

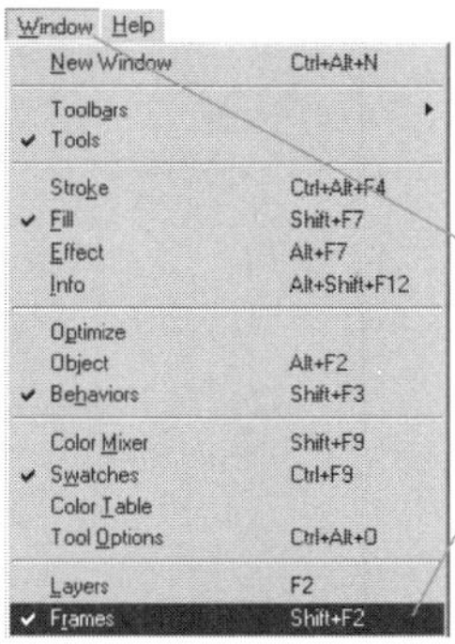

2 Select Window> Frames from the menu bar

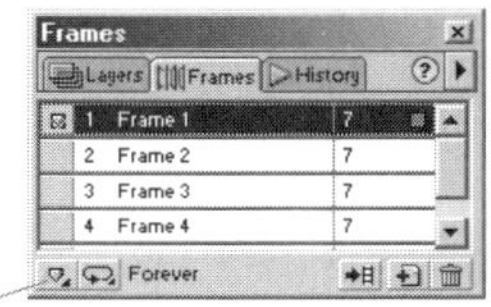

3 Click here to select the onion skinning options

4 Select a frame on the animation's path. Depending on the selection in Step 3, other frames in the animation are visible

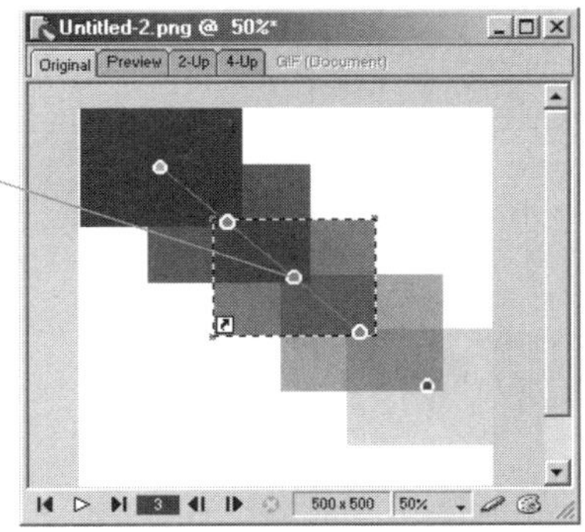

Tweening

Tweening is the process of creating motion between two different points of an animation. If an animation is created as shown on the previous pages, the tweening is inserted automatically. However, it is also possible to create tweening manually, for greater flexibility. To do this:

The type of tweening that can be done in Fireworks is known as motion tweening.

1. Create a graphic symbol and insert two instances of it onto the work area. Select both of them

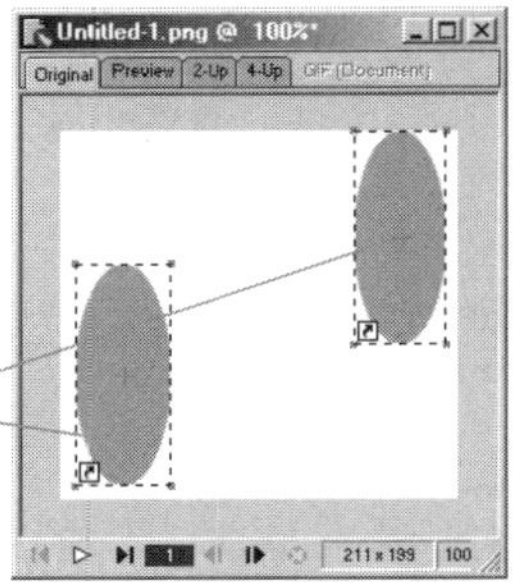

In Fireworks you cannot tween instances from two different symbols i.e. a circle and a square. This is known as shape tweening (or morphing) and a program such as Flash is required to achieve this.

2. Select Modify> Symbol>Tween Instances from the menu bar

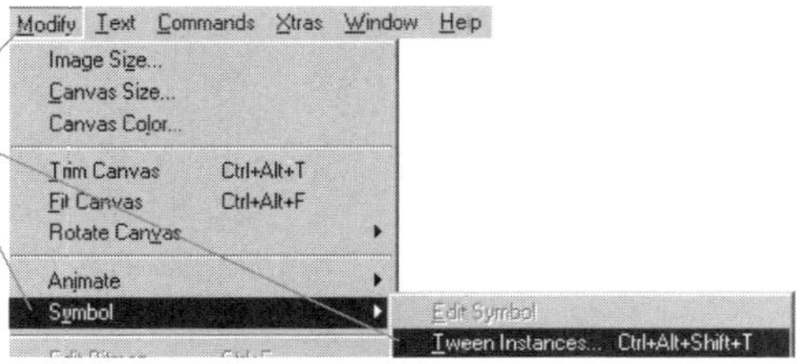

The Distribute to Frames box can be checked at Step 3, in which case the required number of frames are inserted to accommodate the tween. However, this can be done at a later stage and if it is unchecked it enables you to see the full path of the tween more clearly.

3. In the Tween Instances dialog box, leave the number of steps as the default chosen by Fireworks and leave the Distribute to Frames box unchecked. Select OK

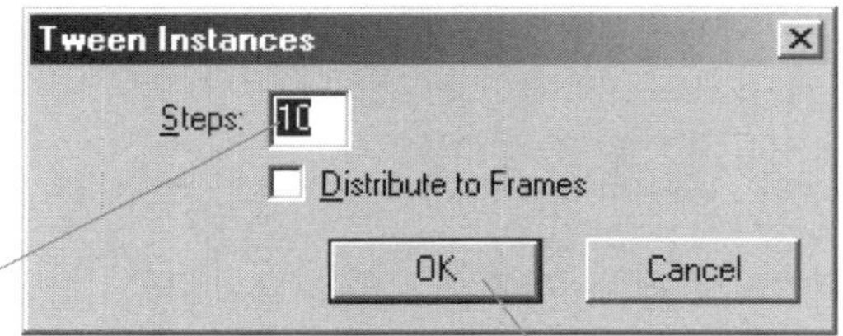

4 To create a multi-directional tween, insert another instance of the same symbol and position it so that the current tween has to change direction to reach it

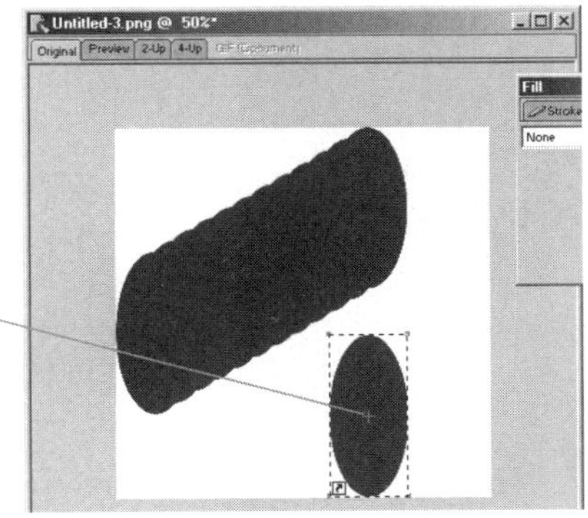

To select two instances at once, click on the first one and then Shift+click on the second one.

5 Select the instance at the end of the first tween and also select the new instance. Repeat Steps 2–3 on the previous page

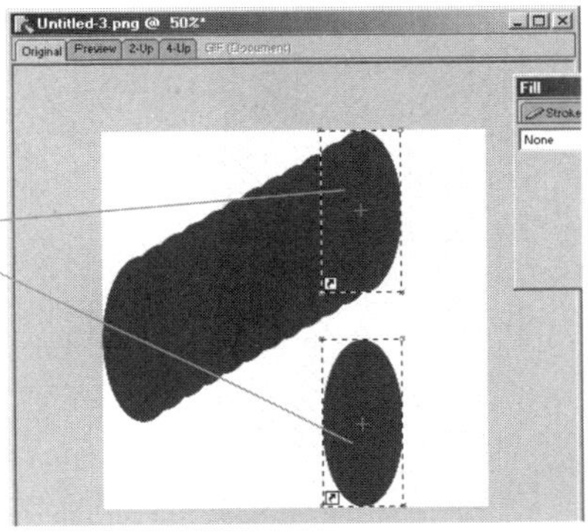

All of the instances can also be selected together by selecting the Pointer tool and dragging an invisible rectangle around all of them in the work area.

6 Select Edit>Select All from the menu bar

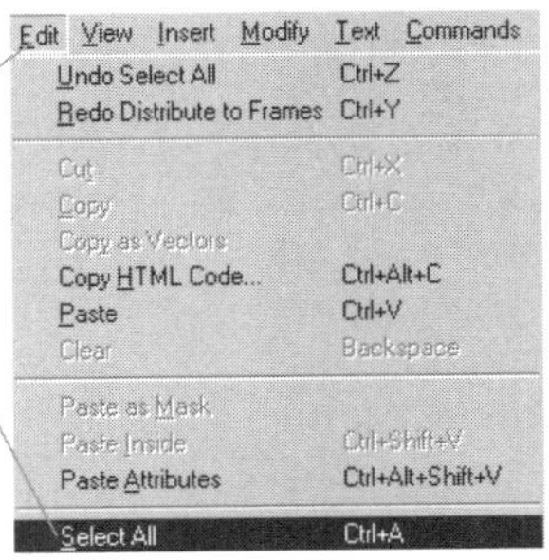

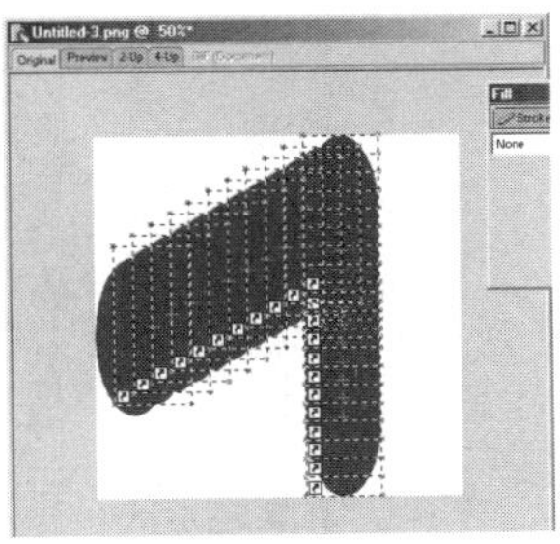

If the instances are not distributed to frames, then the animation will not work.

7 Click here on the Frames panel to distribute each instance to a separate frame. This creates the animation when the frames are viewed in sequence

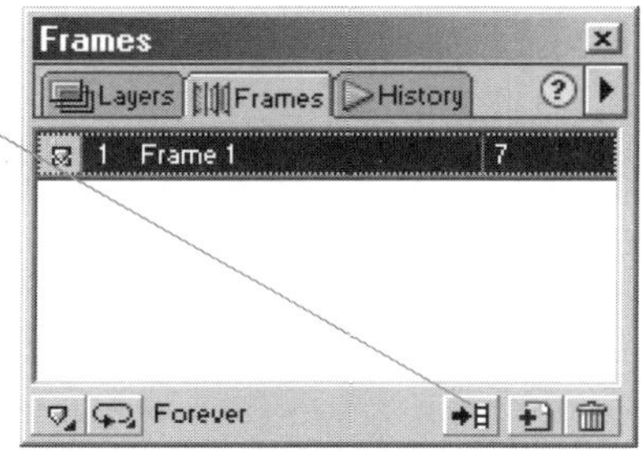

Depending on where you position the two instances to be tweened each time, a curved effect can be achieved for the animation.

8 The animation moves in two directions, rather than just in a straight line

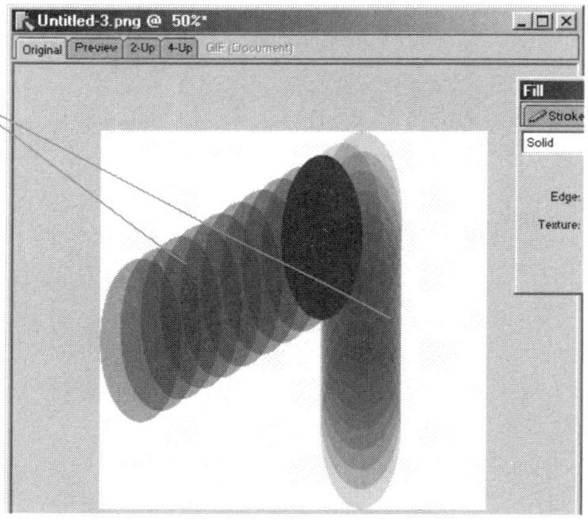

When the canvas of an animation is trimmed, it is done so to the largest area occupied by the complete animated sequence. It does not trim the canvas just to the size of an instance in a particular frame.

9 Select Modify> Trim Canvas to make the canvas the same size as the animation i.e. so there is no wasted space

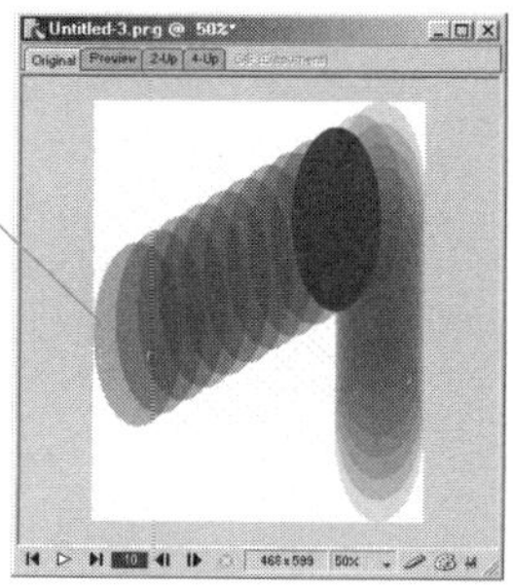

Using animation symbols

In addition to using animation symbols for simple animations, they can also be used for more complex items such as banner ads or animated logos. Once an animation symbol is created, numerous instances of it can be added to a file and each one can have its own properties assigned to it. More symbols can then be created to further enhance the animation. If required, the symbols can be edited so that all of the instances based on them are updated. The following example shows how to create a banner ad using animated text and graphics. It also shows how to edit symbols and change the properties of individual instances. To do this:

Banner ads on Web pages were once seen as the way ahead for online advertising. However, in recent years their effectiveness has been questioned and they are looked at with disdain by many Web users. But this type of animation does not have to be used exclusively for advertising – it can be used for any small-to-medium sized animation on a Web page.

1. Open a new document and select Insert>New Symbol from the menu bar

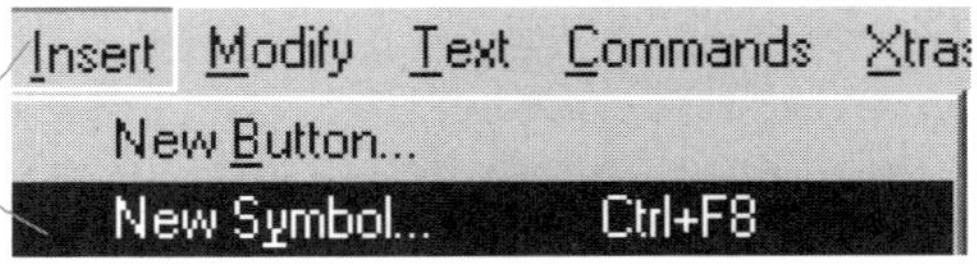

2. Give the symbol a name and select Animation as its type. Select OK

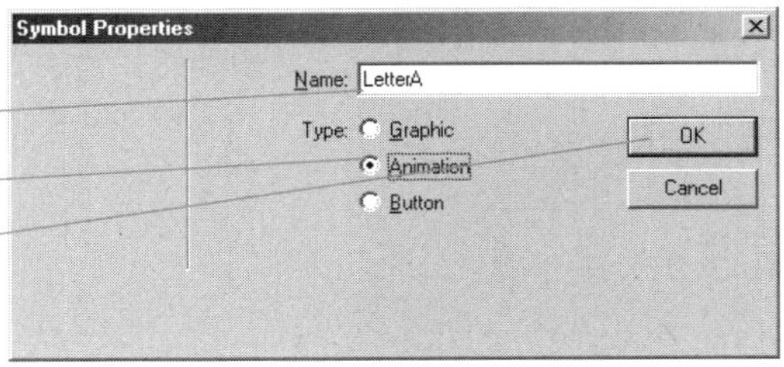

3. Create a graphic in the Symbol Editor

Existing graphics can also be converted into symbols by selecting them and then selecting Insert>Convert to Symbol from the menu bar. If a symbol is created with this method, make sure that all the elements of the graphic are selected before it is converted into a symbol.

4 Select Window> Optimize from the menu bar

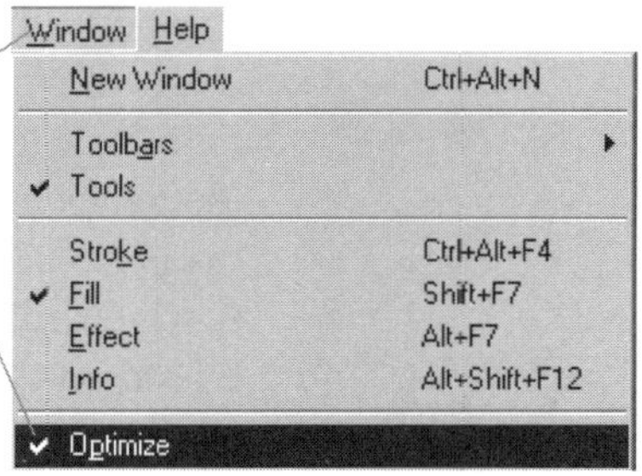

If Animated GIF is not specified as the file type, the symbol will not perform as an animation when it is previewed in a browser, even if it seems to work when previewed in Fireworks.

5 Click here and select Animated GIF as the file type

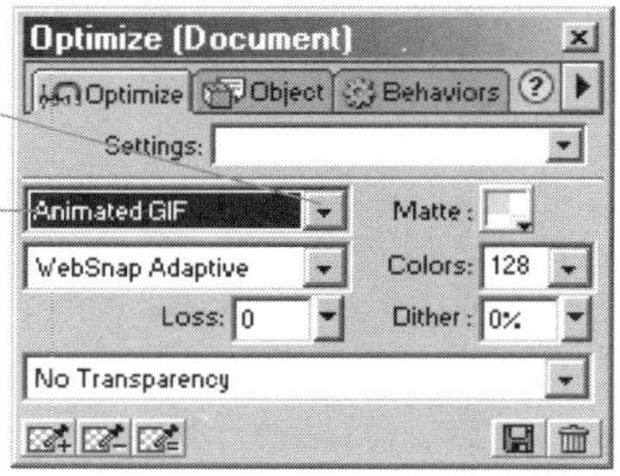

6 Click here to close the Symbol Editor

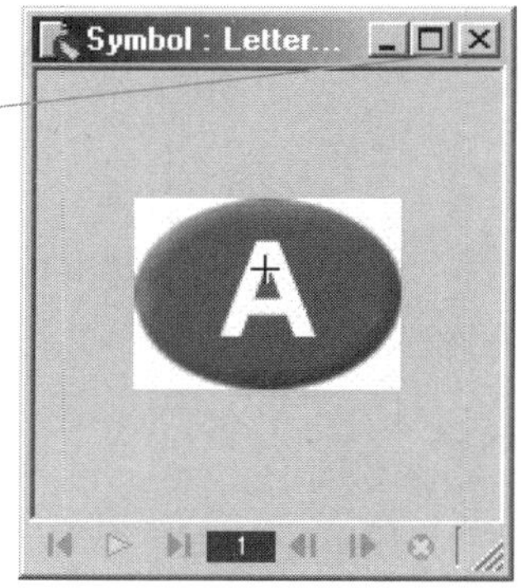

The animation effects for an animated symbol can be added once it has been inserted into a document – see next page.

7 The symbol is added to the Library and an instance of it is placed in the work area

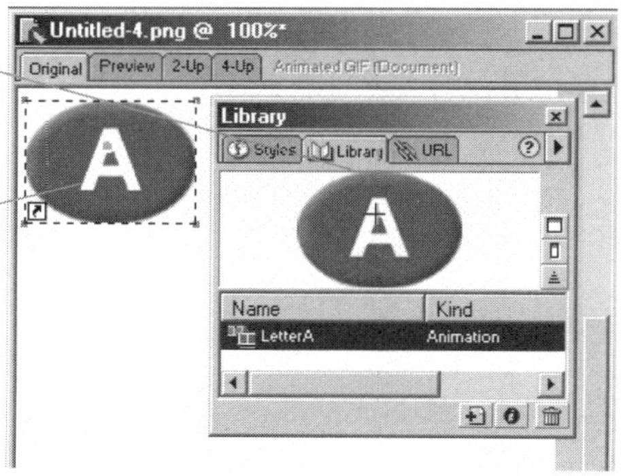

8 Select an instance in the work area and select Modify>Animate>Settings from the menu bar

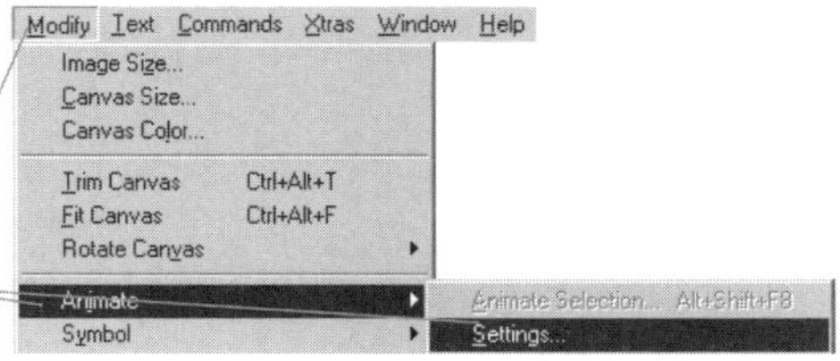

The number of frames in an animation is determined by the number of frames in the longest animated instance i.e. if one animation lasts 20 frames and another lasts 10 frames, the overall size of frames, the animation will be 20 frames. This means that the second animation will only be present for half of the total animation.

9 Set the animation properties for the instance. Select OK

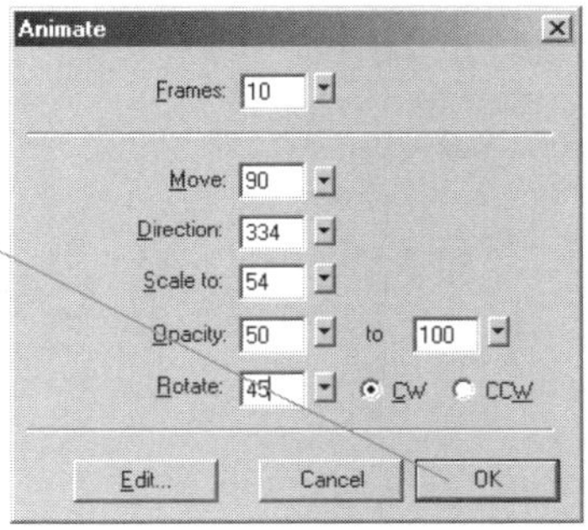

Use the Frames panel to select different frames in an animation and view how it looks at that particular point.

10 Click here and drag another instance of the same symbol onto the work area. Follow Steps 8–9 to animate the instance. Different settings can be used from the first instance. Do this with as many instances of the symbol as required

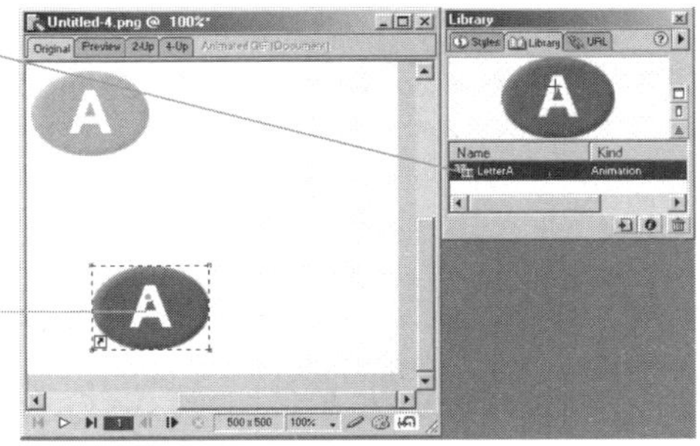

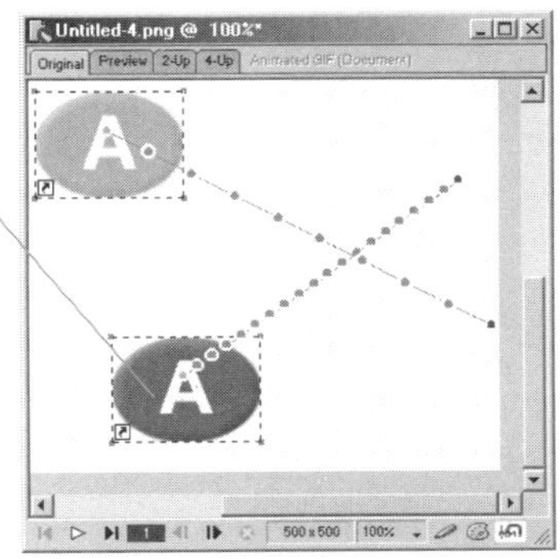

When inserting new instances, they will appear initially in the frame in which they are inserted. So to make sure an instance appears at the start of an animation, select Frame 1 in the Frames panel before the instance is inserted.

11 Create another symbol (Steps 1–7) and animate instances of this in the work area (Steps 8–9)

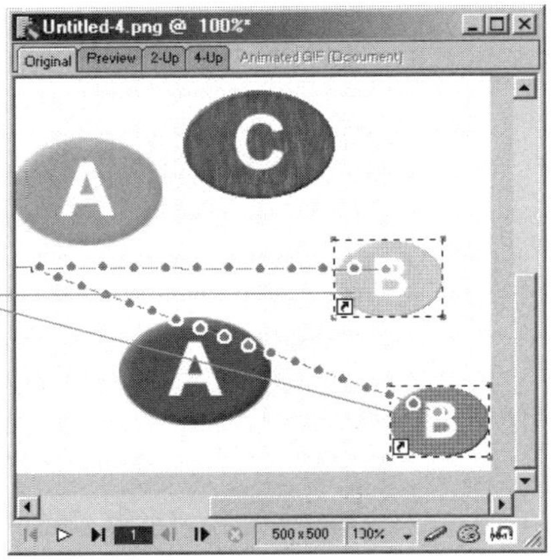

Use the Scale tool on the Tools panel to change the size of an instance. This can be done in any frame of the animation and it changes the instance for all of the other frames in which it appears too. If you want the instance to change size as it animates, enter a value in the Scale to box in the Animate dialog box.

12 Create another symbol and use text instead of a graphic. Insert an instance of this into the work area and animate it in the same way as a graphic

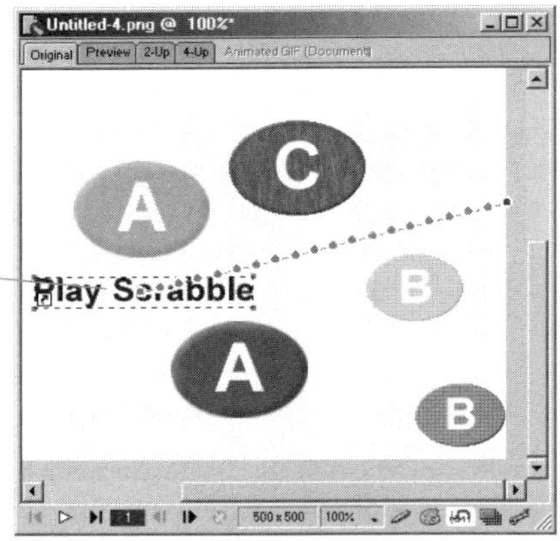

When animating text, make sure it does not move too quickly, otherwise it could be difficult to read.

13 Combine all of the instances into the final animation. Preview it in a browser by pressing F12 on the keyboard

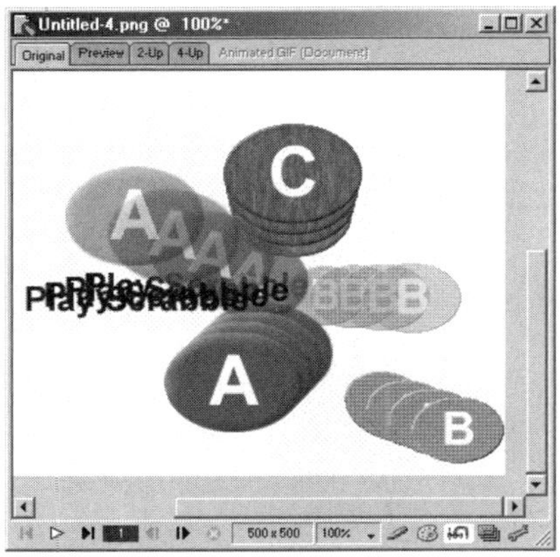

To create a background colour for an animation, select Modify> Canvas Color from the menu bar. Check on the Custom box and select a colour by clicking on the colour palette next to it.

Editing symbols

If an animation consists of numerous instances created from a single symbol, it would be a laborious job if it was necessary to edit all of them at once, for example, if you needed to change their colour from black to white. However, this can be done in a single step by editing the symbol on which the instances are based. To do this:

Symbol Editing mode can also be accessed by double-clicking on a symbol's name in the lower panel of the Library. This brings up the Symbol Properties dialog box. It is possible to enter Symbol Editing mode from here, by clicking on the Edit button.

1 Once instances of a symbol have been added to the work area, double-click here on the symbol in the Library, to enter Symbol Editing mode

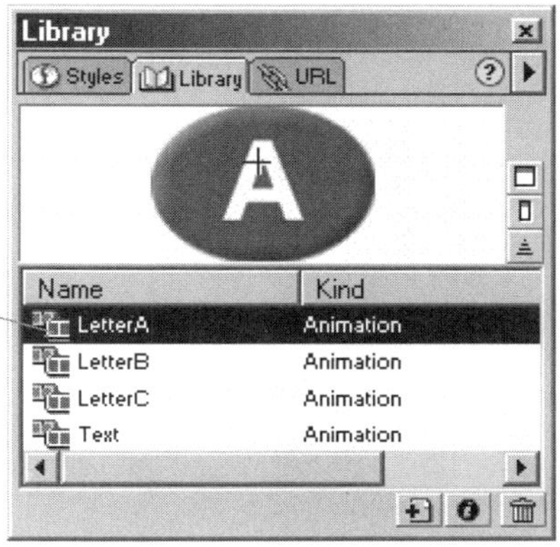

Symbol Editing mode looks similar to the normal work area and tools and effects can be used. It is identified as Symbol Editing mode by the word Symbol at the top left of the window, next to the name of the symbol.

2 Apply editing changes to the symbol and close the Symbol Editing mode

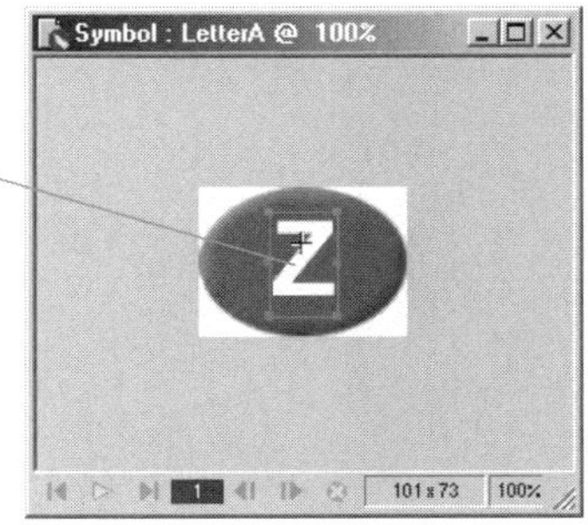

3 The changes will have taken effect on the symbol in the Library and also any instances of it that have already been created

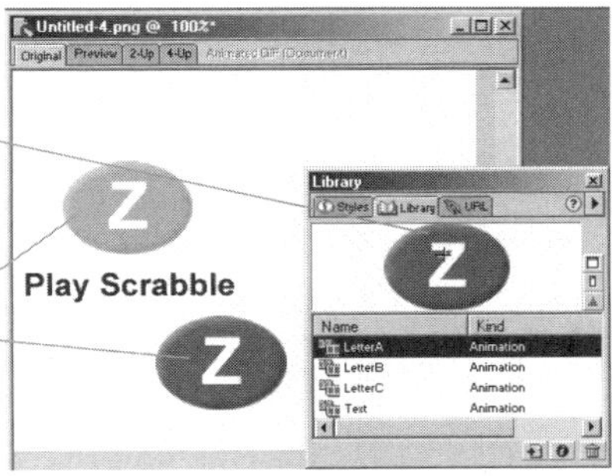

Editing with the Object panel

As has been shown on the previous pages, the Modify>Animate>Settings command can be used to apply or modify animation settings. Another way to do this is the Object panel and, although it does not have quite the same range of options as the Animate dialog box, it can be a quicker way to edit animation settings. To edit animations with the Object panel:

The Object panel can be used to change the animation settings of an instance at any point of its animated sequence. This means that the instance can be selected in any frame in which it appears and changes that are made will apply to the rest of the frames too.

1 Select an instance in the work area

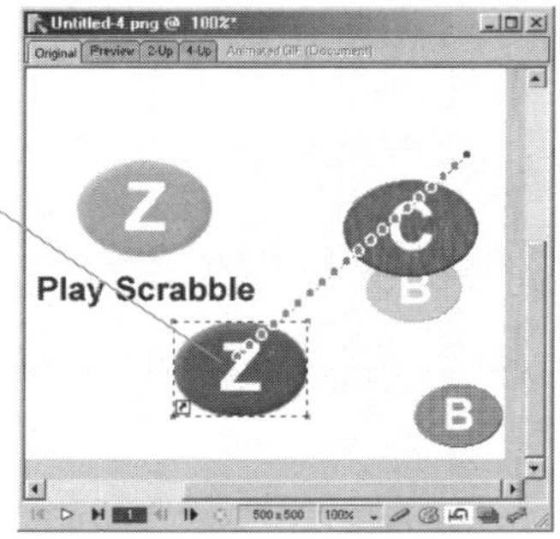

2 Select Window>Object from the menu bar

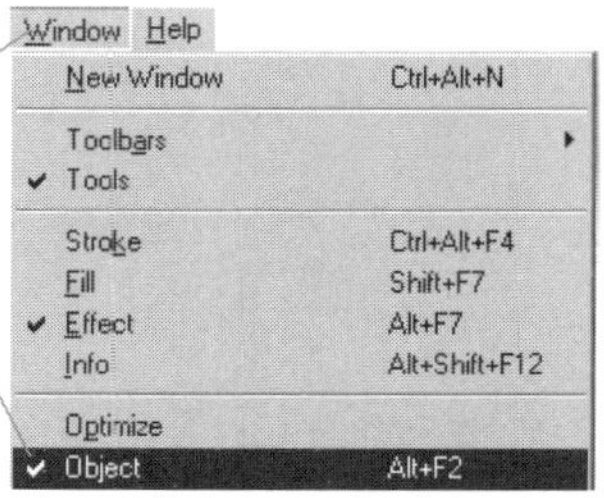

3 Enter the required animation settings. This will only apply to the selected instance. The settings are:

- Frames
- Scaling
- Opacity
- Rotation

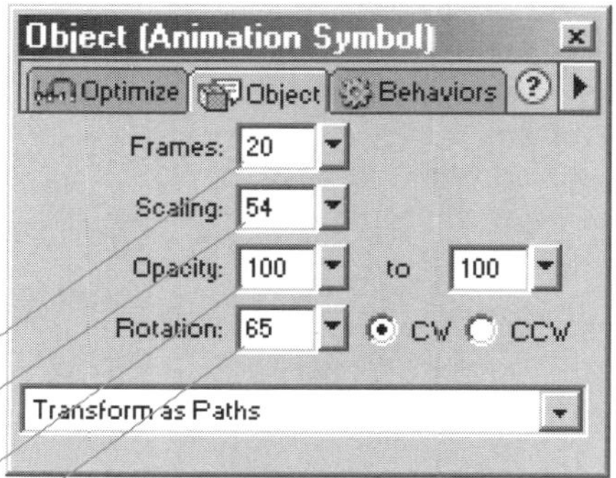

Automating tasks

Fireworks provides the means to perform a variety of tasks across numerous files at the same time. This chapter looks at how editing time can be saved by using automated tasks such as finding and replacing, and batch processing.

Covers

Chapter Twelve

About automated tasks

When working with images you will quickly build up catalogues of various types of images. These could include buttons, rollovers, graphics and animations. During the design process for Web pages or other forms of media, there may be occasions when you want to change an element in a number of files at once. For instance, you may want to change a piece or text, a colour or a URL. This can be done by performing in-built automated tasks. These include:

- Finding and replacing. This can be used to locate a certain item across a group of images and replace it with another item. It can be used with text, fonts, colour and URLs

When you are performing automated tasks, you select the files you want to amend and then apply the task to them. Files can be selected from different directories and they can also be in different formats.

In the Find and Replace panel it is possible to specify elements to be changed

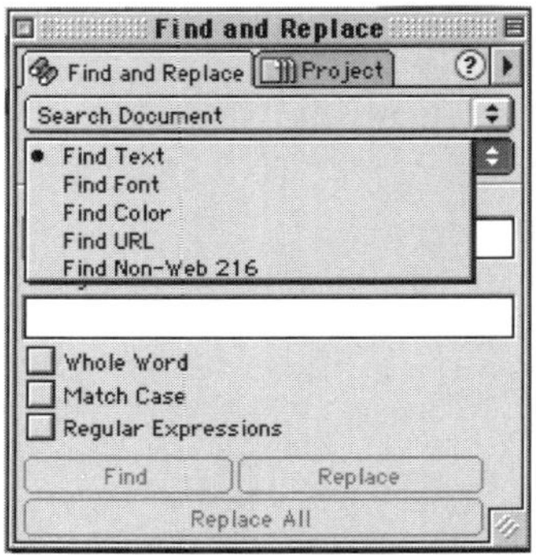

- Batch processing. This can be used to perform certain tasks across a group of images. This includes resizing images, exporting to a different image type and renaming files
- History panel commands. The History panel can be used to store groups of commands that are used regularly. When it is required the whole group can be replayed and applied to another item

The Project Log can be particularly useful if you are working in a team environment.

Another component in the automation process is the Project Log. This identifies files that have been affected by any batch processing and displays a log detailing the changes that have been made. This is a useful way to keep track of files that have been amended.

Find and Replace

The Find and Replace panel is accessed from the Window menu.

Finding and Replacing text

1 Click here and select the criteria for searching for the item

2 Click here and select Find Text

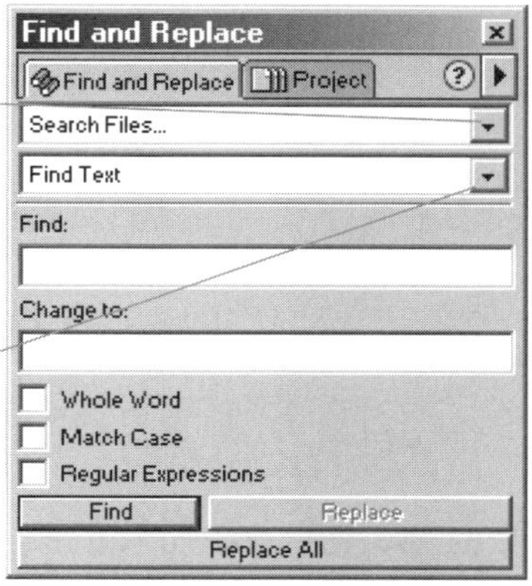

Find and Replace can only be used on PNG files i.e. the proprietary format in Fireworks. This is because images in formats such as GIF and JPEG are viewed as entire graphics, rather than images in their constituent parts. Therefore it would not be possible to identify items such as individual text blocks.

3 Enter the text that is to be found and what is to replace it

4 Select Find

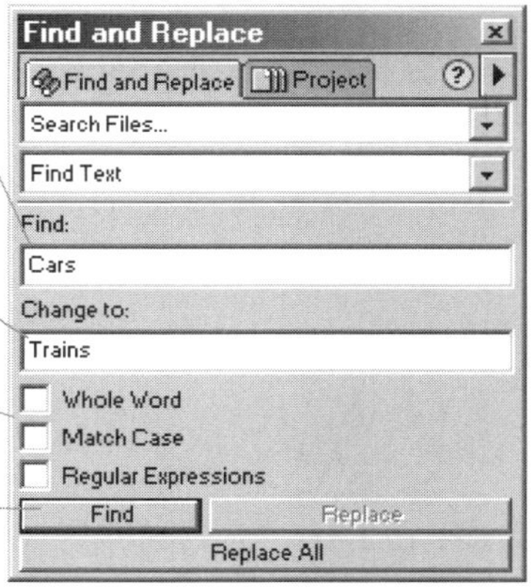

Select options here to refine the text search.

5 All files with the Find text are opened. Select Replace to apply the new text

Finding and Replacing fonts

Any font can be used within images that are going to be published on the Web, rather than just fonts that are available on the user's system. This is because once the image is published the browser views the font as part of the image rather than an individual piece of text.

1. Click here and select the criteria for searching for the item

2. Click here and select Find Font

3. Click here to select a font to change

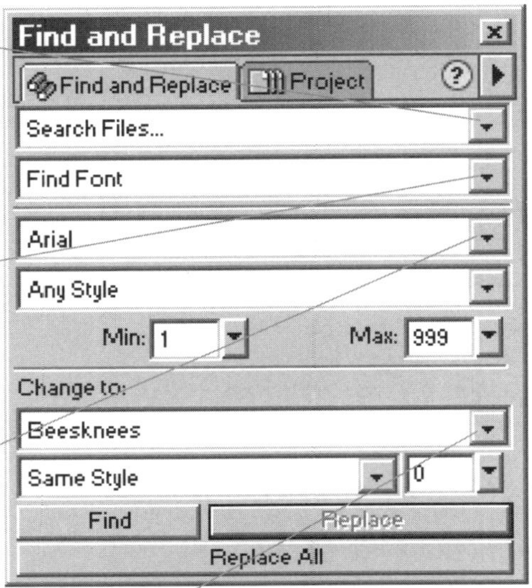

4. Click here to select a replacement font

Selecting different fonts could have an impact on the overall size of a piece of text, as not all fonts cover the same area, even if they are the same point size. Make sure to check that a change of font has not changed the overall design of an image e.g. gone over the edge of a button or navigation bar.

5. Select Find

6. All files with the Find font are opened. Select Replace to apply the new font

Finding and Replacing colour

There is also a Find and Replace option for replacing non-Web-safe colours i.e. colours that are not guaranteed to display in the same way on different browsers over the Web. If this option is selected, non-Web-safe colours are replaced by the nearest Web-safe version.

The Find and Replace colour changes can be applied to strokes and fills together, all properties, or fills, strokes and effects individually.

1. Click here and select the criteria for searching for the item
2. Click here and select Find Color

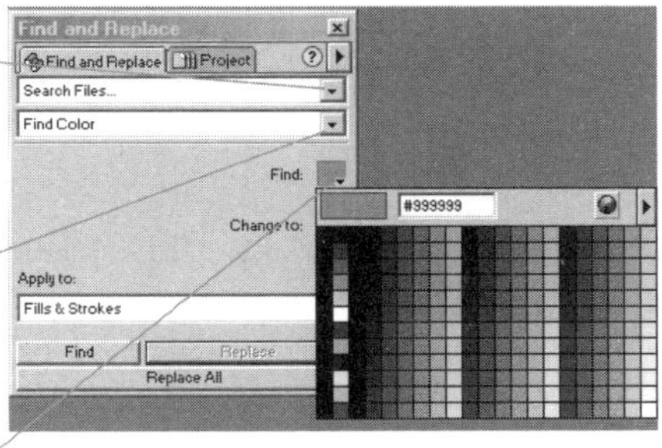

3. Click here to select a colour to change
4. Click here to select a replacement colour

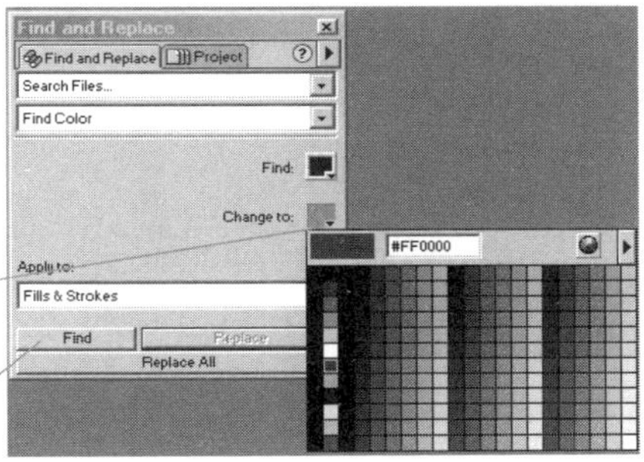

5. Select Find
6. All files with the Find colour are opened. Select Replace to apply the new colour

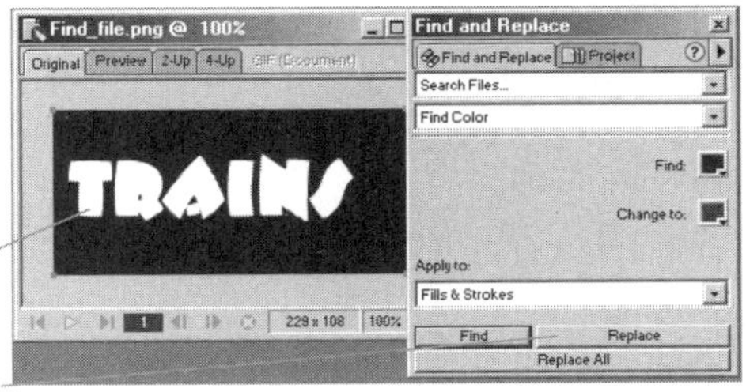

Finding and Replacing URLs

1 Click here and select the criteria for searching for the item

2 Click here and select Find URL

Be careful when typing replacement URLs. Always double-check, because a typo that is spotted at this stage could save a lot of wasted time later.

3 Enter a URL to change

4 Enter a replacement URL

5 Select Find

When searching for URLs, the same criteria as for searching for text can be applied.

6 All files with the Find URL are opened. Select Replace to apply the new URL

Batch processing

Batch processing can be used to edit various attributes of a large number of files in one operation. To begin batch processing the required files have to be selected:

Batch processing functions can be applied to all types of files, not just PNG ones. The exception to this is the Find and Replace batch function.

1 Select File>Batch Process from the menu bar

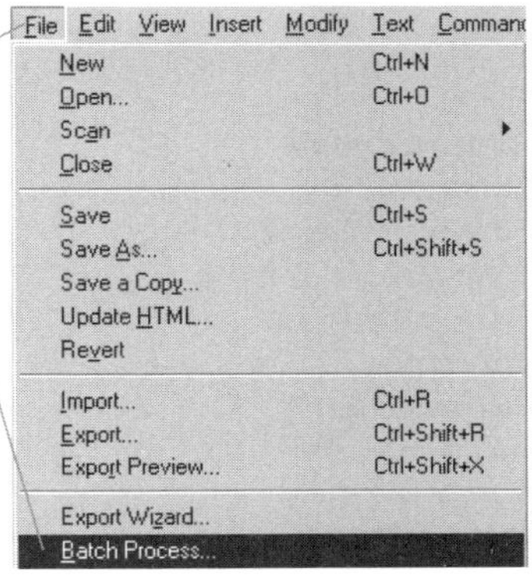

Files for batch processing can be selected from different folders. To do this, add files from one folder, then navigate to a different folder and add files from this one.

2 Navigate to the folder that contains the files to be edited. Select files and select Add to include them in the batch process or select Add All to include all of the files in the folder

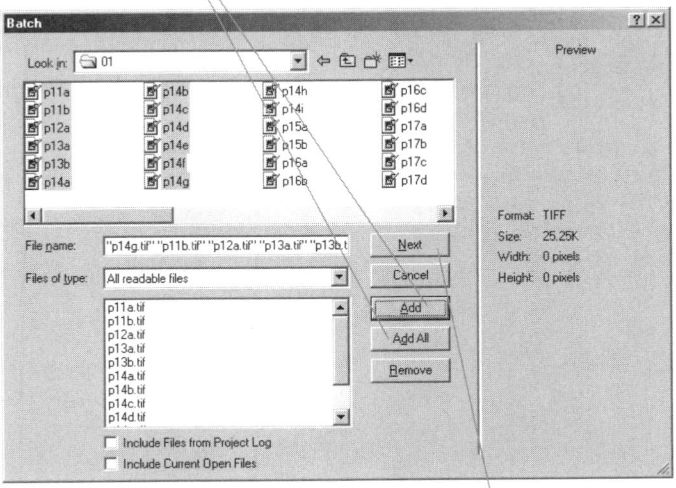

3 Select Next to access the Batch dialog box

Exporting

If you want to convert a batch of files from one format to another, this can be done with the Export function:

1. Select Export and select Add to add this to the commands for the batch process

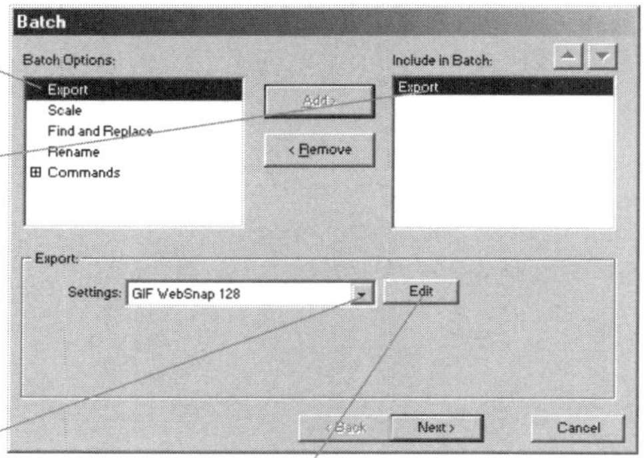

2. Click here to select a file format to which the batch images will be exported

3. Select Edit if you want to export the batch of files to a format other than GIF or JPEG. Select a format in the Export Preview dialog box. Select OK

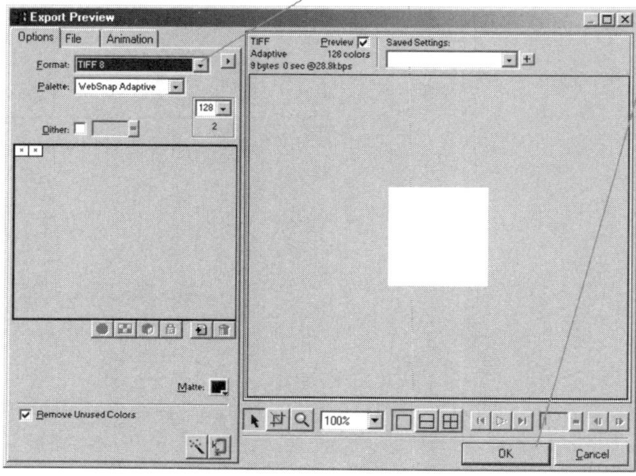

One reason for exporting a batch of files in one format is if you want to use images in hard copy publications rather than on the Web, or vice versa. For instance, you may want to convert GIFs into TIFFs so they can be printed in a hard copy newsletter or similar publication.

Several batch processes can be grouped together at the same time. For instance, a batch of files could be exported to a different format and scaled to a different size, in one operation.

4 The file format is shown here as Custom if a format other than GIF or JPEG has been selected. Select Next

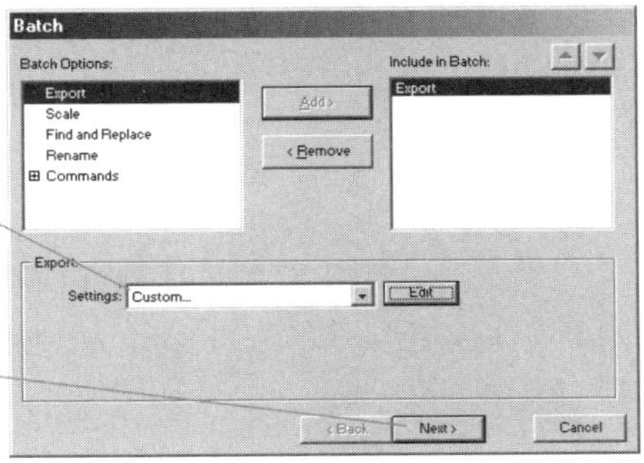

The dialog box that appears at Step 5 can be used to create backup files of the ones that have been changed. For more information about this, see page 185.

5 Select Batch to start the batch process

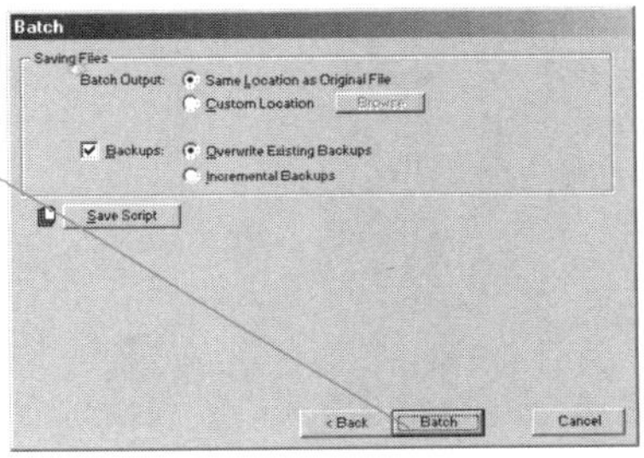

6 The batch process will proceed automatically and when it is finished the following dialog box will appear. Select OK

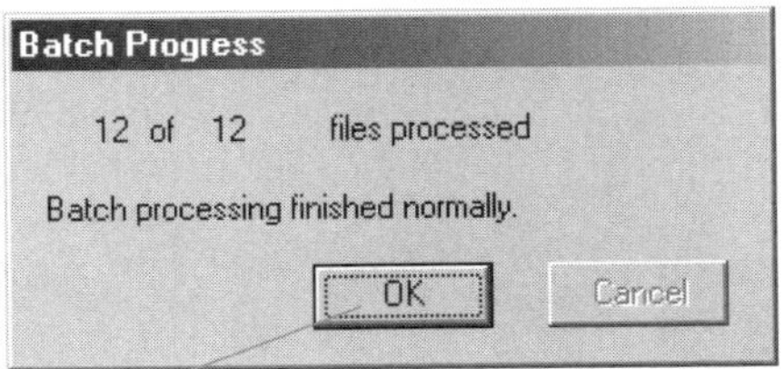

Use the Back button in the Batch dialog box to move back to the previous step of the operation. This can be done at any point before the batch process is started.

7 Check in the file structure to make sure the required files have been amended

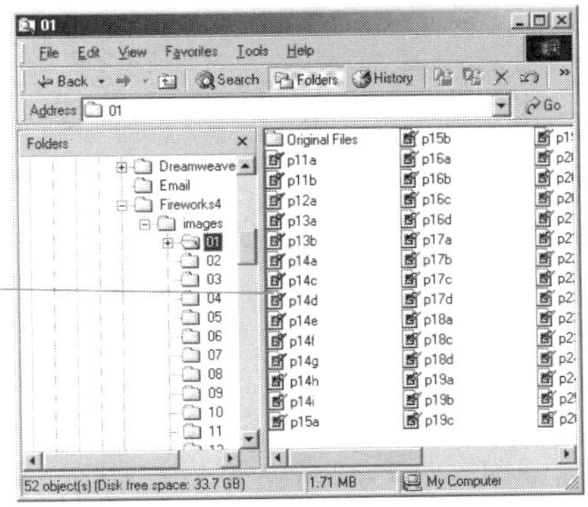

Scaling

Scaling can be used to change the size of a batch of images. This can be used to create thumbnails of images.

Thumbnails are miniaturised versions of a larger image. They can be used as a link to the larger image, so that the user can click on them if they want to see more, or ignore them if they are not interested. This has the advantage of displaying more information on a page and also decreasing downloading time by creating smaller file sizes.

1 Select Scale and select Add to add this to the commands for the batch process

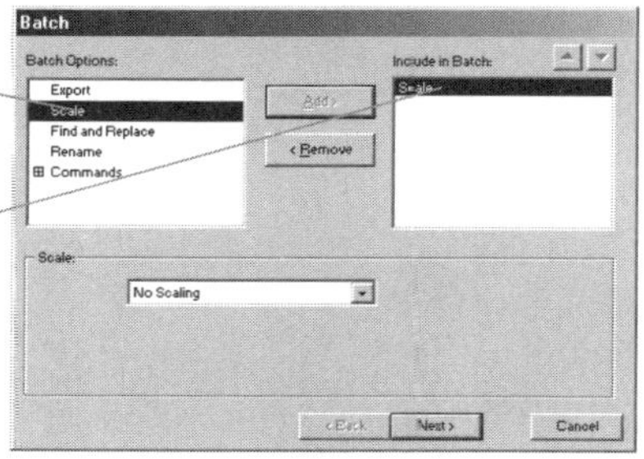

2 Click here to select how the images are to be scaled. This can either be a specific size (in pixels) or a percentage. Select Next

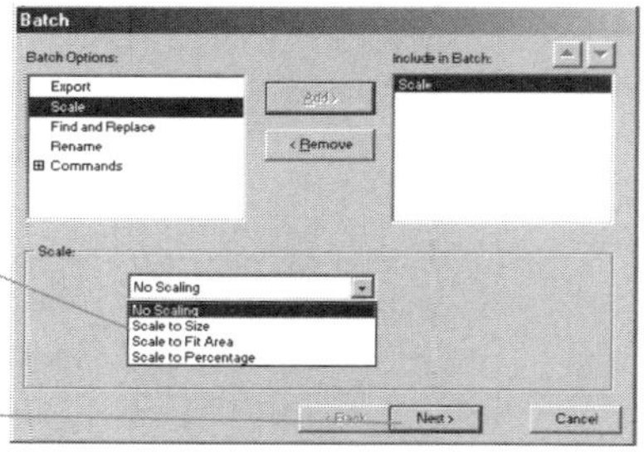

When scaling images that contain text, this can become distorted and appear out of proportion with the rest of the image.

3 Select Batch to start the batch process

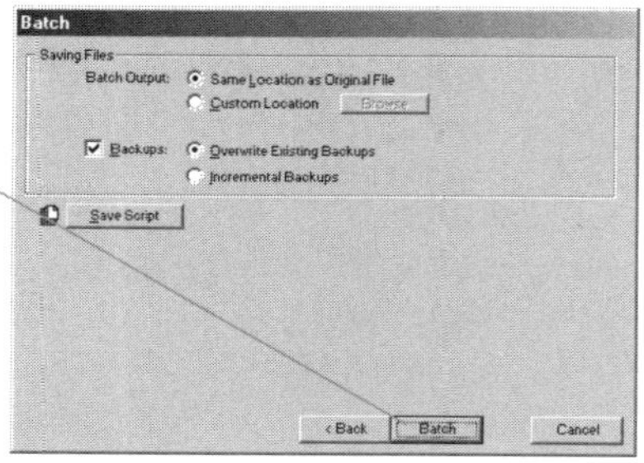

4 The batch process will proceed automatically and when it is finished the following dialog box will appear. Select OK

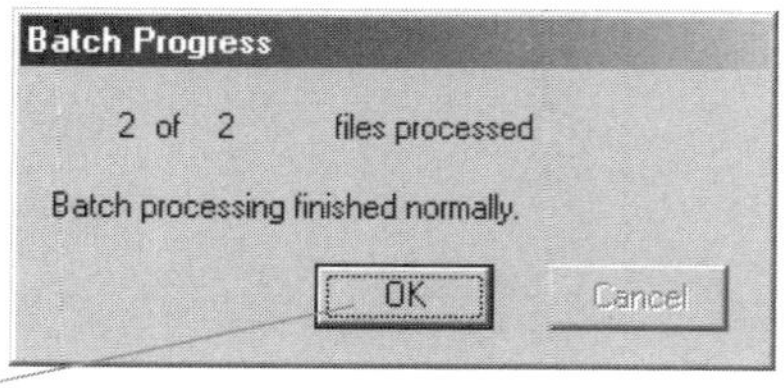

Find and Replace

This can be used to change the same element that appears in numerous files:

1. Select Find and Replace and select Add to add this to the commands for the batch process

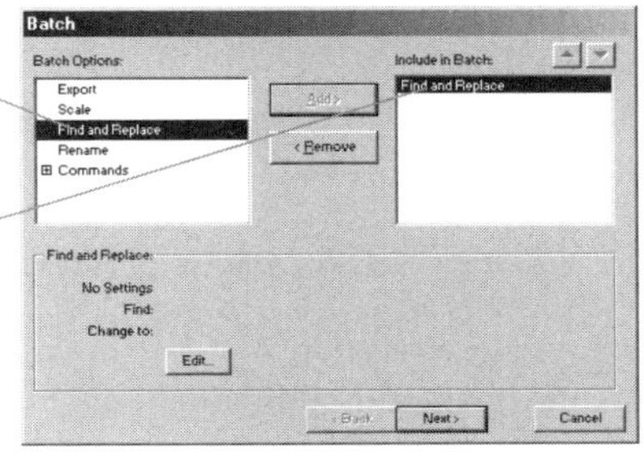

Batch Find and Replace only works with PNG files and certain other vector file formats such as Freehand and Illustrator.

2. Select Edit to choose the required Find and Replace function. These are the same for the Find and Replace functions on pages 175–178. Select OK

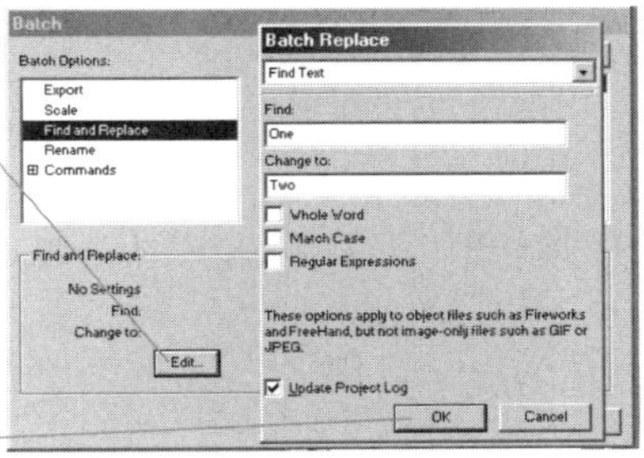

Batch Find and Replace is a good way to update items that appear frequently within image files, such as a company logo that is undergoing rebranding.

3. Select Batch to start the batch process

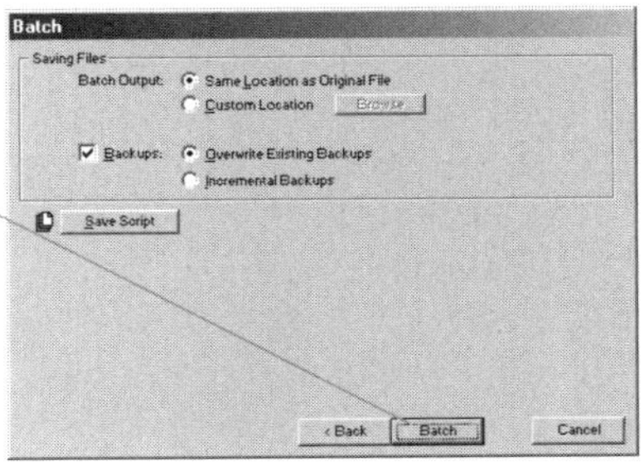

4. The batch process will proceed automatically and when it is finished the following dialog box will appear. Select OK

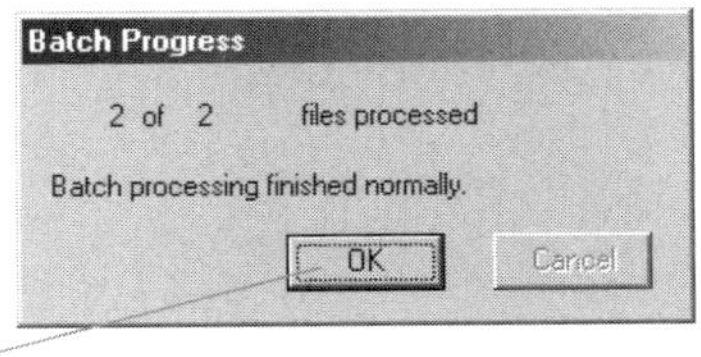

Renaming

This can be used to rename a batch of files by prefixing or suffixing the original name:

1. Select Rename and select Add to add this to the commands for the batch process

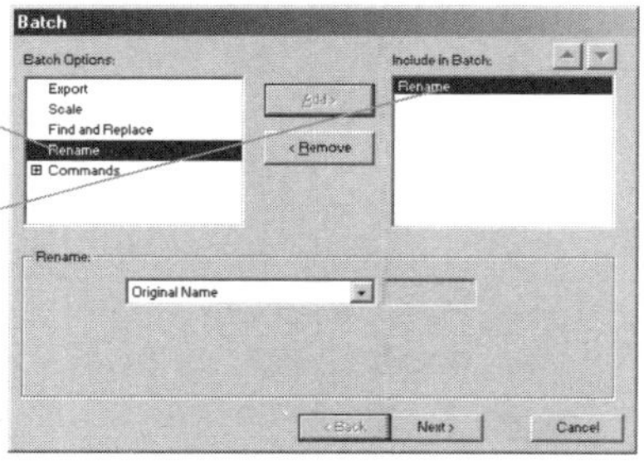

Renaming is a useful option to use in conjunction with exporting files into a different format. If they are renamed at the same time they will be more easily distinguishable from the originals.

2. Click here to select whether to rename the files with a prefix or a suffix. Enter the text in the box here

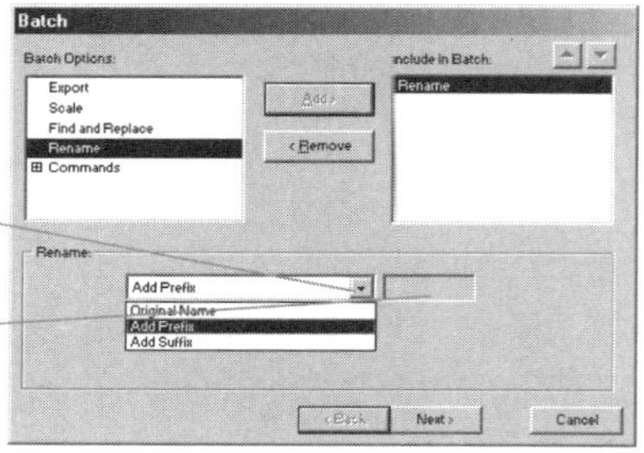

3. Select Batch to start the batch process

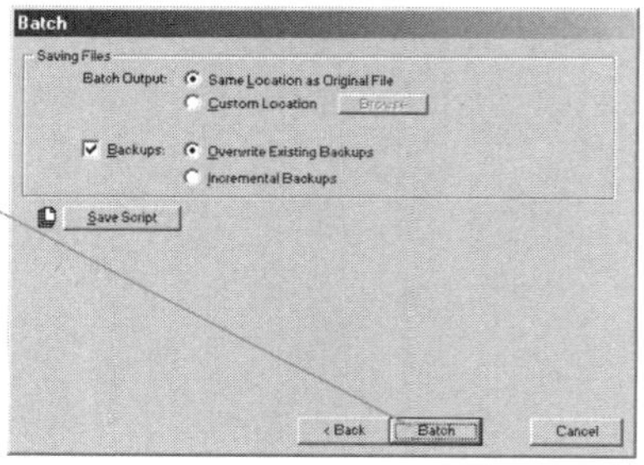

4. The batch process will proceed automatically and when it is finished the following dialog box will appear. Select OK

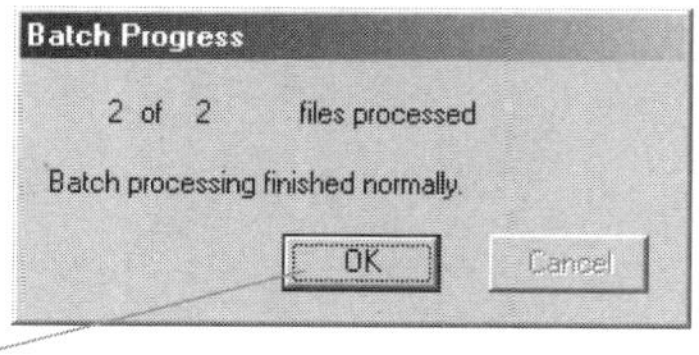

Backing up batch files

When performing batch processes it is important to keep a copy of the files in their original formats, particularly if you are exporting files into a different format. There are various backup settings that can be applied before the batch process is completed. These are selected in the Batch dialog box, before the Batch button is selected:

Scripts can be saved if the batch process contains several actions which you are going to use repeatedly. The script is saved as a JSF file in the same location as the files that are being batch processed. The script can then be opened by selecting File>Run Script from the menu bar and applied to selected files.

1 Check this box to enable backups to be made

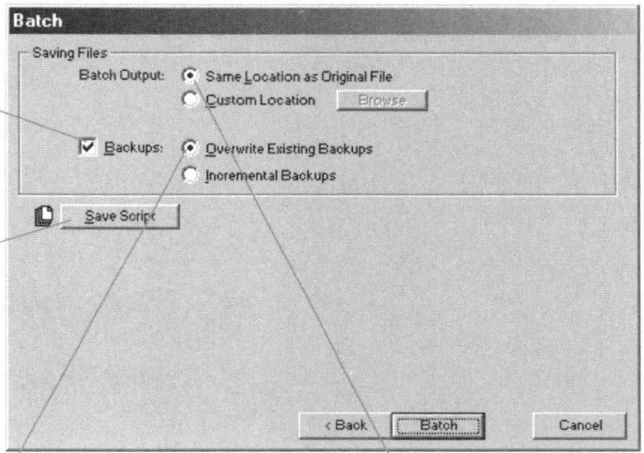

2 Click here to save the script for the current batch process

3 Click here to specify whether backed up files overwrite previous ones or new files are created

4 Click here to specify where the backed up files are stored

Even if no backup options are selected, the original files of a batch process are still saved in the Original Files folder.

5 By default, a new folder is created, called Original Files, which stores the original files once they have been batch processed

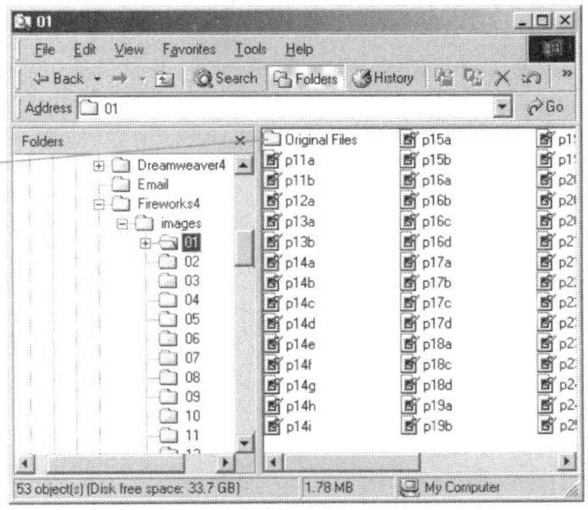

Project Log

The Project Log can be used to keep track of multiple files that have been used in Find and Replace or in batch processing. It can also be used to organise files. To use the Project Log:

1. Select Window > Project Log from the menu bar

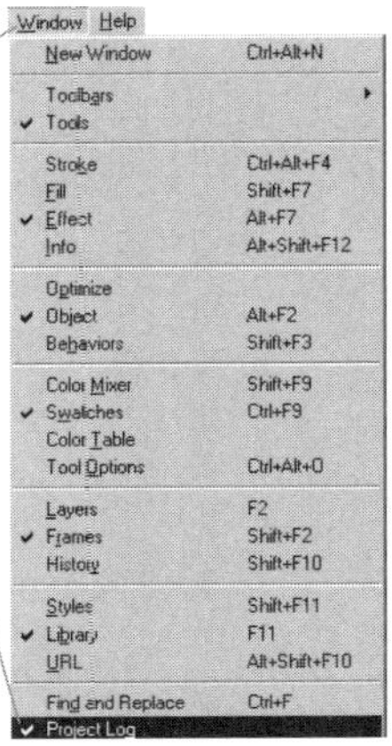

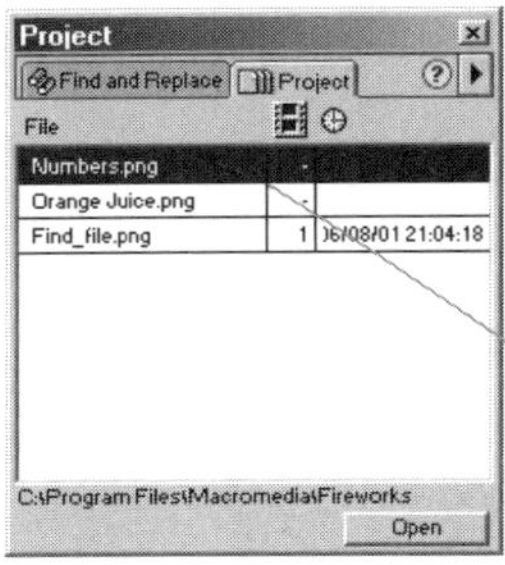

2. Files that have been used in Find and Replace or batch processing are shown here

The Project Log menu can be used to export selected files into a different format, add other files to the log and delete selected files.

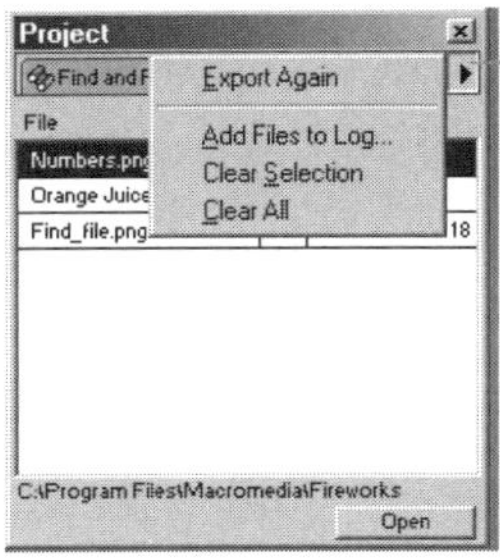

3. Click here to access the Project Log menu

4. Select a file and click here to open it directly from the Project Log

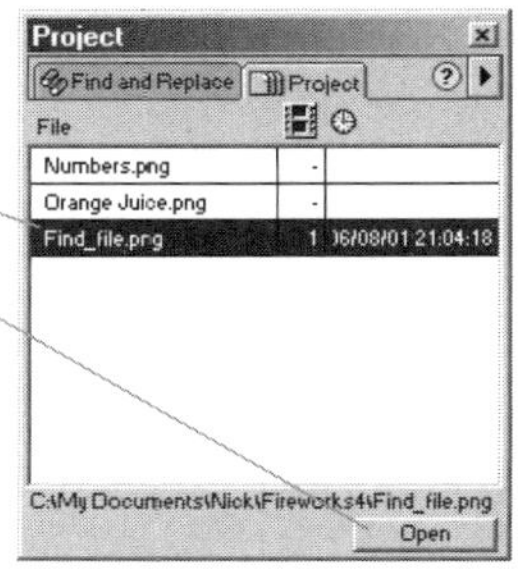

Index

A

B

C

D

E

F

M

N

O

P

R

S